Dear Pe[...]
So h[...]
wonders [...]

the

Praise for Veronica Entwistle's
My Near-Life Experience

Much love my friend
Veronica

My Near-Life Experience is a vital story. Veronica's path is lively and inspiring—a courageous revelation by a woman determined to confront her self-limitations to successfully live the magic of a mystical path.

Joe Vitale
Best-Selling Author, Speaker, Musician, Movie Star,
Law of Attraction Expert, and Miracles Coach

The milestones of our lives don't have to build brick walls. Travel with Veronica in *My Near-Life Experience* to feel the joy and humor of her breakthroughs to her fulfilling expression as a mystic.

John Grey
Best-Selling Author, Lecturer, and Relationship Counselor

In this tour de force, the angst of a young, vulnerable soul struggles with the lessons from stunting childhood moments of instilled shame and confusion. Pouring them into the crucible of transformation yielded a wily and playful but skilled empathy for the human condition—a Wise Woman who can listen deeply as she seeks the soul connection, whether as a trusted friend or as a skilled intuitive counselor. Read Veronica's story and take its positive energy and plug it into your own journey! You will be moved and changed and charged up.

Sue Newman
Photographer, Rancher, and Environmentalist

Not trying to be other than her experience, this gifted writer and personality courageously offers us her life story, attacking head-on the trials of her journey, while retaining her innate nature—a lightness that could not be snuffed out by those experiences. This is an amazing fairy tale of a woman's journey as she climbs the ladder as a spiritual being with the gifts of sight, mediumship, and laughter. That is rare—as she is rare. Yayyyy, Veronica!

Ursela Gurau
Artist

My Near-Life Experience—once you start it, you can't put it down. A touching and poignantly honest journal of an exceptional life as an intuitive is also an historic accounting of the fascinating consciousness-expanding movement of the Sixties and Seventies, which is still going on today. Veronica's constant companion is compassion, as she takes the steps we all must take in life to grow, both emotionally and spiritually. Most important, she also traverses the inner world, converses with those "departed," and courageously stands in her truth as she develops a career in the media, interviewing people who are also travelers sharing their journey into greater realities. I was alternately fascinated, moved, and inspired by Veronica's story and can't wait until her next book. This is a must read.

Linda Schurman
Astrologer, Author of *What Next* and *Fast Forward*,
and Publisher of soothsayer.com

Veronica's authenticity is riveting, a model for healing adversity and coming victorious. Bringing light to the truth of self and allowing Spirit to speak allows her to be a uniquely outstanding therapist. I hope to be a person in her life that honors her work and openness. Thank you. This book has really healed me.

Gloria Wilcox
Senior Intuitive

MY NEAR-LIFE EXPERIENCE

How Do I Know When I Am Really Me?

Veronica Entwistle

Cover Art by Daniel Holeman.
Graphic Design by Christopher Loving-Campos.
Author Photograph by Nicola Kitanovski.

ISBN: 978-1-51157-522-5

INTRODUCTION

We humans are truly amazing multilevel beings. As we travel our deep soul journeys looking for expression and fulfillment, we often live out identities that we morph to fit into the styles of the external world. Yet many of us wrestle inside to meet our real selves or our divine uniqueness while still wanting to fit in to the world. The strange turbulence from the projections and reflections of other people often creates a blur of reaction, confusing what is true about ourselves. As we go along, our identities sometimes posture this way and that in the desire to know ourselves and be known.

My journey was like that. Inside and out of myself, I was yearning to make sense of my life. And as I reread my story, I have to chuckle: Wow! Was that really me? My wild ride through losses—including a nervous breakthrough after becoming a young widow and giving up a child—helped me unearth more of the real me. "Forward into the past," says Doc Brown, the eccentric wizard from the movie *Back to the Future*.

As I excavated the chapters of my life, I saw that I was continuously beckoned by glints of my gifts and my true nature, always calling me in their demand to be recognized. It took great courage but also a deep faith of knowing that no matter what other people thought, the true me I was seeking, the one who knew things and loved beyond this world, was in there somewhere. Always encouraged by a strong inner drive, I was determined to find her. And I did.

Unraveling the mystery of oneself is an infinite process, and the *me* we come to know is only en route to an always emerging self. All of our lives are mazes and puzzles. These days, perhaps, it's better to say they're video games. We have to shift the focus of our listening and feeling to hear the whispers and the loving calls to wisdom, even to freedom and forgiveness, that are there for us. The language can be poetic, blunt, or simply a sensing. Hints can come from higher consciousness, Source, from beings who have passed over, or our own physical promptings. But they are always there — guiding us to a deep, inner home.

May this book be one of those loving calls for you.

CHAPTER ONE

And in the Beginning

I climbed into my little ditch — my studio, my study. It was just deep enough for me to sit in and hide my preschool self. The huge steel grate at the end of it, a little scary, a little threatening, mesmerized me. Mum would peek through the front room window of our townhouse. She and God always seemed to know exactly where I was and what I was doing. Snuggling into the grassy edges and even the mud, I would tune in. Then it began. Scenes unfolded from my life before this life, or in my mind, "where I came from." Their language of lights and colors rolled through my mind — reveries filled with feelings of love, of being loved, of belonging...home, to me.

That mucky ditch is huge in my memory. Years later, I saw that it was small, and years after that, totally gone, covered over with dirt and grass. No signs remain of all the holes my sisters and I dug there with our cousins, on our way to China. I remember tugging my woolly toque down over my dark eyebrows when I was all alone. There I was safe to explore the mysteries of myself — I, the real me, the me who knew I had never been born nor would ever die. The mud, the earth, was the tender loving Presence of the Goddess.

An inner knowing flowed through me. I saw it and felt it as a kind of sweet, rich, chocolate, velvety flow of ancient wisdom streaming steadily behind and beneath the turmoil of our young family. Nighttimes in my little bed seemed so long. I always had trouble sleeping, but I loved to sing — and sing I did, helping to transport myself and my older and younger sisters off to sleep. I wished I could sleep as well as they could. Some nights I felt odd. I knew I was different, and I didn't belong here at all. To the tune of their nightsighs, I would step on to the little doll crib by the window and call out to the stars. I always knew something: I had friends "out there," including a special one I missed terribly, just as she missed me terribly...my friend who was "out there" where I belonged.

Sometimes, lying awake in the dark, I would watch through the open doors into my parents' bedroom. All the lights were off, but against the windows, sometimes starlit, I watched the silhouette of a woman brushing and brushing her shoulder-length hair. Sometimes she was combing, sometimes brushing, and sparks would fly. I couldn't figure out who she was. "Mum, who is that lady who keeps brushing her hair in the nighttime?" Mum just stared at me. Why didn't she see what I saw? Why couldn't anyone share what I saw or experienced? Somehow it was dangerous to her.

Or there were times when I would get up to go to the bathroom, which was a few stairs down on the landing. A couple of my louder memories were of being frozen in place, unable to go up from the landing to my bed or head downstairs, and screaming and screaming. All around me, shapes and figures wafted. An angry adult, usually an aunt or uncle, would come to "save" me. They were on duty in the little townhouse complex, owned by my grandpa, while my mum worked in a café at night. Rigid with fear, I couldn't speak at all or tell them what I saw. To the frustrated adults, I was a lot of work.

The World War II years were defined by that war, by babies being born to anxious young people who needed them as souvenirs of their love or to assure a lineage in a time when many thought they wouldn't live long enough to create families. Or families were created by the excitement of the young men who did live and who came home as heroes. My sisters and I were born in that fervor. Mum was too young and angry to handle her little girl stew, while my dad, her swain, forded his successful provider's stream through the Royal Canadian Airforce, the big grocery store Safeway, college on a GI bill, and ultimately a great job as an optometrist, helping people see. Little did we know then how my "seeing" would be a powerful issue, even a problem for some. It would take seventy years and my father passing before, finally, he understood we were both trying to help people see.

As I watched Mum carefully, especially when I was very small, I tried to help her, to tell her that I knew who she really was. "Mum, you are so sad. It's okay."

She would cry. "Crazy! You are going to be locked up." Mum's rage rose in waves, pounding, not on the beach, but on her little girls. "Something to cry about!" she would holler as she flailed at her children. There were times when I cried and cried for her, "seeing" intuitively that Mum didn't mean to be this way. She just lived with so much confusion. Anger and confusion.

Mum burst often with scary rages. "If it weren't for you, I wouldn't be this way!"

It's hard to be a child; for me it felt particularly hard to realize that I knew a lot, but wasn't supposed to. I worried about it a lot. I felt enshrouded with a mantle of relentless power, and I writhed inside. In those days of "children are to be seen and not heard," most of us hid behind our cloaks of guilt and shame. I thought I could help. I could fix things. "If big people would only tell each other what they really feel, it wouldn't get so crazy." Oh, ho — is that a false dream! We used fears and "boogeymen" and stories of heroes fighting danger to develop enough of our imagination to topple mean authorities in the battles of our inner legends. One great aspect of my family is that we loved performance, and we frequently acted out all kinds of stories using these fairy tales or movies like *Cinderella* to control and design our lives and our inner being. That was a rich part of our world.

"Don't lie. Don't ever lie," the nuns and priests, our parents, and our aunts and uncles taught. But the vast difference between what was known and what was said was so confusing. "Lying is evil," they said, and yet abundant lies seemed to form webs of social behaviors throughout our home, church, relationships. A divide deepened in me, somewhere between my inner self — deep, old, and wise — and my outer self — confused and exhausted, always failing and never knowing why.

No one spoke about empathy, about seeing things and feeling other people's feelings. When mum was enraged, to me she looked like "the big yellow," a weighty ball of dark yellow. I swallowed her anger in the form of stomach aches and vomiting, even dizziness and fainting. The doctor, the first one in an ever-elongating string of medical people who

4

checked me over, said, "There's nothing wrong with her. It's psychosomatic."

"See? You just made it up." Enraged at me, Mum stormed as my tummy stormed as the bus rolled and lurched across Vancouver.

I was so restless. Unknown to me, or anyone else at that time, I was feeling everyone else's energy. That din of sound and feeling would build up, and I would burst into tears and cry uncontrollably for a few minutes. After the tears washed the mélange of feelings away, I'd burst into song. Crazy?

Creative, perspicacious, chatty....I was sent to school a year early; really, this was to ease the load on my mum. I was meant to do first grade twice, but I ranked first and helped the other kids. I was on my way! Walking the six blocks home with my older sister, I would tune in to Mum's energy. Was she mad today? Or was she all right? Will we get into trouble? If I could see and feel that she was angry, I would be alert. The watcher in me would step forward. I remember reaching up for my sister's hand. She was tall and I was short. Under pressure, her huge brown eyes would go blank. I would watch, alert and wide-eyed, to prepare to protect us from Mum's erratic wrath. Though we girls weren't always able to get along, we formed a tight little army.

Deepening within me was a split between my inner, that *me* who saw where I had been before, the *me* who was wise and strong and ancient. I loved God and prayed hard to be "good," but I was branded as "bad." I'd slither around the floor wetting my pants while Mum hit and kicked, then she'd scream even louder because I did wet my pants—all because I invited my aunt for coffee instead of tea, or whatever the current sin was. I knew I was "bad, bad, bad" and "crazy." But I also knew that when I used a breath, a special breath, I could drop out of any pain, not feel a thing.

A couple of the nuns often hit us with straps for being "bad." One time, a time that tightened up the knot of shame and "badness," a handful of us were taken into the cloakroom and asked about our sexual desires. We admitted the evil truth: Our little gaggle of four-, five-, and six-year-old girls had peeked at our cousin's willy. The jig was up. It was game over. We were going to hell for sure! She kept pumping us for information that we didn't have. We weren't quite sure what she wanted, just that we were being caught at a terrible deed.

As I said, I had a deep knowing. My perceptions, or wisdom, or maybe we could call it my magic, were wrapped tightly in a spiraling cocoon, maybe nurtured by God at times, infused enough to stay alive. That cocoon of perceptions and knowing was safe, but for me, it became harder and harder to find, like a sacred vessel in a tabernacle. Being smacked around by either Mum or the nuns—and for me, rambunctious, restless character I was, that was most days—dulled my senses and split me farther and farther away from my wisdom. They thought they were disciplining us. But the perceptions they thought they would beat out of us grew stronger, and many of us learned to pop out of our body/mind.

It was similar to what Beethoven did with his music, you might say. Late at night, his drunken father would drag the young Beethoven from his bed to play for his guests. He must have transcended the pain as his works grew in number and remain gifts to our world even these days.

Their words told us, "Be a good girl! Be like me!" I decided, very young, "Not a chance!" Their angst told us, "Remove yourself from that reality! Look around! There's inspiration out there."

"Hi, I am glad to see you," the nuns would say when we arrived at the church or at a conference. I could "see" inside of them — the nuns, teachers, even parents — and know that they didn't mean it. They were lying, as usual. Inside they were unhappy and annoyed about seeing me or us or whomever. I remember Sister Patricia hugging me to her cowl, which creaked under the load of starch that kept it still on her grand, black-pleated bosom. Thank Heaven I resisted a wild temptation to bite her breast. I was small, but my oversized teeth were my greatest defense.

Then, Margaret, the fourth daughter, was born with a severe case of spina bifida and had to live in the hospital. We three sisters thought of her daily. In those days, however, children weren't allowed in a hospital, so we couldn't go see her. She was a part of us, though. My mum, at this point only twenty-eight, was exhausted, but she rode the lurching bus to visit her every day. I often tried to figure out what Mumma was thinking, with her husband, my dad, so far away at university in Toronto, poor on students' income, her little girls *bad bad bad*.

After six months of a painful life, still in the hospital, Margaret passed. The morning that she died, I answered the phone. Although the caller didn't tell me the news, I "knew" what the message was as I handed the phone to Mum. That chasm opened inside of me. Deep, dark, and drowning, those chocolate streams of my knowing pushed the truth down there, far too deep to express, even for an inveterate communicator. I don't remember what Mum did, but soon, my older sister and I walked off to school as usual.

Despite being only six at the time, I remember that cold February day so clearly. I felt oddly disconnected, knowing something had changed. The sister, so present in our world, yet whom I had never met, was gone. There was a big hole. I was relieved to be going to the familiar world at school. There I got playfully silly. Pointing to the picture on the back of my storybook, I giggled as I whispered to my friend in front of me, "Hey! The pig's tail comes out of the crack of his bum."

Suddenly, a voice yanked me out of my laughter. "Veronica, come up here!" Sister Patricia's voice was slimier than Mum's. "Come up here to the front of the class, right now!" My stomach flittered as I walked through the stares of the grades one and two students. Remember being young and saying, "Don't look at me"? I felt like that. They all knew I was guilty of something. Sister Patricia, as usual extolling the spiritual virtue of truth, put her heavy hand on my shoulder as if it were the sword that dubbed a knight, and taught the class, "Today God has taken Veronica's baby sister because Veronica is a bad girl."

Oh, no! Mum is going to kill me. I writhed in shame and fear that I had a terrible power deep within. I was eighteen before I admitted to my mum that Sister Patricia had said I'd killed Margaret because of God's payback. Mum was horrified. "Why didn't you tell me?" she asked. But I knew she couldn't have handled it; worse, she might have been hurt and furious. I was only six, but she was mired in her grief and who knows what would have happened.

The split inside me widened. Sometimes I think of it as a cartoon: innate wisdom shimmering in an ever-decreasing cyclonic blob as it spirals off into the universe. It was an odd split. At times I was in a trance, not connecting with who I

8

was. Oh, I got good grades, but spinning inside, even later in high school, I got lost in hallways between classes.

One day, while we were still living in the townhouse near my ditch, I was sitting in the corner of our kitchen under the laundry rack. Mum had just pullied it down from the ceiling, then pullied it back up, laden with freshly washed clothes as if they were liquid, dripping off the rack. I watched intently as the ringers of our washer licked and squished more clothes. Mesmerized, I mimicked the motion of the ringers with my arms. I always wanted to know how things worked, including machines and especially people.

"Mum, does everyone have a little brown-and-black velvet me inside? And if they do, why don't we all talk about it?"

"Oh, my God, you're crazy!" Poor Mum burst into tears. "They are going to lock you up!"

At other times, suddenly, without warning, I would sob or faint. It was about thirty or forty years before I understood enough to turn my healer's focus to empathy, subtle energy, and the radiances from the myriad of energies churning from all our emotions and attitudes. My outbursts were my clearings, often fast and furious, followed by singing and more singing—still my favorite release. Obviously, I wasn't an easy child. We didn't know any intuitives back then or maybe it would have been easier for Mum to understand me...and herself.

I also remember watching her flail in her rage, and I knew that that wasn't who she really was. In my tears raining from all the trauma, I would also cry for her. Her gap was also huge—a distance between who she really was and this enraged being stumbling around on the earth plane. I tried to tell her I loved her, but she couldn't bear that and would shudder.

As the years went on, I struggled inside with the impossibility of being me, being good, responding to experiences I had no language for, and the insanity of the authorities and world around me. What did it all mean? I was highly emotional, and suicide kept popping up as a reasonable choice. I just didn't belong here. We've all heard so many say that—usually from the so many who are here on this planet to soothe the raging jealousies and greeds that keep us embroiled.

But I loved my reveries. For instance, aside from the depth and uniqueness of each person that I could see sometimes, and which intrigued me even as a wee person, I was fascinated by noses. I would stare at people, obsessed with noses and why we have them in the first place. They were interesting—all shaped so differently, puttied onto our faces, posturing this way and that, just like the people who owned them. I would stare, mesmerized by Mr. Man or Mrs. Lady, the teacher, priest, or Mum, always aware that there was a deep being inside of each one, a different self, and I often wondered about this jutting ID card. Why did noses have to be that way? That seemed so strange to me. I knew you could understand so much about people from the noses they chose...or picked? Periodically, even now, I slide into that familiar trance, an altered state, and "read" how noses reveal aspects of their owner's deeper inner drives, usually depending on how they point, portals to their inner self.

Actually, you can read any part of the body to understand people. These days, I have had enough experience looking into people—their gifts, their demises, their dharma, their solutions—to read the messages in the shape of their noses, their points, their direction. Somehow, I knew that where I lived before they didn't have noses...at least not ones that stuck out of their faces like that. How smart we are as tiny people!

But there was no way out. I couldn't take my own life really, because, back in my ditch, my little "study," I felt myself alive as I relived so many scenes from where I had been before and how beautiful it was. These precious experiences were "feelie movies," as if I was tuned right into the experiences with all their sounds and feelings, the relationships, and most of all, the love. I didn't know what it all meant, just that suicide as I thought about it later, couldn't provide what it seemed to offer: a way out. My visioning seemed to give me the feeling of being on an adventure, trying to figure something out in this thick gel called life. That "knowing" helped me quell the urges that, like entities, plagued me during my late teens up through my mid-twenties and pressured me to do things like yank my steering wheel fast enough to pitch me over a cliff. This battle continued for four or five years. I literally, at the most extreme times, fought for control of my steering wheel.

God and/or my mother lurked in every bush, always watching and judging, it seemed, like Santa Claus with his naughty-or-nice list. Clouds of shame enshrouded any enthusiasm about myself and my creativities. There was a hopeless numbness in me, always a desire to be good, but what was right? What was wrong? I often felt odd as I watched the world do its crazy dance—each one of us blindly cocooned by thoughts and feelings or that blinding empathetic steam from reactions all around us.

I loved God, as I said earlier. Truly. With all my heart. I know I was born with that. I loved God right from my earliest memories. But I remember, hands on hips at about six or seven years of age, looking up at some ubiquitous, billowing clouds over Vancouver, talking to my personal

11

God design. At that point, He was a man in a white business suit, with a long beard, and — if you can believe it — had the measles! I said, "God, I love you, but you are silly. You hire mean people to be mean to little kids. What's the matter with you?" There was no answer. By then I had learned in catechism classes that if your prayers aren't answered it means you aren't a good girl.

Well, I had also learned by then that hell and God's vengeance was just a pig's tail away, and I was on a perplexing trail. No matter how good I thought I was, or wanted to be, I was in trouble. I even looked like mischief. Maybe it was my freckled, turned-up nose and wild hair. Or my fast movements and rapid articulations. Or those spontaneous bursts of emotion, both tears and giggles. Teachers would take one look at me on the first day of school and point me to the front seat of the room — especially as the years went on. I was restless, talked and giggled a lot, and had to keep busy. But I was a good student. And Lordy, I tried hard to be a good girl.

Church times were different. I loved it, what with all the incense, candles, and otherworldliness. It wasn't quite up to my ditch, but it was transporting. I mused often, such as: Did you know the soul is like a white t-shirt? It would be stark white at the beginning, but all these *bad bad bad* marks of sin were indelible stains. Oh yes, we had confession, but we might not get to the depth of whatever we did. Then that dirty, white t-shirt would be gray. And once it was gray, there was no getting it clean. Bleach wouldn't even help. But we were going to be saved. One day, my teacher Sister Isadore said, "If the Bishop ever comes to hear your confession, bring up every sin you have ever done, everything you can think of and do a super-duper job of confessing." Apparently, he had a special stain reliever, a special dispensation that would make everything cleaner inside of me.

One thrilling Thursday when I was in the fifth grade, it happened. The Archbishop of Vancouver was actually coming for a visit, and he was going to hear our confessions. Even lining up to kiss his ring was awe-inspiring. I trembled as I waited for my turn. This was it! This was the time I could be all cleaned up and become good. Once we had the special blessing/gift from kissing his ring, we were ready for the all-time roto-rooter confession. Eagerly, I entered that magic box, truly vaulted by dimensions of time and space, angels and saints. Not quite like Dr. Who's magic police box, this one smelled like wood oiled with incense. Making the sign of the cross on my chest (daren't say breast), I began, "Bless me father that I have sinned." I felt like I could almost hear him think, "Oh boy, did you ever!" and off I went — through the seven deadly sins, the ten commandments, the stations of the cross I roamed, confessing something about each one. "Father, forgive me. I have been hating my parents. I wanted to kill my sister. I lied to my teacher about my homework and to my mother about practicing piano. I slept with my cousin, and he's a boy." Actually, it was camping together at age six and literally just sleeping, but I thought that was a sin. I tried to confess about how I didn't honor my mother and father and how I always tried to wiggle my way past my Mum's explosions with little and often ineffective lies. Exaggerating and expanding, I sounded like a master of sin at age ten. I was dead set on cleaning up this murky path to hell, burning out my vagrant intentions or anything that stood between me and Heaven.

"Young lady, you are mocking the sacred sacrament of confession. Do you understand me? You must take confessions seriously."

"But I...." Going blank, my focus flitted. My stomach twirled as my soul shook. "But Archbishop, your Holiness...I just wanted...."

Like most adults I knew, he wouldn't even let me explain. He wouldn't hear how desperate I was about this confession, how worried I was, how I wasn't sure what was true anymore because no one told the truth. He just frowned and gave me a whole rosary and some novenas and the stations of the cross. There I was kneeling at the altar to say my penance about ten times longer than the other kids. What a whispered stir that caused! They all knew I must have been "really bad." And I was so worried that I would never be cleaned up inside.

Later, I realized that most of the friends who I got a great kick out of wouldn't be making it past the hell bridge either—not if it was that slithery a trail through very simple feelings in life. Oh well, somehow it will be all right. At times, I kind of thought of hell as a warm place to gather forever.

CHAPTER TWO

Shades of Authority

So I grew up. I thought our dad, the fun character who infused our home with music and laughter during his visits from college would save us once he came back for good. He would realize what was happening—that Mum was not all right—and he would soothe her and save us all. He didn't. He wouldn't. He couldn't. Always loyal, he had to believe her complaints. I guess I did, too, at some level, believe that because of my curious, perspicacious nature I was bad. We four kids had shared the fantasy that he would save us, but by fourteen I was angry. I remember the day I announced to my sisters that he wouldn't. I just knew it. He never planned to save us. From then on, I was furious with him. I couldn't trust him to know us at all. I remember, though, that he and I would occasionally have intense discussions about ideas, history, psychology, and the world. I liked those times. By then I really knew that life was exhausting, unfair. Mum told me later that some of my earliest conversations (and heavens, for me as a chatterbox, that could well have been in the womb!) were about things just not being fair. I was dizzy and lost and lonely.

But the heartier side of my family life was our singing. My dad taught my sisters and me, while we were still small enough to share a bathtub, and later my younger brother, to sing harmony. Dad played his violin, guitar, banjo, gut bucket, slide whistle, accordion, whatever he was exploring at the time, while we soared with songs that rose out of his childhood, ours, and whoever's. Singing was our family's way to enjoy dishes or housecleaning — one of us upstairs, one in the basement, two on the main floor, merging our voices. We even filled the car with songs as we traveled. I still thrill at the rare occasions when we attune and harmonies flow again.

And I loved the chanting at church. *Kyrie Eleison, Kyrie Eleison.* Even as teenager, I loved this ritual. The smoking dishes of incense burners swung on long chains that clicked and chirped with birdlike sounds. The thin smoke wafted, and our young voices were woven into colorful rituals. My spirit flowed free with the sound mingled with the smoke from the candlelight and incense, drifting around the vaulted ceilings from choir loft to sanctuary, filling the hair of the priest and altar boys, then back to us again. That part of mass was literally enchanting.

I can still conjure the Presence I loved back then — feeling, smelling, expanding in It. For a few years, that is all I wanted: to be enfolded by the Mighty Love of God, that Being I still call The Presence. I dreamed of being a nun. That would take care of my "badness." But it was not to be. I was poured out of that soup. In school I often got an A in religion and a D in behavior. A puzzling guilt and shame kept hacking at my peace. As the years gathered up more interests, fun, diversions, and certainly more questions, the essence and enchantment of church faded. But I tried digging just a bit more. I set up an appointment to meet with our priest after confession one Saturday night.

"Father, why is it the same punishment to miss mass or murder someone? In both cases we go to hell."

"Well, that law was created in the fifteenth century to control the people in the villages "

"But Father, it's 1958. What about now?"

"You can't change laws."

Hmmmmmm. I felt the same emptiness as I had when I heard my sister Margaret died. My inner self dropped down...to where? To where? There was a hollow space inside me, and I left the church for good...in a chariot. The beautiful, yellow, 'fifty-seven Fairline 500, with all its transcendent promise, awaited me. Actually it was my boyfriend's mother's car. Its bright wheel-well lights— purple, my favorite color—flashed on the hubcap spinners. It was more suited to cruising past the Dairy Queen on Main Street. Parking-lot gravel sprayed behind us, or maybe it was shrapnel from my blown-up faith. I was very torn. What was true? What was the love of God? Was that what love looked like—punishment and laws from the fifteen hundreds? That sure wasn't right to me. It would be decades and many miles before I dropped my fantasy of a fair, nurturing, or spiritually driven system and awoke to the greater truth: that systems of religion, politics, and economics were created and organized to maintain the flows of power, to keep people or societies in line. I couldn't have believed that then. I still, after all my experience, believed in a God that was nurturing us all and living in the higher echelons of the realms of power. The illusion was my escape.

I loved people, but at the same time, I was frightened by them. I was perplexed, but also fascinated by the crazy distortions of people's interpretations of one another. If someone has a defense, for example, it emanates reactions. Or if people had abuse—physical, mental, and/or emotional—as a small person, they attract more as they grow older. That would be a crucial part of the transformational work I would learn. I hadn't yet learned about what I laughingly call "projectile thinking." But I would learn how whole societies simply pass on base behavior on empathetic and energetic levels.

"When I am big," I'd decided at about four or five, "I am going to learn how big people work." I was perplexed and determined. Maybe I could be a doctor!

This learning is still the only game in town for me, after many, many years of in-depth intuitive counseling with all kinds of "big people." People in pain. People wanting to shuck elusive patterns. People wanting to evolve. We cruise through our inner selves, around the gaps or blocks that threaten our deeper goals. At times we excavate identity and purpose, then continue on through realms of potential. How powerful we can be when we pull away old programs.

But I was still in my early training for that profession, also known as late adolescence. After all those years of moody confusions, Mum's rages setting the scene, me crying at night, at fifteen and the start of eleventh grade, I got a new hairdo. It was an "in" short hairdo with kiss curls alongside my face and shaggy little bangs. Voilà! Suddenly I was invited out by a boy. My first date! He arrived at the house with his own special hairdo, his James Dean *Rebel Without a Cause* greased flattop, wearing a glittery vest. He looked like the epitome of my parents' fear for their daughters. I fell in love for a while, and our relationship became my emotional base for the next five years. I knew I shouldn't marry him. I often planned to break up with him, but in the aura of my parents' haranguing, I would turn to him again and again to snuggle. He was fun and smart, but definitely not a high achiever. Soon I was in his group — a lively, fun-loving, ice-skating, jive-dancing, motley crew. We shared our interests in drag racing and snuggling, me often with a book on the seat. He preferred comic books and, it would turn out, women.

In retrospect, betrayal was inevitable. Betrayal is like a snakebite whose poison evokes transformation.

Around twelfth grade, there was a new girl in town whose brother was in our group. No one liked her, but I did. It was a harbinger of naïve patterns of trust I would carry in my life for about fifteen more years. "Come on, Jenny," I welcomed her. "Join us! Be good to her, everybody." I set it up. That summer, my seventeenth, I went to visit my grandfather in Los Angeles, and during that two weeks I was gone, my boyfriend and Jenny began a relationship. I didn't know for six months after my travels that they were getting together each night after I was dropped off at home. My parents kept me on a very tight curfew of midnight even until third-year university. I just went out earlier.

A girlfriend alerted me to it with a barbed sweetness. "Everyone is laughing at you, and no one wants to say anything. Maybe if you would change your hairstyle....." Is it always about a hairdo?

Well, maybe it is, as that hair went into reaction and almost fell out in the ripping storms of my rage and hurt. It was as if every hair on my head, and on my body, was buzzing. I stormed downstairs to my bedroom, dredged my drawers and cupboards for everything he had ever given me. Sweaters, perfume, photos, heart-shaped chocolate boxes flew around the room, smashing against walls, unceremoniously dripping pieces of red hearts or sparkly wrappings. Stuffing from my treasured furry skunk and other snuggling animals floated through the air as I hurled them one at a time, crying and screaming. For once my mother wasn't angry. Instead she was compassionate, kind, and worried. She reached out to hug and console me. But it was hopeless—kind of like soothing a Tasmanian devil.

I hopped into Mum's car and sped to Jenny's folks' house. *Blap blap blap!* My horn called Jenny to the door.

"Hi," she smiled sweetly at me.

My bushy eyebrows practically rattled as I intoned, "I would like to see Ted."

"Oh, he's not here." She acted amazed that I would even expect that he would be. I rolled my eyes as her words clanged. Whenever I hear that "clang" inside, I know someone is lying.

"He had better come out here." My voice iced the space between us.

She went inside and, soon, there he was—my Prince Charming: long-legged, light-brown hair pomped, blue eyes softly contrite but looking small and ringed behind his thick lenses, blonde eyebrows arched, lime-green jeans. His arms were outstretched in a white flag offering. He strode to the little car.

"Let's talk," he smiled. I didn't smile. In fact, just as he walked in front of the car, I revved up. He laughed as he lifted his long leg over the hood before I could hit him with my mum's Triumph Herald. Thank you, God. I heard recently that he is now a jail guard. Well, he sure protected me from going to jail!

He begged and begged forgiveness. We stayed together, kind of, but inside it was over for me.

In 1960, launched by high-school graduation, I went off to the University of British Columbia to become a schoolteacher. I'd get to work with kids! Maybe I wouldn't have to grow up. My moods swung wildly. Feelings of dread vacillated through me, poking at my numbness. I was spacey, not quite present. My brain speed was doing a kind of pulse, zooming and slowing, but we didn't talk about that back in the early Sixties. I rarely slept well, which made me weepy and added to my being spaced out. The doctor gave me a prescription for sleeping pills. I tried them, but I told him, "When I take these pills, I feel strange. You know, uncomfortable and even more awake."

"No, you don't," he said. His assertion that I had no idea how I felt, so I must be wrong, made my mother angry at me, as usual. I disappeared farther into myself. What was I? Obviously I wasn't what I thought or felt like I was. I felt quite crazy and incapable of being anything "right."

Plus I had my recurring visions, more like a slithery shade over my sight, which implied that the person I was talking to was a different person than I thought and with different intentions than I had assumed. A happy-seeming woman would become gray and threatening. A young woman would become an old, wise, enlightened being, or perhaps a cynical, even enraged indigenous person. These spontaneous visions kept me fretting that there was indeed something terribly wrong with me. I didn't know whom to ask. Now I realize that these were introductions to different lifetimes, either with that being or the influences from beings that we shared. Or they showed hidden motivations. Mostly they were warnings of coming deceptions.

But it would be many years before I cracked that code. I learned by being deceived! I had to learn to look at it consciously with my third eye, the intuitive's telescope. I did not want to be locked up in a mental hospital as Mum had so often threatened. In time, I would begin to explore the dance between nutrition and trauma, the one fracturing the other — the influences that make so many people's behavior erratic, reactive, and unstable. This was all in addition to being a creative with an urge to transform, which none of us acknowledged back then.

The interpretations of our actions were flung at us as if we were not supposed to have odd quirks. For example, my sliding visions or other reactions to food, especially milk, brought, "You are just doing that for attention." "That" might mean being nauseous or getting rashes. "How could you?" family members would ask. Guilt. Panic at the control I couldn't find or even understand. Then there was the time I was caught necking in a parked car. "How could you?" Again came the dizziness, feeling lost, such loneliness. Could it be because everyone did it?

Through my boyfriend, I found fast cars and sex; through myself, maybe through my drive to understand "how big people work," I found deep literature. The literature lasted the longest. It salved my drive for some meaning, some sense of how life could really be different. Where is the truth and where is the transformation? In the books I read extensively, I found some answers that soothed my curious soul.

But I was split. A part of me was very numb, kind of in a trance; another part of me was always in a panic. I always knew I had been different in some other space and time. I remembered some of it, though it was harder and harder to rekindle those wonderful experiences of my ditch days. What did it all mean? Why couldn't we talk about the little brown-and-black velvet me that flowed streams of knowing deep inside? She was always there, but through the years I didn't always pay attention to her. In the family, I was the disrupter. If I were a cowboy in a bar, I would be the one

22

turning the tables upside down as the pitch of the silences rose. The gap between how people felt and what they really meant tore at my body and mind. I acted out their silent rages. As I mentioned, I cried for relief; then I would burst into song.

And this, they said, *was bad. You are crazy. You are bad bad bad.* I look back and, outside of hitchhiking through Africa at twenty-one, which scared my parents (although they may have been relieved if they had known I consciously chose Africa instead of suicide), I don't think I was ever really bad. Oh, I broke some speed limits, but carefully. Oh, I had premarital sex. But it turns out we come from a long line of people who had sex! And that sex wasn't even very good, but we didn't dare ask anyone about it. I remember that by then I could not fathom bad or good. It made no sense. You couldn't talk about what was real. That wasn't okay. But you could slither around the floor as a four-year-old, being kicked by your mother because you were "bad." That was okay.

These days, many talk about conspiracy theories. Yes, there was a conspiracy. We were living it. The tacit agreement echoed itself in, "Don't talk about it." The Catholic and other religions were corralling our numbers. Today it would be like getting us to click "like" so we could be drilled and pounded, shaped by its edicts. The bullying in schools, a subject emerging globally these days, was predominant in most levels of authority in the 'forties and 'fifties. We didn't have social networking amping up its muscles, but it was there. The potential strengths of parents and folks who did not sort out their pain stayed suppressed. Women, even Rosie the Riveter, post-war, squeezed back into the corset of convention to be polite, safe, secure. So the poison went inside, into the core of our beings. Authorities of all types bullied us with shame. But it turns out I wasn't the only disrupter, as realms of frequencies that, in my view, contain human thought and feeling burst or maybe tore open the minds and expectations of so many.

It was time in the universe. The evolutionary revolution, dedicated to finding our way out of our trance of deceptions that were both personal and political, was brewing. The awakening was booted along by our Sixties' form of social media: music. "You shake my nerves and rattle my brains" — and shake we did in the irresistible delight of Jerry Lee Lewis. We saw that, indeed, "Times they are a-changin'," one of many reflections from the minstrel of change himself, Bob Dylan. Then there were the piercing and heart-ripping guitar riffs of Hendrix, the hot, gravelly tones from Janis Joplin, and gifts from so many others that burned out our inner confinements. Mahareshi Mahesh Yogi joined the transcendent scene with Transcendental Meditation, and we all got our secret, never-to-be-spoken mantras. But more about the waves of that emergence a little later.

My first two years at UBC were struggles with studying, my mother, and flailing around in that relationship with Ted. I was immature. The betrayal pushed me farther into that feeling of peering down a hallway at the world. When would I connect or belong? Or would I ever? My inner self still observed from her ancient stance. That question still pulls on me sometimes, but can be answered by deepening more and more to my ancient one, the one who had never been born nor would ever die, to connect more to being "in the world but not of the world." I knew how to talk all right, but I also knew a painful gap between talking with people while feeling a deep, aching emptiness. That gap yawns between what we try to share or dig through and what people can hear. I would hearken back to that little girl in the ditch who wondered if everyone has the little brown-and-black velvet me inside. How sweet, smart, and forever she was. Why couldn't people talk about that inner space?

I went "home" through literature courses, especially Russian and British literature with their rich, passionate characters. Vicariously, I rode the wild waves of their experiences, so often described from their deeper inner nature, plunging with their devastations, rising with their successes, and careening emotionally through the intrigue and entanglements that love and life's adventures can bring.

Long conversations with fellow students were explorations of the infinite human space as we mined and mapped glintings of the human process...profound characters painted by D.H. Lawrence, Dostoevsky, the Brontë Sisters, Tolstoy, or Herman Hesse. It was a rich, dreaming process.

I studied poetry by glazing over and holding the book in front of my chest first, then reading it. After that meditative process, the spiraling gyres of William Butler Yeats or Wordsworth's daffodils seemed to emerge. Images would light up and metaphors would sing. There was a fire inside of me, but it always seemed to be under water like a Great Lake between my passion and the earthplane reality.

I came home late one Friday, the night before my final French exam, during my second year at university. The day had been long with university classes and then selling sweaters at the Heather Shop until nine. Ted picked me up. Off we went to Vancouver's best burger joint, the White Spot. The triple O, their famous hamburger goo, dripped down my favorite purple mohair sweater from my sumptuous mushroomburger, but it was worth it. A good night kiss, a snuggle, and I was feeling good as I arrived home about eleven PM and headed downstairs to review my French notes. Lo and behold! All of my drawers had been dumped. Lingerie, papers, sweaters were strewn about my room — the huge mess tore at my skin. I threw my head back and screamed.

Mum and Dad both ran to the subterranean rec room bedroom I shared with my younger sister. Mum waggled her rage: "Your drawers are a mess! You live in a pigpen!"

My stutters were tormented. "Finals, Mum. I'm in the middle of finals."

Her searing rants shredded my lifetime of behaviors, filling the room as if with strips of audio ticker tape. She topped it with, "And, you're not leaving home 'til you are twenty-one!" Dad, always loyal, just stood there supporting his wife.

So much for living at home to save my folks and me some money. I picked up the essentials and went to bed, tired, anxious, sleepless, and hopeless. I squeaked through that French exam, but I resolved to make it through something else. Desperate for my own life, I managed to pass my third year of university, took the test for my teacher's certificate, and headed for a teaching position in tiny Squamish, British Columbia, nested in the virgin mountain wilderness destined to become the famous Whistler Mountain Ski Resort.

It was 1963, the year that Kennedy was shot. Like so many of us, I was personally traumatized by those shots that spilled Kennedy's blood all over his wife's pink suit in Dallas. It broke us out of a trance of possibility. The invincible world leader, he had seemed like the voice of possibility, an icon of youthful power and wisdom, even truth. Where were you when that news ripped through our lives? Those shots were personal.

That fall, in one of the most spectacular settings in the universe, I moved in to my own tiny teacherage studio for thirty-six dollars a month to teach first grade. The freedom thrilled me: twenty years old, reading about existentialism by Jean Paul Sartre and Theodore Dreiser, listening to Joan Baez over the PA at school in the middle of the night, playing badminton with one of my fellow teachers, and taking hits of diet pills in the endless attempt to be thin.

I had so many questions. *Who am I? Why do I still have a huge distance from myself? Why am I shaking, afraid, and so unstable? What is my life?* I knew I wasn't the same inside as outside. Other people seemed to believe that they were. *Are they really?* And, always, *who and where is God?* My questions were distorted by the diet pills, I quickly learned.

I loved my class, which was filled with busy, lively, invigorating children. But I was feverishly straddling realities, my inside observer knowing that I was as old as life itself. The outside of me was thrashing wildly, however, trying to keep focused on the demands of the world, my budget, my car, my family's judgments that had primed my inner self to take over for them (to pick at myself incessantly in their absence), and God, the Great Accountant in the sky. Also, there were hormones, those testy, little critters that incite attractions and passions. There was so much to deal with.

"Squamish?" Mum's taunting voice had been incredulous "You signed up for a job in Squamish?" My excitement flushed into worry. "Alright then, go ahead, but if you are going to live there you are not allowed to come home on the weekends. When you are gone, you are gone."

Further alienated, and oddly deadened, I said, "Okay, Mum." So I flowed around her fence—I went home each weekend and stayed with my boyfriend's aunt who lived beside his family in their duplex. Of course Mum found out. Enraged, she vented, "How could you do this to me?"

"To her?" I was exhausted, dizzy, and confused about how to be a good person, how to please her, how to be proud of my work. I was also dizzily aware and a little scared of "being different." That death-defying gap between my inner drives and how I was presenting myself externally grew even larger.

There was a tiny health-food store on Main Street in Squamish, and there I timidly first put my toe in the world of what was then called "quackery." I took notice of a few things to eat and how they made me feel afterward. Visions still swooshed through me at times. I would feel unsettled and afraid, always afraid, that I was crazy...or, worse, that somehow I was like my Mum. Interesting foods—odd breads made of things like rye grains—began to center me. Yet it would still be many years before I was confident, or maybe desperate, enough to make the choice finally, truly to center myself on the inner world, to become the real me from the inside out.

Talk about my inner world! That February, I had life in me. I was pregnant. Actually Ted and I were, but I wasn't sharing my inner being yet with him or anyone. It wasn't exactly the immaculate conception. But maybe it is "immaculate" to need to be close, to be familiar, to be loved and nurtured, and to feel possible. Ted had gone to Los Angeles for a year to work in order to buy himself a new chariot, a Corvette that he could bring back over the border. Mum and Dad had been so relieved that he was gone, hoping I would find someone with more ambition, but here he was—back with his dream car. And here I was—pregnant.

I also needed a doctor for my rampant eczema. Metaphorically, my skin was screaming as it was splitting, bleeding, always dry. Years later I learned that skin problems can be a sign of strength, meaning we don't take inner distress into our organs. Instead, the skin reflects or actually releases that angst. My organs must be happy!

My friend Elinor, a fellow teacherage resident and grade-three teacher, gave me the name of a family physician in Squamish for my skin problems. I told Dr. Max about my missed periods He conducted tests and, indeed, I was pregnant. But he launched my change from the inside out. This was truly a birthing, a turning point. Dr. Max did something I had never experienced: he, a man, actually talked with me for a time. "Who are you really?" What a question! That very question gave me something—something of myself. No adult, no one in fact, had ever asked me that. "What it is you would like out of your unique life?"

"Dr. Max, I don't want a baby right now. I can't bear the idea of marrying my boyfriend and living in his folks' basement. I don't think I could bear it." I knew that.

The rest of the questions rose like fragrances out of the overgrown garden of my experiences. He set up an appointment for me to have an abortion the next Tuesday afternoon at four-thirty in Vancouver. My classes ended at two-thirty. It would be a backroom thing with the requisite four-hundred dollars cash in my purse.

The weekend stretched on and on. Monday morning, I sent a sealed note upstairs to my girlfriend. "Elinor. I missed my period. I am pregnant."

Soon she was tapping on my classroom door. Her face looked blanched. "Are you sure? This can't be true. Not you." My nickname in the teacherage was "the nun," as my fellow teachers seemed so much more sophisticated than I was, what with my states of withdrawal, blushing easily, giggling, holding back, being wrong, and my all-around immaturity. To them I was lost and overprotected.

"It's true," I whispered, my head hung in shame. "And I just can't marry Ted." We rushed back to our classes.

But later that day, drinking tea in her suite, I asked her, "Will you please drive me to Vancouver tomorrow after school?" I told her what it was for; it was a huge request.

"You'll die!" Her huge hazel eyes were flashing with terror and compassion.

"I would rather die." My eyes darted around inside of myself, that cavernous, echoing world of fears of being wrong, of home and family, even including God who was busy hurling us downstairs to unredeeming flames. My self-esteem was precarious. I felt drained and impossible. "I can't marry Ted. He has no ambition. He reads comic books and wants me to live in his parents' basement. I just can't do it." It all felt so shabby and sad to me, or as if I were drowning. I simply had to push my way out of the mire and the relationship in which I was terrified to be trapped. I was different. I knew I had to be. What does that mean? I had to figure that out.

"Don't do it. Please. It's dangerous." Elinor cried, arguing and pleading with me. "Don't do this dangerous thing."

It was 1964. I had less concern then for the beauty of the spirit of this child, or why this child wanted to come through me at that point. We were at the brink of the women's liberation movement. I was reeling with anxiety and the familiar presence of shame that was always used to corral us in,

"Oh, Elinor." We were both crying by then. "I am so cornered. I have to do this! You know, Elinor, I really would rather die."

Still weeping, she said, "Alright, I'll drive you. Just be ready. We'll head down as soon as I'm finished with school tomorrow. I just don't like it."

That night, Ted raced up and down the road by the teacherage in his latest pride and joy, the Corvette. I'd finally told him, and he, too, was crying. "Don't do this! I'll marry you. We can live in my parents' basement."

I felt cold and untouchable. "Please go away, Ted. I can't marry you. I just can't. Please go away." Finally, I heard his Corvette's engine growl its turn as it left Squamish.

In the rhythmic dramas of my life, wonders have never ceased. In a spacey trance after school on that fateful Tuesday, I picked up papers and crayons, shoved desks around, and hung up errant jackets. Then, without warning, my great beloved friend, Divine Intervention, grabbed my belly. At about two-fifty came intense cramps, a flood, and relief—a miscarriage. More powerful than a hairdo, The Divine consistently declutches my stunned self out of fear and shame and onto greater vistas.

I learned later, as my sight and knowing emerged, that my child, the being, like many miscarried or aborted spirits, was serving my journey by awakening me. But at the time, I was too frozen in fear and shame to allow myself to acknowledge her spirit presence. I just knew I *had* to do something or drown. At times, I feel her deep, forgiving love. Her presence was to send me on my way. And for her, apparently, the journey we shared sent her on her way as well. It was a herald (Hark, shall I call her Herald!) of the approach I would take to mothering. For me, it has always been a wake-up call, always the choice of the being wanting

31

to come through. Is it to complete soul events? Even my animals have "come to me" unbidden. My gratitude grows in the light of the path they generate in my life.

That evening, in lieu of our wild ride to Vancouver, Elinor and I celebrated with steak and sweet wine. We were always dieting in those days, but this time it was the grapefruit, steak, and wine diet from Elizabeth Gurley Brown's *Sex and the Single Girl*. We giggled and chatted in relief while, in a kind of productive penance, I happily writhed with intense cramps.

My life was changed. As I recovered, a little renewed, I read greedily. Our apartments were lifted by more lilts of Joan Baez's voice filling our hearts and our heads as we commiserated.

Back I went to Dr. Magic, Dr. Max, for my post-miscarriage checkup. He continued to turn my thinking and feeling, as if on a lathe. I had never experienced anyone ever safely looking into my eyes and even my soul. He saw something there. "Life is huge. It's an adventure. You need to be who you are. Expand and love." I remember how I felt, gears changing inside of myself. I was deeply touched. I followed his prescriptions. Ortho-Novum 5 birth-control pills were the latest thing. He prescribed them as much for my hormone-driven bleeding hands and menstrual difficulties as well as for birth control. He added, "You need to meet a man who is a world traveler. At least have an affair and an adventure. And," he emphasized, "read, read, read....wonderful books like George Bernard Shaw's *Man and Superman*."

> *I had become a new person; and those who knew the old person laughed at me. The only man who behaved sensibly was my tailor: he took my*

*measure anew every time he saw me, whilst the
rest went on with their old measurements and
expected them to fit me.*
— George Bernard Shaw

I have never forgotten Dr. Max. There he stands like a
sentinel, a point of reference in my legend, when my
direction gets foggy. He gave me permission to know me
and be me. Oh, life didn't just flow on, past the guile and
shame so easily doled out to keep us in line in those days.
But he was the starter gun, and my unraveling process
began. I felt better, stronger, richer about being myself. I
remember him often — even now, fifty years later — as a
beacon. I hadn't yet learned to manage or even honor my
gift of seeing into people. Nor had I learned about the
miracles of subtle energy. But he showed me something I
constantly use today, after finally dropping my shields of
defense — most of the time, anyway: the art of really looking
at people, plus knowing that we can often be healed or
partially awakened by simply being seen and known for
who we are. Rarely spoken, this is an amazing truth that taps
innate love. His focus and words ladled out empowerment
while helping me catch a glint of the true value of being
myself.

And back to that cure-all — now that I was single, it was
time for a new hairdo! A current guru was Clairol. "Blonds
have more fun," the alluring ads dared us. Wooed, I was. I
bought the potions and soon, there I was — a blond! A blond
with black, bushy eyebrows. Well, as a blond, I looked like
a hooker, a tart, with my hair crackling and crunching under
its paperlike brass yellow. The three types of peroxide I
used — just to be sure — could have burned my head bald!
My teacherage mates howled with laughter as they saw me,

a brazen lock sticking out of my babushka, as I sneaked out of the school, darting past windows to borrow Elinor's car to head to Vancouver and have my hair dyed brown. Later, in tribute to Marilyn Monroe's famous blondness, I would hear, "Hey, Marilyn!" in the parking lots or the halls of the teacherage.

It was 1965. The Sixties had arrived, with more and more following Dylan's words while the sexual revolution perked. *Ms. Magazine* and books like *The Feminine Mystique* tore the lids off our containers. Liberation was probably what I was after then, although I didn't think of it like that.

The gap between my expanding world dreams and my self-deprecating shame pulsed. I longed for something "out there" — something I missed terribly. Belonging? Maybe it was France? I had always yearned to be in France. I had no real experience, but, dreamer that I was, living in the sensual realities of Durrell's *Women in Love*, Theodore Dreiser's *The American Dream*, more existentialism à la Sartre, some more wit from George Bernard Shaw, and several ancients texts, I grew.

The kids in my class were great, as I said, but they couldn't close that gap in me. One of my greater joys came from eating lemon-meringue pie and drinking coffee at the local Chinese restaurant, the home and business of the family of one of my first graders. They spoke no English. The whole family needed English lessons. So I went regularly after school and, right there in the restaurant, I taught English to her grandmother and father. "Catch the ball, Spot. Jump! Jump!" Guided by the pictures, we joined the old first-grade primer's stars, Dick and Jane, laughing as we all

34

"jumped" around that tiny Chinese café saying, "Jump, jump, jump, jumping." It was such fun, and the family was breaking through.

The haze of desire clouded my life. There was no going home. My longings were flamed in those winds of change. I wanted to be connected, to be alive. I wanted to be in love in an endless romance; to experience great adventures; to feel, see, and know all my senses. I also yearned deeply for some kind of spiritual connection. I read about yoga, including a couple of classics on the subject, but everything I read about the ancient philosophy and exercises seemed to demand celibacy. I had already nixed Catholicism with its inhuman sexual rules and slippery slope to hell. I did read the entire Bible from front to back, though, with a drive to know God. And I continued reading English and American literature.

My desires drove me deeply to question life and myself. Still, at times, I had a desperate struggle with the idea of suicide. But what if reincarnation was real? I explored different philosophies of life and a bigger and bigger world. I felt impossible in my own world. The world could be bigger, and it could be mine! But how? An urge rose to see places like Africa—frontiers that were huge in my fear and fantasy. Kenya, I thought. Elinor and I planned a trip to Europe together. But then she fretted, "We need to teach another year to be more secure."

"Okay, okay." I tried to accept her reasoning, but my dream dropped with a thud.

What was security to me? Teetering on the edge of life and death inside, I still knew that I somehow had to come alive. The school year was almost over. With a hearty thrust and no real credentials, I applied for a vacant position for the fall as the high-school French teacher. Maybe it could be my route to passion and to broad adventure. "If no one with the appropriate credentials applies, you can have it," the principal encouraged me. I knew I could do it, and I would be closer to a lifelong dream of traveling to France. When the degreed French teacher showed up a few weeks later, I had a brief moment of loss for my awakening wings. Kismet's plan was greater, however, as it often is — much greater.

It was my love life, not a new hairdo this time, that carried me across the threshold of change — as the *I Ching* says, "Across the great waters." A date for my twenty-first birthday was set up by new friends. And so it was that I met Steven. He was a physics major who was driving a Palm Dairy truck through Squamish twice a week delivering dairy products. I was in awe. Physics? Lordy! Wasn't Physics the ivory tower of intelligence? Shaky and scared but excited, I heated some chicken-noodle soup for our lunch meeting, trying to ignore my teacherage mates skulking in the bushes eager to capture the first wisps of our romance.

Knock, knock! I opened the door to a tall, dark, handsome man. He looked ivy-league, but casual. His clear, warm, blue eyes held a mesmerizing hint of a question in them that would last for about nine more years until they iced over in disillusionment. His smile was huge. A quirky scar on his right cheek spiced his wide grin. I was so nervous for our one-hour date. But his hands shook as he reached for the bowl of soup I offered him. Awwww. He was nervous, too. I was immediately calmed.

"So you're the Good Humor man!" We laughed and imitated the old "Third Man Theme" from the tiny ice-cream truck that trolled the neighborhood for kids. "Do do do do do...Come get your ice cream....Ice cream anyone...Ice cream on your block!" His humor was fast. He had just graduated from UBC, and at the end of that summer and his dairy delivery stint, he was headed to Europe for a world tour.

So here he was—Dr. Magic's prescription: an adventuring, revolutionary man with a wonderful sense of humor. He grabbed my hand and led me out of my narrow, defended structures.

Chapters of my life often extol the panic and tragedy of people not living into my plans, not letting me be sure of my world. But in retrospect's brilliant reframing, I feel the advantages of my losses—badly wrapped gifts—turning my life on its lathe. My spirit would fortuitously turn around obstacles to meet emerging talents with vibrancy or to release karmic detritus. I knew so little. But I was learning. And my adult life began.

CHAPTER THREE

I Want to Know What Love Is

That summer was tumultuous and transitional. The days were filled with love, fear—all the components of a lusty novel. Living in student digs together in a beautiful, classic 1920s Vancouver house, Elinor and I went through a kind of swinging-door situation, endings and beginnings with her men and mine. Ted and I did our final dance in July at a huge party I had promised I would go to with him. He drank a lot, which was unusual for him. Then he drove me out to his parent's lovely home. They were away for the weekend. My resistances melted as he wheedled and flattered me, and our love, throughout the whole drive there. Then it got crazy. I remember my panic as I dangled against the wall in his mum's kitchen, pinned in place by his large hands around my neck. As I said, I am a good watcher, and I watched, terrified, but poised inside, until he looked weak. I kicked and pushed as hard as I could. He fell to the floor. I grabbed his keys, raced down the long flight of stairs—in my spike heels—to his car, and sped out of the driveway.

I raced up Granville Street, one of Vancouver's main city streets, to the university district, but I was stopped by the police. One of the headlights was out. Ted was bearing down in his mum's car. "Please, I have to get home." I gave my address to the officer. "My boyfriend is beating me up, and now he's following me. Please, I need to get home!"

The policeman was respectful. DUI's weren't the fashion yet, but I hadn't been drinking. "Go. But be careful. Get that headlight fixed...." His voice trailed off as I sped away.

A second policeman stopped me. "Oh, Lordy, help me!" My heart pounded. Again, the same plea released me.

That scene was a nightmare as I darted down roads and alleys to avoid Ted. A bright turquoise Corvette with its "hot" engine is hard to hide, but I knew how to drive. Its turns were tight and fast; I lost him briefly and pulled up in front of the house. I jumped out of the car and ran, but the Corvette started rolling backwards. It was horror-show material: I ran back to it as Ted's mum's station wagon was closing the gap. I pulled the brake like a huge zipper, and off I dashed again. Stilettos aren't as good as New Balance or Adidas, but run I did, fast, and almost flew up the three flights of stairs to the apartment where Elinor met me at the door.

"Help! Elinor, help!" I was crying. She started smacking my face the way they do for hysteria in movies. A cold rage rose in me. "Don't ever, ever hit me," I said fiercely. "Don't ever!" I didn't know yet that the energy patterns, attractions to being hit, are established in many who are beaten as kids. I was learning...school of hard knocks? Hahaha.

We went inside and leaned against the door as Ted raced up the stairs. We had no phone. Over the balcony I climbed, awakening our neighbor. "Help, please!" She called the police for me. "We'll send a car immediately," they said. Ted was threatening to break our door down. I remember calling through the door, "Ted, please leave. The police are on their way. They will arrest you." Once I could see the flashing red lights nearing our home, I suddenly lost all emotion, and with the resilience of youth, plus a practical joie de vivre and a coldness that people experience in degrees after physical

39

abuse, I proceeded to wash my hair. After all, I had a date the next night with Steven. Oddly calm by then, even cool, I was still aware of Ted's steps receding down the steps just before the police arrived, and I was relieved. Despite his craziness, I couldn't bear that he or anyone else I was close to would end up in jail.

The next day, I saw Steven's Palm Dairy truck rolling up our road for a surprise visit on his route. His bright smile faded as he shifted down and aimed the ice cream truck to move right on past Ted's Corvette, still parked on the road, a precious relic from the debacle the night before. Quickly I leaned over the balcony and hollered, "He isn't here." He parked and up he came. We shared a fine cup of tea steaming with drama. That night, with make-up covering the bruises on my neck, I went with Steven to a sumptuous party in North Vancouver. And again my life expanded.

Our ensuing visits were rich. We talked of Steven's pending European trek and shared lively discussions about movies, dreams of our future, or the meaning of life and ice cream. We'd roar—I laughed more than I ever had with a man. "Sparkling repartee," he called our one liners and rapid quips.

One heady, sensual day, lounging on the grounds of the University of British Columbia overlooking the sparkling oceans, among prolific and fiery-colored fuchsias, rhodo-dendrons, and rose bushes, Steven asked a question that was a presage of our relationship. "Do you think there is reincarnation?"

Though we had roamed through subjects like philos-ophy and our own personal experiences, I was cautious about admitting my own vagrant perceptions. I questioned myself so much and wasn't yet ready to try it out on our relationship. Oddly, it wasn't my perceptions that worried him. It was the fact I had been raised Catholic. He'd even stopped calling for a few weeks, then returned because, of course, I am so entrancing! But that day, excited, I answered, "I do. I don't know what it is exactly...but there is something. I have always kind of known it. Even when I was little, I could remember where I had been before. You know, when I was little."

"I have always known I am going to die young," he quipped with those questioning eyes. His smile was infectious, his eyes were bright. Neither of us knew yet how much of a portent this was.

"Hmmmmm....well...I always thought I would be a lonely old lady." It has occurred to me, as the years unfold, to change that belief. And later, I would learn that loneliness is an urge to find one's true nature with all its time-released expressions.

"If I do die young, or maybe you do....If either one of us dies young...."

"And *if* we still know each other...." I remember how careful we were not to act too eager or entranced. Our words sidled around a possible commitment. "*If* we still know each other, and if one of us dies, and there is something on the other side, let's connect."

"Okay, deal!"

His laugh was always ready. "I'll tip over a lamp in your living room. I'll mess up your hair!"

I laughed, too, but then shuddered. "That might just terrify me. Let's not scare each other."

"Okay, okay. How about a tapping on the front door and then a tapping on the roof?"

"How about calling one another's name?"

We lolled on the grass. "Rooonnnnnnnnnnnnnnnnniiiiii.....
Ooooohhhhhhhhhh, Ronnnnnnnnnnnnniiiiiiiii!"

"Oooooooohhhhhhhhhhhh, Steven! Steven, come find me!

"Oooohhhhhh — tap tap tap!"

Our spirit sounds soared through the air, like scary movie spoofs. When we stopped playing around, we decided to make an official deal, listing ways we could be in touch. Tapping on the door. Tapping on the roof. The voice, too — calling one another's name, letting each of us know what the other was experiencing over there, wherever "there" was.

Throughout that summer, our relationship bloomed while I added to my Bachelor's degree by studying American and British Literature. I flipped rapidly through *Moby Dick* and other great novels, and writing essays was an enticing and rich busy-ness.

Near the end of that summer, Steven threw a party. His folks were away for a few months, and he and his brother were batching. I offered to go and get the house ready. As his dad was a minister, they lived in the church manse. The doors were locked. I couldn't find the purported hidden key, so I went up a ladder and climbed in an upstairs window carrying my overnight bag. The neighbors must've loved that! The house inside was a mess, what with two busy college boys working, playing, and enjoying their freedom with parents away. I played the classic feminine role I had been taught: I tidied up the huge mess and set everything up for the party.

Fraternity brothers and fellow physics grads arrived at the door, launching the party with the tune of "Jesus Loves Me." Their loud and hilarious mockery fascinated me as it was quite a stretch away from my Catholic world. The next-door neighbor kept coming out and shaking her mop, squinting at the action. I stayed overnight with him, which sounded so romantic and risqué, but, really, it ended up just looking after him when he became violently ill from partying. And the worst part? I left behind my favorite elegant black-lace lingerie. Later, I saw it in a drawer his mother opened, but I just didn't have the nerve to tell her it was mine.

As summer moved on, Steven earned enough money to go to Europe. After my first year of teaching, and especially after meeting Dr. Max, I ached to travel, too, and whined as Steven talked about his plans. "I wish I were going, Steven."

"Oh, shut up," he jibed. "You're twenty-one. Either go or don't go. You don't need anyone's permission." Thus came another dramatic shift inside of me, a palpable easing of something deep.

An old question still hung in the air for me anyway. Suicide is definitely not going to work to bail me out of this feeling of being disconnected, useless, so why not go to Europe? If I could go anywhere I want to, if I could stretch out and explore, why not go to Africa? Unable to talk with my folks, I needed to find something — something that meant something deep inside, something about me and my life. Steven and I made another plan. We would meet periodically on our travels and be touchstones for one another along the way.

I fantasized about a European and African tour, eventually Thailand, elegantly clad in suits and hats, carrying leather suitcases with small, elegant stitching on them, traveling on trains and boats. Huge expanses of possibility awaited.

My imaginative life always has its practical switch, and this was no different. Elegant traveling fantasies à la black-and-white movies and old novels were quickly shucked in Scotland, the first port of call, and updated with a backpack for a hitchhiking adventure that merged with Steven's. And our romance, with all its odd traits, began. We traveled together. Hitchhiking was easiest with a man-and-woman combination. It was easier for him to get a ride and safer for me. Sometimes we argued and fought over stupid things, usually over our intensities or expectations. But the commitment was there to travel, independently but together, supportively.

One day, he was walking ahead, with his huge rucksack on his back. He put his head down to read his map. Bonk! He walked right into a lamppost. He fell backward, pulled down by the weight of his pack. Talk about stupid things — this was one. I resisted chuckling as I made sure he was all right.

He pulled himself up. "Why didn't you stop me? What's the matter with you?" he tossed at me.

"Uh...uh..." No answer. I had been dreamily drifting past the old lampposts and buildings that were hundreds of years old, lost in my reveries. The argument was a no thing, typical for us

The wonders of ancient tombstones, the old castles, and Scottish family history — for example, a whole area full of Campbells (my maiden name) in Scotland, and other morsels — were a little daunted by the cold restrictions of old, stone hostels that really never did warm up, no matter how many thick, gray-wool blankets we gathered.

Then, down through England, I met cousins and aunts who looked like, walked like, and shared gestures and mannerisms with my siblings—my first experience with the language of DNA and lineage. I checked out the dates on graves, to see how old they were. Canadian civilization was still so new.

It was so damp and we were freezing already, although the winter was only beginning to encroach, and the dearth of household comforts glared. We kept hitchhiking south, lumbering and zipping along in, alternately, large or tiny cars and then the cabs of trucks through Belgium and Switzerland—where the cold was handled much more gracefully.

One ride we got was directly to Athens from...I don't remember now. I think it was Yugoslavia, where I slept standing up on a crowded train and breakfasted on wonderful walnuts that were sold through the windows of our train. Before that, though, we met another two couples who, like us, were hitching to Athens. We decided to race. We placed a little bet and off we went. Steven and I would surely win. It seemed like we had greased thumbs. Immediately we were picked up by a truck driver with a large empty truck. We had it made.

It would likely be an eight-hour ride—an easy win! Soon, however, our truck was bouncing out into the wilds, ultimately to a farm. And there the driver and others began a long process of killing cattle and loading them onto the truck. That macabre process took about six hours. We all slept in the cab, the snoring Greek truck driver, Steven, another snoring hitchhiker, and me awake through the long, chilly night. In the morning, off we went. Looking for a bathroom was interesting. In our only common language, I finally brought my toilet-paper roll out and waved it. The

45

driver, a good-natured fellow, immediately pulled over and gestured at some bushes.

Across Northern Greece and on down to Athens we went. We met our challengers almost twenty-four hours after they had arrived. Regaling one another with the hilarious shifting details of our plans, our experiences off the beaten track were worth it all.

Once in Athens, I was entranced. Something inside of me stirred, deep inside. That something was from the Acropolis. I would leave our hostel where Steven loved to swap travel stories with other travelers, and I'd hang around on the steps of the Parthenon and the Acropolis. You can't do that these days. As I say, I knew this place. I could feel the feet — centuries and centuries of feet — their action somehow carrying them to wisdom, currents of energy from their collective movement still sweeping through the stone temples. I felt so ancient and alive.

"Are you crazy?" Steven razzed me. Maybe I was!

Then, I met George. On a ferry from Piraeus to the tiny island of Poros, I was approached by him. He was an older man who was exotic enough to scoop up all the attention. "George," he said, introducing himself as he held my hand while bowing regally. My travel companions stepped back. He was much older, probably in his late forties, mustached, and very mysterious with his black cape blowing out behind him.

"You are so beautiful...." (Actually, I was pretty normal looking.) "I would like to put you in an apartment here in Athens, so you could be in my movie. Your eyes....." As he wooed me with compliments, Steven made gagging noises. My dreamy thrill made him and our other traveling friends roll their eyes. But I was entranced. I had a lurking fantasy to be seen and known, a fantasy on a par with my earlier dreams of elegant travel with matching luggage and beautiful hats. How exotic. I would love to be in a movie.

"How strangely here is mixed virtue and perversity," he wrote mysteriously and manipulatively in my journal. He wasn't quite like Dr. Max, but he did look deeply into my eyes. He could have emerged from an Agatha Christie masterpiece. I didn't swoon, but was headed in that direction when he added a new compliment: "You have the most beautiful hands."

"Hmmm...."

I looked at my hands, cut and bleeding with eczema, and quite, at this point, scarred. Just like my grand dreams of elegant travel were eclipsed quickly and practically by a rucksack, I awoke from my trance. I shook myself off as Steven and the other travelers we had gathered en route scattered the pieces of my reverie with their teasing, mocking me and the fantastic stranger in the black cape. The movie maker and the naïve Canadian traveler. I had to giggle. The ferry docked and soon our little troupe was dancing in the streets with the Poros locals, laughing about my "movie career" and my "Greek god visitation."

Talk about virtue and perversity, the overnight ferry from Piraeus to Alexandria delivered us to Egypt's ancient majesty and the lure and lore of the Pharaohs, Queen Nefertiti, pyramids, and magic. Yet we were jolted into reality at the sight of the seething slums with people defecating all around great antiquities like Pompeii's Pillar. In a huge and awe-inspiring museum, leaking water dripped steadily from the ceilings, etching holes in enormous stone statues of Pharaohs. Disturbed, it reminded me of stories of water torture. In Alexandria, the beautiful port of our arrival, the sights and smells were still and pungent, suspended in the heat and humidity—like the incense from my church days, but never wafting. The whole place was thickly sensual, beyond Athens even. I loved the warmth and sunshine. At that time, I was reading *The Alexandria Quartet* by Lawrence Durrell with the intoxicating sounds, sights, images, and emotions he wove through the lives of his four characters. Durrell's sensual poetry with its rich detail almost suffocated me as I soaked in the heady, pungent, warm air in an altered state, not sure when I was reading or experiencing.

We "did" the pyramids at Giza. We didn't go inside, although many have since our time, but we did ride three hours each way on horseback to see Saqqara, the step pyramid, with a one-eyed, sickly guide who claimed that he came from an amazing heritage related to great pharaohs. He had had bilharzia, an illness from parasites in the Nile that silvered his and the irises of the eyes of so many.

Steven and I had now added Tom from L.A. to our travel team. And Tom had been feeling sick. His fevers spiked. We all, along with a few of the other travelers we met at the U.S. embassy, as we lined up at an outside window for peanut-butter sandwiches, trooped to a clinic where the doctor told us that Tom was indeed quite ill with hepatitis. We all had what seemed like enormous gamma globulin shots, and then we waited for results. Hanging out in Port Said for weeks, waiting for a go-ahead from his embassy doctor, was fun. In the daytime we researched visas. At night we went dancing in "sheeka beekas," bars where the women were plentiful. In our scant shared language, I finally caught on that all the other women were prostitutes; otherwise they wouldn't have been allowed to be there at all. But it was fun and unique. We danced the twist and laughed. Boldly, the women would pull at my clothes to see what kind of lingerie I wore. It seemed so innocent, more of a sharing and learning. We usually laughed uproariously in the process.

We also learned to change money on the black market. I was the best at finding the greatest exchange rates for Canadian travelers' checks and striking incredible bargains in open markets. We drank copious cups of chai from vendors whose chants and clanging teacups sang out relief from the parching heat, but those promises couldn't really deliver. I had many marriage proposals from vendors as a visa to Canada sounded pretty good to them.

We planned and replanned our travels. Steven and Tom dreamed of China and the romantic Trans-Siberian Railway. I was stretching my boundaries into warmer and extreme worlds like Kenya...oh, Africa. I had some kind of soul pull to Kenya. Just the name resonated deeply in me.

Together to and from the embassies, we enjoyed three things:

1. Peanut-butter-and-jelly sandwiches in an American hamburger bun out back of the U.S. Embassy.
2. Swapping information with fellow travelers about places to go, connections to make, routes that were great, and some that weren't advisable as we waited for our peanut-butter sandwiches.
3. Exploring Visas for Russia, Africa, and China; how to travel there; what to expect, to enjoy, to watch carefully.

"You know, Africa looks darned interesting."

Tom snorted.

"Hoy!" I added, excited about my own latest discovery. "There's a ship, the Pierre Loti. It leaves Port Said to cruise down the Red Sea to Mombasa in just a few days."

"Hey, Tom, the doc says you are almost ready to head out again!" Steven said coming out of the clinic where each of us had been tested.

"And look. We can go fourth class," I added about the Pierre Loti. That fit perfectly into our wanderers' budget. Excited, we lined up for our tickets.

Fourth class was only for soldiers, however. It was basically hammocks in the hold of the ship. No women allowed. I would have to book a semi-private accommodation, which was far beyond my budget. The guys decided to go anyway. I put my head down on the café table and sobbed. It was my dream to go to Kenya and Tanzania. How bizarre. They could go and I couldn't. I was so frustrated. My dream had actually seemed so close, but now it was so far away.

I went off for a walk, contemplating my possibilities. Why did I want so much to go to Kenya? I just did. It was a soul drive. How could I earn some money in Port Said? I paced the hot, sandy shore, my mind swimming in its waves. That's it. I would get a job there, even for a short time. I couldn't belly dance and sure didn't want to prostitute, but I would find something.

When I returned to the café next to the ship's docks, by the consulate, Tom said, "We are the Three Musketeers."

"We have a plan," Steven added. "We'll add up the three fares, one semi-private and two in the hold"—they groaned and exaggerated their victim stance, rolling their eyes—"and split them evenly."

"Really? Oh! Really? You would do that? For me? Oh, thank you, guys. Thank you. What can I do in return?"

Tom chuckled. "Okay, kid, find me a woman, a single woman. Oh, and you can exchange our travelers checks, you always get the best rate."

"Okay, Tom. It's a deal."

So we three, the hot and sweaty Musketeers, boarded the Pierre Loti to head down the Red Sea. Alas! I couldn't keep my whole deal with Tom. Oh, I got the exchange rates all right, but the only other single woman was my roommate — a kind and plump Danish nun. Destiny blew the deal. So while I ate great food, they had basic slops. We were living in completely different castes, my two friends and I, and could barely connect as we went down the Red Sea to Mombasa. The trip seemed endless, but I think it was less than a week in the Equatorial heat. Finally on land, with my ankles swelling to elephant size in the heavy atmosphere and new diet, we hiked along the mysterious beauty of the steaming coast of Kenya to a campsite town called Malindi. The ocean was lined with spectacular white-sand beaches, and Tom body surfed in the waves. For a short period, we camped and lolled on the beaches and dined on fresh lobster we bought for a "shilling." Then, as often happened throughout my travels, I had an opportunity to make a little money: to run the campsite for two weeks while the owner took a trip. So I rented out the tents and managed the little café, a fun job made even more interesting by folks arriving from all over the world for short stays.

I waved good-bye to my travel buddies as they began hitchhiking the long trek to Nairobi while I shored up my finances. A couple of weeks later, my Arab boss arrived back and fell in love with my orange hair, the work I had done, and me. After getting to know me better over a good two days since his return, he invited me to be his fourth wife. By then I knew what he wanted — he would have access to Canadian Immigration if I married him. I awoke in the middle of the night to him crawling into my tent, intent on sucking on my toes. I was horrified! But his four-hundred-pound self was easy enough to push back. Right about then, good old Divine Intervention arrived again, just in the nick of time, in the form of two British servicemen in a little plane camping two nights en route to Nairobi. "Would you take a hitchiker to Nairobi?" I asked.

"Sure! Come along."

I stepped off the little plane in Nairobi just as Steven and Tom straggled into town after their weeks on the road. The caste system was still alive and well in their tales of hardships and delays.

On we went, hitchhiking, truly living in the moment, meeting great people—fellow travelers, locals, bush people—miles and adventures carving paths into our inner selves, working as we needed, moving on. Having a woman with them still made the hitchhiking easier for the two men and, in turn, they protected me. With our backpacks, hostels, and taking the cheapest routes possible, I felt a determination to keep going. The many exotic miles along the Rift Valley, seeing craters, and stalking cheetah with cameras in a game park soothed my inner pain. My rapport with places was highly intuitive. For example, I knew East Africa, as well...its beauty, terrain, and vibration. I was "at home." Something in me awakened, a presence of self and being. Africanization programs aimed at restoring the continent to its native population were pushing forward, however. My skin color looked pretty colonial—or, as they called it then, neocolonial. This was the time when the Canadians who had been setting up the armed services in East Africa and even embassy folks were being sent home. I knew I should move on.

As I look back, I recognize that I really was touring my soul's journey. I only knew it through feeling strangely at home in odd environments, such as the areas around Mt.

Kilimanjaro or roaming among the long grasses beside the roads along the escarpments of the immense stretches of the Rift Valley as we awaited rides. Drivers always picked us up. Sometimes, though, it could take six hours for anyone to come by. Sitting on the side of the road, playing hide and seek in the grasses, I felt so safe.

Steven's middle name was Ernest. And he truly was. During one of those wait times, Tom and I were sneaking through the long grasses, hiding and tickling Steven with the soft end of a six-foot grass wand. No cars or trucks had been by for hours. He turned around, annoyed. "Stop. Can't you see I am hitchhiking?"

I razzed him again. "Ernest... You really are Earnest. You are..." We laughed.

Sometimes as we waited alongside the road for the next car or truck to come along, we'd have time to wash and dry our clothes in a little stream, which would dry quickly in the sun. Majestic Masai warriors—utterly awe-inspiring— would stride out of a seemingly empty vast space. The red wool-and-mud hair gel kept their long hair organized in well-turned tresses. They would come up and fondle my outrageous orange hair and pat my shoulders laden with my large backpack. They seemed unaccustomed to white women who carried loads and certainly to ones who carried large packs. They stood around us, and effortlessly, with quick flicks of their long spears, pierced the dry, red earth. It seemed as though the spears were greased. Steven and Tom were green with envy. Nodding, beckoning, gesturing was our shared language with a few Swahili phrases thrown in: *Wopi naquendi?* "Where are you going?" Or, *Jambo, mama. Ilubuni?* "Ili, lady. How are you?" Their bodies were lithe and their gestures rhythmic. One day, again by the side of the road with the bright green grasses waving about a foot high, one of the trusting Masai handed Steven his spear. Steven grinned. He was thrilled. He flicked it airily, as he'd seen the Masai do. Bonk! It hit the earth with a thud and fell over. They all laughed. They knew it looked a lot easier than it was!

Periodically, women would stride out of the horizon, often carrying heavy bundles of wood. Dangling around their shoulders were gourds decorated and readied for carrying milk and water and the jewelry they made to sell. Rings and rings of beaded necklaces were fitted tightly all up their necks, maybe layered six inches up from the shoulders, in the unmistakable fashion of Masai women. They offered us gifts of gourds, necklaces, and elephant-hair bracelets, which were knotted or decked with glass beads. Blatantly and innocently, they pushed and pulled at me, fondled my hair, touched my pack. *Kidogos?* "Do you have children?" 'No.' Then they gifted me with hollow gourds for when I did have my children—my *kidogos*—so I could carry milk in them. They were gracious and kind, staring boldly and laughing easily. We had no fear of them.

Some of our rides brought us close to people we would never have met. One was in a huge truck. Waving his hand, the driver directed the guys to go to the back and me to climb into the front. Next stop, we picked up a young mum with two wee children. One, it seemed, was not quite two while the other was an infant. She plopped the toddler onto my lap. No question. His eyes curious, comfortable, bright, and cute, he stared up at me. He stared back at his mum. He stared at me some more. Then he moved his hand up and down my arm. His hand was so much darker than mine. His eyes widened as he kept looking, comparing, then looking up at his mum again. His curious question seemed to ask, "What's with her skin?" She burst out laughing—she laughed and laughed. It was contagious. I started, too. Then the driver joined in. That might have been my most fun ride.

A Mercedes picked us up once. Three of us, with backpacks on our knees, sat patiently in this beautiful car. My leg was pressed up against a gas can for about three hours. My calf muscle, like memory foam, kept the imprint of that can for more than twenty-four hours.

Once in Nairobi, though, the innocence of my beloved warriors was totally gone. In the city, the Masai seemed angry, even scary.

Steven had more money than I did, but for each of us, a penny saved was another mile we could go. As we traveled, we played Hearts, always for money. We never actually collected what was owed to us, but a part of the game was that when we changed countries, the money changed to the new country's face value. That meant that at times our winnings were worth a lot. Like today's instantaneous stock markets, though, they could be thoroughly devalued in a simple border crossing. It was fun.

We also had another contract: no falling in love. But in the middle of these exotic scenes, of the challenges of travel, of sleeping in grasses or on beaches or in an infrequent motel, of long hours on the backs of trucks, of absolutely relying on the courage and ingenuity of one another, I fell in love with him anyway. I felt guilty and anxious about it. There was no avoiding my love, but we had made a deal!

One day, I was really homesick and rustled through my pack, looking for a picture of my sister and her family. I blurted out, "Steven, I have to talk to you about something."

He paused his research with his maps and looked up at me from his perch on his rucksack, expectantly, that familiar query brightening his eyes.

"I am falling in love with you."

"Well," he said, "we'd better separate. I think I'll head to South Africa with Tom."

"Okay," I agreed. My heart sank, but a deal was a deal. "I need to make some money so I'll get a job here in Dar es Salaam. I will try teaching school."

As I look back, I was brave for a twenty-one year-old white girl in the heart of Africa. Or maybe it was because I was still in my trance. Such a long way from home, I felt oddly safe—in some ways safer than at home. No one here was projecting old, critical attitudes onto me...not so far, anyway. I was exploring myself as much as the new terrain. We met and were embraced by embassy folks from Canada, Germany, the U.S., and other countries. I babysat and was offered other jobs by these expats. I applied successfully for a teaching position, a seven-week term in a kindergarten (what Africans call "reception age") class. I was invited to live with some of the Canadian embassy people. Steven and Tom took off for South Africa, down past Victoria Falls and who-knows-where else.

I planned to head for India after the seven-week teaching term. Teaching was hard. The combination of bush kids and high-end embassy children was overwhelming and exhausting. Both of the groups of kids came from the higher end of their culture. The bush kids took scissors, tools that they had never seen, and turned them into tools of pounding and tearing as well as into bird-puppets. I was in awe. They rolled around on the floor in response to music and color, giggling and just being in tune with life. The British embassy kids were rather elite, sitting at their desks doing everything "right." Obviously they had advantages of reading and writing at home. I felt unable to bridge the gaps and accomplish the curriculum with these two distinct groups so I asked for some guidance. To my surprise, the headmistress said, "I wouldn't touch that class! If you are having problems, you must see the Minister of Education." But he simply said, "You are a teacher. You must teach. Good-bye." I finished my seven weeks and resigned.

During that period, I had also developed a friendship with three young men, two from Greece and one from Ireland. We played cards and explored the city. Then, as the end of my teaching term approached, an attraction began to develop between the freckled, young Irishman named Jerry and me. We began to make new plans—plans to wander together; with our hosteling consciousness, we'd tour Ireland and then possibly head across Europe to India. Or would we head across the Indian Ocean to India and then travel back? We didn't have to know yet. We were just tossing our ideas around. At that point, and still, I was fascinated by India with its gurus and teachers and extreme societies, but it was reputed to be dangerous and especially brutal for women. Still, I had a strong pull to know some of the extremes of human existence, and I also think a major part of my soul's journey was that pull that attracted me to places I knew "somewhere in time."

Life has its ways. A sudden long-distance phone call came for me from what was then Rhodesia; it was Steven. I was being courageous and independent, but I had missed him and missed sharing our adventures and explorations. "Hi, Steven. What are you doing calling? This is expensive."

"I love you," he said. "I miss you. Will you marry me?"

Without hesitation I said, "Yes. When will you be here?"

"In a couple of weeks."

Oddly disconnected and practical, I said, "Okay. See you soon. You had better say good-bye, Steven. This is expensive."

Thoughts of Ireland, my new freckled crush, my pending new adventures evaporated into the ethers where they rested "out there" in the realms of alternate realities. I periodically wonder what ever happened to Irish Jerry.

Soon, Steven and Tom and I hitchhiked north, catching a last ride out of East Africa in a Land Rover, on our way to Juba, the beginning of the Nile. I remember turning to look out the back window of the Rover. There, in all its majesty, was Mt. Kilimanjaro with its lit peak. Three giraffes loped across the road. "I'll be back," I believed as my heart swelled. Well, it hasn't happened yet. But there's still time. Soon the Nile River and our epic steamer/train trip would challenge our soft, Western ways. On barges for a few days and then trains, we careened through dusty deserts and the full length of this toxic but beautiful river. The steamer pulled into ports along the way, delivering and picking up goods. For the horrifically impoverished people in those ports, meeting the steamer, one coming from the north every twelve days and one coming from the south every nine days, was a big event. Sad, bony faces crowded the docks. One of the crowds celebrating our landing was pretty much all crippled and sick people with massive buck teeth and parts missing. I couldn't stop crying. I knew something there — an awareness far beyond my mind. What is it that hurts an entire village?

Next stop, we were back on the train again. In the Sudanese desert, our train broke down. The winds were strong. Temperatures soared between one-hundred-and-fifteen and one-hundred-and-twenty degrees. We seemed stalled on the edge of forever. There was nothing in sight through the dusty air. But then, lo and behold, there was a shimmering ball on the horizon. As it drew near, it burst into the silhouette of a man on horseback who galloped toward us as we lingered there outside our broken-down train.

His smile was broad. His missing teeth left interesting gaps. Where did he come from? I know the world is round, but to actually see the curving of the horizon and someone coming over it is still amazing to me now, but it was even more so then, as I was so used to being surrounded by the gigantic presence of the Rocky Mountains. He hopped off his steed, his diaper-like white pants draped around him, a sparkling bejeweled dagger emphatically hanging off his sash belt between his legs. Was he real or just one of my visions?

Tom coveted that dagger. "Man, I want that...."

I watched, stunned, as Tom started a bartering process through gestures. Reminiscent of the settlers with the First Nations in the U.S., he cheekily offered a piece of string. I rolled my eyes. Then he presented a series of things he found in his rucksack. His jackknife. A shirt...and on it went...'til both my erstwhile travel companions simultaneously looked at me. At this point, I was pretty scrawny; the cut-offs, which I had traded for my wool sweater with a woman heading north as we were entering hot weather, were barely staying up. My hair, always prone to bleaching, now was blaring its "blonds-have-more-fun" message. Topped off with a color mélange of brown dye and cooked in the African sunlight, I had the greatest red/orange streaked-out mop. The natives loved it. Both boys gestured at me and our conquistador lit up. Me! He would take me in exchange!

They were just kidding around, but I could just imagine galloping off forever — to what? — over the horizon, which looked more like a sandy void (dark matter, only beige?)

behind my would-be swain. I growled, clung to their arms so hard I am sure I hurt them, then bolted to sit inside the boiling train where I felt safe. Was I? I thought I was. Tom didn't get his dagger.

The train started up and soon it was another phase on the barges again. The heat was intense. When I had to pee, there was almost nothing, a tiny bit of brown liquid. My arms had crystals of salt on them. There was little or no food, but what was served was interesting — like odd pieces of meat and potatoes mashed with tiny bugs throughout. I don't know what the meat was, but we ate it. What else could we do? The *limonada* was sweet and weak, but it was wet. We were ready to drink the Nile, though we were well aware of the bilharzia from its parasites. We continued on our journey, alternating trains and steamers. Actually, steamer sounds exotic. It wasn't. In fact, it was a group of barges loosely strapped together careening along the Nile, often banging into the shores of the long river, creating mini earthquakes.

The heat was steady and fierce, so, combining forces with some Peace Corps and CUSO workers who were en route home, we created tents on top of the barges where we could be out of the sun and lie down. Our tents were made of whatever we had — sleeping bags, towels, big shirts. They looked as motley as we did, but they worked. We had all learned to innovate, to make things out of nothing. That was one of the greatest gifts of this period: knowing how little we needed to get by.

Near the beginning of our journey, at Khartoum, we were joined by an elegant French couple, who kept asking for "First Class, please." Here it was. The only first class was in the tents we had created on top of the barges! We tried not to laugh too hard. They were devastated, but soon the Fancy

Frenchies, like the rest of the travelers from so many countries, settled in with us all and even ate, with gusto, the mashed potatoes *au bugs*. At least they had been cooked.

Back to hairdos...unfeminine, unpretty, I continued to be shocked every time I passed a rare mirror. My hair was wild and, as I said, strangely orange. "Arrrgghhh!" Still the freckled kid with the wild hair looking like mischief! I whimpered inside. What happened to all my plans to travel with pretty clothes and elegant suitcases? And my world-traveler lover? What a dream! I just needed to brighten up. I grabbed my well-worn rucksack and headed to the women's bathroom, with its holes in the floor for toilets, and started my do-it-yourself elegance. I plopped my rucksack on the floor at the side of the large room near the crude mirror made of metal. I didn't look around at the other women at first, busy as I was dredging my pack for accoutrements of charm and beauty. Hmmmm, spike heels? Probably not. Eye makeup? Eye liner? Black lace bra and underwear? That would help. I stuck my feet one at a time under the trickley tap, sloshed my body a bit with my facecloth, then began my paint job.

When I looked around, it was obvious that my feeling was shared by several women in veils and voluminous black dresses. As I carefully penciled my eyeliner, they were as meticulously etching turquoise scallops around the edges of their feet and their mouths with a kind of paste. We stared at one another in appreciation. There was a camaraderie that day in the hold of the barge. It was as if we were discussing our lives, supporting one another. It was a movie scene, subtitled in our hearts and minds. It felt affectionate and was a true lift.

Steven and I dreamed and mused. "Let's get married on the Nile Steamer," we tossed back and forth. "We can sell our story to National Geographic. We can keep going, through India and then to Australia."

But, being the eldest son, Steven couldn't do that to his dad, the minister. Finally, we worked it all out. Steven would earn his PhD at UBC. He would be a university physics professor. We would have children — two of our own, then adopt kids from other places such as Africa and South America plus, perhaps, Indigenous American children from either hemisphere.

Inside of myself, I was feeling that I was being found, being designed. Later, I would be someone, a full-fledged woman in my own right. Right then, however, I was observing my being, once removed. I didn't want to give up on a life that gave me a constantly changing feast. I know my points of view had shifted radically through the stretches in thinking that were provided by my travels. I knew that I was safe anywhere and could always make my way.

I was very in love with Steven, but there was a huge part of my heart that questioned going home to get married. But I didn't feel well, not energized by tromping through ruins in North Africa. We were tired. Could I keep being inspired and continue that feeling of exploring, of finding a new country in every day, a new me in every reflection? We finally knew it was time to book a flight from Tripoli to Montreal, then hop the interminable three-day train trip across our vast country to Vancouver where we were truly going to land.

Feelings swirled in me. I was getting married. Like going to Africa, maybe it could take care of my hopelessness about life. My world quickly got smaller. There were arguments all around me about what a wedding should be like, the colors we should wear, who would be invited, my role as a fiancée or a wife. Suddenly I was in charge of all the mundane, whilst my prince charming, my travel mate, basked in his success and studies. I started teaching fourth grade. The days seemed long.

Out of the blue, or really the postal service, I received a response to the application I had made the year before for a teaching position in the international schools system: *Dear Miss Campbell, We are pleased to offer you one of two teaching positions, one in Switzerland or one in East Africa.*

I wrote back: *Thank you for the opportunity. Both places fascinate me. I am sorry though, I must refuse. I am about to be married.*

Sincerely,
Ronni Campbell

As I fretted through the details of my wedding plans and all the controversies that arose in discussions of color and style, I wondered, was this the right thing? It was, on every level.

CHAPTER FOUR

Paroxysms of Evolution

Steven received the fellowship he was counting on to do his PhD in biophysics, working on heart research studying rattail arteries for membrane permeability. I found it all rather frustrating — teaching and working hard, doing all the housework in a propelling angst to do marriage right, and respecting his learning. The hustle-bustle just seemed too much for me.

My past, with all its self-esteem issues, was pushing up into my life, and it was more than I could deal with. Here I was back in that environment again — home. Added to that was a whole different kind of adventure going on. Starting in 1965 and for the next few years, styles morphed or emerged from the sophistication of black sheath dresses and pearls for dress-up to expression in wild jeans, even bell bottoms with huge flowers on them. We were married in October that year.

Over and over again, I've learned that if we don't take care of the childhood pains — with all their programs and triggers from traumas — the disappointments that arise naturally through the years can be incapacitating. For me that was so true. I would flip out, become enraged, and find myself unable to sleep (well, in truth I'd always had sleeping issues). Sometime in 1966, I think it was springtime, I started to weep. At one point, I wept nonstop for weeks and weeks. Steven pushed me to go to a psychiatrist. I needed help, and we both knew it. I went, reluctantly. There was still a kind of stigma then, but just maybe someone would be able to be with me, be with the vagueness, the holding back, and the kind of innate confusion I had been living with, which separated me from feeling life. What my doctor didn't know, but I found out later through articles and other women, was that the Ortho-Novum 5, the birth-control pill Dr. Max had put me on, caused huge emotional breakdowns for many women. But we didn't know that—not then, anyway.

On one visit to the psychiatrist, I found myself summoning up the courage to tell him something about me. I had been hiding behind my trance, my fear of being bad, my fear of being crazy—really, the fear of being me—so I had not admitted much of what was real for me. "Dr. Stephenson," I started, "sometimes...I know...things."

A fine shiver warned me as he picked up his pen and paper. "Reeeeeeally, Mrs. Holtby?" With an odd twist of an "aha," he started jotting notes. Quickly, I shifted my words into a kind of blather. "I mean, I am quite smart, but I need more education because I don't have enough confidence to do the work I want to do." The movie *Girl, Interrupted* came out twenty years later—a movie about a young woman who was put in a mental hospital because she was emotional and too rebellious to conform. I writhed during that movie. That was my huge fear, that if people knew what was going on inside my mind, what with visions floating up and obscuring the consensus reality, they would know I wasn't okay. Okay, who is okay? Who is actually okay inside? Isn't that where our demons lurk? And how many seemingly crazy people are actually catching some of the more brilliant lights of life on this planet? And inside myself, even talking with Steven, we thought just having a baby would make it all better. As I write this, I chuckle.

While living on the UBC campus during the late Sixties and in the dynamic ferment of the revolution, I began to dabble in self-awareness. I heard that there were ways to release ourselves from our past from within. There was gestalt therapy, "t" groups (a popular forum at the time), plus all kinds of self-help and improvement meetings. Added to that was the zest of marching against the twisted dominations of authorities. Our generation was just beginning to understand their hypocrisy, and protesting and iconoclasm started to erupt everywhere we turned. I took the inner-revolution path and Steven took the outer. He didn't deal with "driveling pap," as he would call my girlfriends' and my touring our histories. Then there were those who used drugs—dropping out, turning on—and explored the freedom of sex. That wasn't us. Maybe we'd do a bit of hash, which helped me sleep. But we were sure we could change the world and bring peace to the planet... ironically, stormily!

One of the therapy styles, gestalt therapy, includes dramatic interactions with aspects of oneself. We moved back and forth on chairs—"the hotseat," it was called—as we performed roles. It unearthed huge dramas and hidden vulnerabilities. The process launched my inner four-year-old and truly undid me. During my half-days as a professor's research assistant in the chemistry department, I was drifting, childish, vague, unable to function normally. It was only a starter step to dredging my subconscious. Some of my fellow explorers were more extreme, acting as if they were babies, sucking their thumbs and whining. Others were doing primal screaming, and others were having more free sex. We wanted to help the world, to contribute, to have peace, to see the end of separation through finances or social status. I don't think it helped much.

I made enough money at the chemistry department to augment Steven's fellowship stipend. Then I got a raise. I went to see our friend Phil, a writer who kept a shoe hanging from his ceiling beside a plastic rose and an upside-down clock. He lived like legendary Left Bank literary geniuses, in poverty in a basement suite intent on writing novels while smoking strong, harsh, non-filter cigarettes. He reminds me of my fantasy for the elegant stitched suitcases and hats I thought I would feature while travelling! We all went to his den for inspiring conversation and philosophical challenge, often late at night after the pubs closed.

"Phil," I said with my burgeoning understanding of love and sharing, "here is a little money. I got a raise and my expenses are covered. I want you to have this." From my heart I offered him the money with my deep urge to contribute to the arts.

His response surprised me. "I don't need your money," he said fiercely. "Go home and spend it yourself!" Sharing isn't always easy.

The next phase of our Sixties emergence was dramatic and brave. On shaky legs, armed with shards of shattered illusions, we gathered our angers and intelligence and began to merge with rising groups to take action for peace. The Viet Nam War spiked campus attention, and most of our close friends, all male physics students like Steven, well-funded with fellowship grants, began studying North Vietnamese newspapers and our own Western world news. As the discrepancies between mass-media news and the underlying truths of dominance and resource manipulation were becoming obvious, our anger boiled. We were catching on to the realities of controlling interests. We responded: Marching. Vocalizing. Joining rallies. Be-ins. Love-ins. It was a wild and colorful time. Our uniforms consisted of jeans (to be in the worker's world!), straight hair, or wildly colored jeans and tied-died shirts—everything a statement of life, bursting free of the market constraints. And it is hard work to constantly sort through your integrity. In those days, in earnest support for the farm-workers union and Cesar Chavez's great work, none of us ate a green grape for a number of years. We recoiled at the thought. Nowadays, I am happy to gobble far too many of them, as I can find organic.

Steven joined the underground system for running draft dodgers through the PEACE ARCH border, often able to get them landed so they could set up a home in Canada. There is an old camaraderie between the U.S. and Canada since we are, as often as not, related. The underground was carefully orchestrated. We would house soldiers for three days max, and then they would move on to the next site. More and more came through our little townhouse. I cooked up a storm, and as best I could, I tried to hear them, to soothe them, but their pain was far beyond our experience. The icon had smashed for them, and they were lost and broken, not even sure that they could ever go home after running, even deserting.

That was great service. I am still proud of it and proud of Steven to be as committed as he was. What a challenge! Friends and family were divided, and some were simply oblivious. I remember odd snippets of our experiences, like coming in from my job at UBC only to see the latest guests on our tiny patch of front lawn. They had dropped acid there and were smoking pot. Lordy! And here we were a very short half block to the RCMP station! Warning. Warning.

"Hey, you guys. Get in the dang house. Get a grip!"

One hot, hot summer day in 1967, we had a hilarious experience thanks to the underground. I woke up to someone knocking loudly on our door. After bouncing down the stairs in my babydoll pj's, I opened the door.

There, in eighty-plus-degree weather, was a fellow with a fedora, brim pulled down, trench-coat collar up. "Good morning, ma'am. I'm looking for Dennis Smith."

"No one here by that name." It was a lie, but it was a part of the game.

"We got word he's here."

"Maybe last month. By the way, nice outfit. Subtle." I giggled at his obvious detective guise — right out of a sleuth movie. He growled as he skulked away, brim still down.

The Sixties activists wanted peace in the world. We were, as I said, awakening to the reality of deceptive and aggressive political forces engineering opportunistic wars, which is still going on. We were bitterly embroiled, at times ironically heated, with our efforts to install peace. Steven was studying in great detail and espousing the words and actions of Che Guevara, Castro, Chairman Mao, and other revolutionaries.

"Up against the wall!" he and his friends would say to people who disagreed with their extremism.

"Stop saying that. Good grief, you guys! We're working for peace!" I found it grueling to fight with them over peace.

Then there were the lyrics from Sixties songs — "Something happening here / What it is ain't exactly clear...Singing songs and carrying signs / Mostly say, hooray for our side" — by the Buffalo Springfield, Jimi, Janis, the folks of Woodstock, and the master, Dylan. On and on it went, awakening us with barbed and ironic messages of dissent — Country Joe and the Fish: "Be the first one on your block / To have your boy come home in a box."

We absolutely knew that if we could talk about the ills of our systems, everyone would get it and welcome peace. Not so. In my family alone, even though we were Canadian, there was a split over it all. We didn't speak for months. But, in truth, that was (and still is) my family's style. We were being angry and forceful, my parents said. We were just too young and impatient to understand and get in step with their ideals. They couldn't hear us grieve over the blindness or acceptance of the flagrant corruption. "'Twas ever thus," my dad said. That 'twas...until the Democratic Convention in 1968 when my mother, watching the violence on television, suddenly turned around. "What on earth is going on?" Shocked, triggered, she began to understand.

Steven finally got his PhD amid the flames of the revolution. After five years of juggling membrane permeability in rattail arteries for the hallowed halls of heart research, and through activism, marching, landing draft dodgers and deserters, and gathering with others for peace, he actually finished his thesis. What a relief!

Around the time of his thesis defense, his brother Bob called. "Hey here is an opportunity to change the world — a community development job! You get to help and organize natives and Métis." The Métis were originally the product of early French settlers and Native Canadians, now a huge group in northern Canada. They lived in no-man's land. Not native and not white, they were shunned by both and certainly, like most crushed beings, not able to support a quality of life with their own taxes. The job, like the U.S. Peace Corps, in Canada called the Company of Young Canadians, would be an opportunity to fight city hall. Steven and his CYC cohort Bob Parrish would work to stall the twice-yearly floods so people could maintain their little community of shacks along the edges of the Fraser and the Nechako Rivers. But we recognized that there was an agenda. Prime Minister Trudeau apparently wanted to siphon off the vitality of the revolutionaries by putting it to use in real problem areas.

"Dear God. Not this job. Please, please, please," I prayed and prayed diligently and fervently. The challenges of student life were ending and, with them, the revolution, which hadn't quite succeeded. Now there would be a promise of a new couch and a gentler life style, I'd hoped. The draft dodgers, the money issues, the dream of getting into the world...."Please God."

They—whoever "they" are—say that when our prayers aren't answered, the result is better for us. At least God thinks so. But by that time, I was sure God needed therapy. Steven was offered the job, a two-year stint, with two-hundred dollars a month for him and eighty dollars a month for me. Out of it we paid one-hundred dollars rent.

My dad quipped, "Great! Nine years of university and you get two-hundred dollars a month and to live in a slum."

Soon, there we were, once again, just as with the draft dodgers and deserters, beyond our capacities and experience. Our hearts went out to these people, especially the unceasing supply of children who, even as young as age ten, were prostituting and welfare-bound. They were untutored on the inner ambition and personal power.

I watched from our little, white house on the river as my neighborhood writhed in poverty—alcohol, smoke billowing from cigarettes and wood stoves, ratty clothes, ringer washers being hauled up and down the bumpy roads by girls in spike heels, miniskirts, and back-combed hairdos, their little ones flocking around them. Knowing the battering and the hopeless futures of their men, as often in as out of jail, violent in frustration and alcohol, I remember weeping to Steven: "We are supposed to help them build dykes, stop flooding, grow stronger. But they can't see their way out of it. It'll take a good three generations of work to get them going." I just knew. I was like the proverbial minister's wife, reluctant as I was to be there. What a challenge! Steven immediately spoke in the local style, double negatives. I was apparently my usual self. Appalled, Steven asked me to stay home from meetings as my language was too intellectual. I did. But I was confused at first. Suddenly, though, they began visiting me. Some wonderful lifelong friendships began from this unlikely group. We created so many meetings to attend. I began to teach knitting—not a strong suit, but I did it. I also taught a little about nutrition. My new friend Rose, a bright-eyed, skinny-legged redhead whose mother was the activist who had called the CYC for help in the Cache, met me over copious cups of coffee. We started commiserating about what was needed among the people there. Half of them were her relatives. Plans emerged. We were both to attend city-council and political meetings, gathering the residents of the Cache around different problems like what to do for the old or for the young, or about school or welfare. Off we went. We coached one another on the protocols of "uptown" meetings with political city-council people and "downtown" meetings with the Métis. Rose had a depth, intelligence, and deep spiritual light that surpassed many who were more socially "set." Today, I still admire her unfolding service to Spirit and her amazing consciousness as she mothered the Métis' organizations for years, helping build a strong system throughout northern Canada. And the richness of our friendship keeps growing to this day. We worked hard to help the folks there find equal footing with the uptown folks.

The rivers rose every other season. In 1971, the water filled many homes, flushing out chairs and clothing, old lamps, and other bits and pieces, to float down the street rivers. It was a huge, expensive mess. It was my first experience with major flooding, and I was unprepared for the acrid odor that took over our little, white house on the river with its dirt basement. The smell remained for quite some time afterward in many of the shacks and homes. But the local folks were accustomed to ugly, smelly inconveniences with their outhouses and taps that promised but didn't always deliver water.

Steven and Bob set up a dyke-raising bee along the river. It was a community project, like the old barn raisings. People from all levels of the city pitched in to help. I did the traditional woman's role of providing sandwiches and coffee to muddy, sweaty workers. The shoulders of the Nechako and Fraser Rivers were broadened and heightened. We were proud.

Domestic violence was another problem in our little community. It was almost a ritual by the time cabin fever took over the people — usually around January and February, dark days of cold weather and the drifting, choking smoke from wood stoves and more. Alcohol, like a torch to dried twigs, sparked fights, and women would be beaten. Sometimes even the men were, too. Our neighbor was put in jail for beating his wife terribly. But she waited and pined for him to return.

Another one of the local women also became a very close friend. This loving, smart poet had one arm missing at the elbow. She had lost it to her lover's gun and was still with him. She would show up at meetings joking, "I will be the secretary. I am the only one with a short hand." Her laugh was contagious. These people laughed easily, shared whatever they had, and supported one another even when they were battling. The fiddling champ of British Columbia lived there, as well—a part of the clans. Weekends were sometimes rich with dancing all night, toe tapping, little kids and old folks in the middle of it all. But they needed support for the frustrations that would build.

"We need a place for women to go," I stated, "to be safe, especially in the winters. They can't leave their crazy, abusive lives without somewhere to go."

I went to the city government, boldly and alone, and asked for funding for a transition house. To my amazement, the problem was recognized as real, and I was told, "Yes." With a growing number of women from both sides of the real and proverbial tracks, we initiated and set up a new transition house for abused women in Prince George. Also, I ran an abortion underground, connecting women who needed abortions with doctors who understood when their personal doctors or families couldn't help. Sometimes, I question my focus on abortions during that time, but I had been aghast to see the hard lives of so many of the kids born into squalor and low expectations. The arguments pro and against didn't, in fact still don't, include how we would nurture educate, feed, clothe, and inspire these children.

I was beginning to bloom, to feel a creative aliveness in myself. So many women joined us; they helped with our transition house, raised money, and collected signatures in support of political issues, secondary sewage treatments, and better conditions. They even sent a delegation to meet Trudeau in Ottawa to plead with him to stop the U.S. from testing nuclear bombs in Amchitka. I was sent with that delegation After we received notice of our appointment with the Prime Minister, our enthusiastic blitz enabled us to raise enough money in just a couple of days to go. I became a fixture in the mall, collecting signatures or funds for projects, so much so that when my younger brother moved to Prince George, someone asked him, "Is that your sister, that girl with long hair who is always in the mall collecting signatures?"

My spiels were apparently fetching, and I often fundraised money from right-wing folks for left-wing projects. "You are impossible to refuse," they would say. It was a small town, and faces were quickly familiar. Our profile from work in the Cache was high. I loved it—the activity, the continued feeling that we were "doing something."

Change was in the air. I hadn't become pregnant yet. Although my hormones had been under scrutiny for years, it turned out to be Steven. He was so hurt and horrified. We put our names in for adoption, which we had planned to do since our African travels.

But I was so busy, finally so alive in my own work that I wanted to take our name out of the adoption process. Steven was busy with strange hours and travel in his community-development passions. I knew that if we had a child, Steven would still be busy, and I would be reined in, doing more of the domestic role. During that time, I also appealed to the Leaders of the Company of Young Canadians for a support organization for wives of workers. We were often on our own while our husbands were "in the minute"—on duty or call, traveling, or being supported by mentors. We ran the home front, usually with a dearth of money or comfort. One of the mums in another zone had become so depressed that she attempted suicide. I jumped into action, wanting to develop a support group for the spouse supporters, but there was little interest from the organizers. As far as my own development went, I already felt stifled and self-deprecating enough to question everything. My growing projects were bringing me to a turning point, a new strength inside of myself. I knew more domestic engineering while Steven was gone or "busy" would crush my new drive. During a three-week camping trip, I worked on him, enticed him, begged him, and cajoled him. He was heartbroken, but finally he relented and agreed to remove our name from adoption. He was so dedicated to the greater good, he didn't even want to use the resources required to have our own washer/dryer arrangements or to be consumers at all. I knew it would be quite the challenge for me, both inside and out.

In the final half-year of our program, a number of major events happened. First, as we drove home after our camping trip, back into the little community on the dusty dirt road alongside the river, the kids surrounded our car yelling, "They have a kid for you. They have a kid for you!" Steven whooped while I went inside and hid in the bathroom, head in hands, knowing I was in for it. In a few weeks, we met a little native girl named Naomi. "Well-adjusted," the officials said. "Happy."

And in three more weeks we were parents. She was a strong-willed, beautiful child. We met among a gaggle of tiny residents in a receiving home in Hazelton, British Columbia. My heart changed as I met her. We had been told she was three and a half. When we met her, we found out that she was five and a half. "Uh, oh. This could be hard!" I said. But how could we refuse this little one with her huge, wooing, "pick me" eyes?

We bought and moved into a small house in town, just in time to bring her to her new home. I quickly fell in love with her, but was also resentful that my expansion could be short-sheeted now.

Second, the New Democratic Party came into power in British Columbia. Third, the women's group found a location and funding for the transition house. In February, as the bitterness of cold, northern weather was still clamping down on Prince George, the transition house was installed to catch the victims of the fury of cabin fever and alcohol-fueled rages.

Fourth, Steven was promoted as the Director of the CYC for Northern British Columbia. We would have a real income! And with that, we were moved to Victoria, the capital of British Columbia, along with a flock of idealists like us— rebellious, young, intelligent, keen on making a difference.

Oh, just like during the Sixties, we knew we would make a huge difference. And we, the four of us—by then we had added a Métis teenager, Janie, to expand her opportuni-ties and for her to help with Naomi—arrived in Victoria when the flowers were already doing their luscious spring-time dance.

Our time in Prince George had been rich and productive. Although the people had all pulled together for the dyke project, we ultimately lost the battle. Soon after we moved to Victoria, another huge flood came that was too costly for the city to bear. The Cache was bulldozed, its little community scattered, finely sprayed to various neighborhoods of Prince George. The goal was that the squalor would be spread out, thinned out, among the many flavors of life in that city. A few years later I returned. Like the great ditch in which I explored other realms as a child, or like layers of civilizations in Egypt and Israel, around the world, it is totally gone now. In spite of all the depth of our experiences there, our little, white house is also gone without a trace — footprints of the great strides and bubbling times of organizing possibility for our little community lost, as if to the sea.

We were so happy to be back down south, still working toward what we considered would be idealism, following our revolutionary times from the Sixties. But I was frustrated at being a mum figure, especially being almost a single mum. Janie didn't last long. She missed her roots. I loathed the idea of ever being a single mum, and this would be preparation for two intense stints at that very role. Karmic, you might say — there was something I had to learn here.

Steven was the Caucus Executive Assistant with twelve-hour days, after which he headed straight to the pub. Like many of the other women, I was on domestic detail. But no grass grew under our feet: we set up co-op babysitting, women's ministry meetings, consciousness-raising groups, and fun times. Once again life was busy. That was a time in my life, and perhaps in the British Columbian government's history, that contained some more of the most vital women I have met in my many years. My confidence flowed in and out, but my determination to be active prevailed.

When our little Prince George house sold, we decided to buy in Victoria. Steven was away when I found our home — a traditional, 1909 Victorian three-story house. Its wood pillars were huge, square oak. From the beveled glass windows, some high, some octagonal or rectangular shapes, slid spectral illuminations of daylight along the walls and across tables, chairs, and our old, tatty couch. I loved the hugeness of shapes inside and out of this house.

The woman selling it chose me out of three offers that came in. I wanted to include some of her furniture, such as her piano and an oak table in the deal. As we bargained, she said, "My dear, if you are ever widowed, you'll know that money doesn't matter. I just like you." Interesting.

We moved in, settling Naomi in her new room upstairs, with the ceilings slanted under the roof. There was another room up there, an enormous space that I called *my* room. Its door was closed and hard to pull open. Entering was like stepping into a vaulted place. Stretching myself out to fill this wonderful space, this niche of my own, I dreamed of writing in this room.

As Steven was usually gone with the legislature's demands, especially on travels to meetings, and I was still quite the insomniac, I would watch television in the room we had anointed as the TV room. Often, I heard footsteps come down the long staircase from the upstairs floor. I checked. All was well—no visual sign of anyone.

Around that time, I started going to monthly "tea and a reading for seventy-five cents" gatherings at the Victoria Psychic Society. At first, I would walk up to the meetings, which were just past the legislative buildings, alone. Just the comments that I had a great smile and "eyes to see if I would use them" were uplifting. Eagerly, I included my friends in this secret until, soon, so many were going that I could barely get in.

We started to have gatherings at my house, bringing in Ouija Boards and tarot cards. But then came a strange learning curve. The Ouija Board would carefully spell out a name, "Archie." Archie had been the owner here; he had retired, then subsequently died in this house he loved. There were other names, as well. We chatted with and challenged our Ouija friend. I would ask it questions, but when it moved too slowly, cheekily I would chide it: "Oh, come on, Weeeeg." Apparently Archie or whomever didn't like my attitude. It started to be creepy. Odd. A bit scary. One day, as I entered my living room where two friends had their heads bent over it as it spelled out their answers, the planchette fell off the board. After several more times like this, it wouldn't work if I came in to the room at all. Then it would fall off if I even considered going into the room. My women friends were panicking. Feeling a warning of sorts, I strode into the room, grabbed the lettered board, and after saying, "I'm going to take you over my knee," I did—I cracked it over my knee. The last thing we needed was to be infested with crazy influences. But we were learning more about reverence and choosing higher spiritual resonances.

Over time, other things also began happening: Steps from upstairs creaked all the way downstairs, then back up again. That heavy door to my upstairs room would open, then close. The couple that were living here had wanted this house for their retirement, and Archie obviously was still refusing to give up that dream, even though he'd passed over. My brother, who doesn't love the occult, was visiting on one occasion, sleeping up in that room. The next morning, he shot out of our house. I found out later that he had heard Archie. The door had opened and closed. The stairs had creaked with each step. It was too much for him.

Alone at night, I actually enjoyed Archie's sweet, kind spirit. He comforted me. Naomi always slept well there and never commented on it at all. I don't think it was an issue for her. I liked him and he liked me—that is, until I challenged him a bit later.

Some of our fun times there were like period pieces. Several of the women, including mothers of Naomi's friends, and I would get together and have afternoon tea in the old-fashioned British style. The charms of Victoria made the setting perfect. Dressed up with flowered hats and flowing clothes, we sipped sherry out of tiny glasses, poured steaming tea into bone-china cups with forget-me-nots, roses, and old villages on them. I remember Naomi peeking around the corner, looking at us, and turning a finger around the side of her head. "Are you okay, Mum?" Our kids thought we were crazy. But then kids often do, don't they?

One day, under the tutelage of my opera-singing friend Pat, we all made ourselves up to look old—eye liner marking all our wrinkle hints, skin tint over it all, and blusher. We truly aged forty or fifty years and acted like it. Even getting to the phone in those pre-cellphone days took so much longer in that role. Around that time, Steven returned from his latest trip, and we decided to age him. It wasn't possible. His face would not age. He had wonderful laugh lines and many natural etchings on his skin, but no matter what magic we wrought, he just didn't look any older.

"Oh, Steven, you're no fun," we teased him, unaware of the message he was sending us.

He tried to play with us, and finally he said, "I'm just exhausted."

One summer day a few weeks later, Steven and I met for lunch in the heart of Victoria. It was one of those beautiful-sundress days. I felt all glowy and in love as the waiter served our salads and filled our wine glasses.

But we were at a new turning point. "I have to talk about something," Steven said. "This job is killing me. Chairman Mao himself couldn't change this government. It's the machine...the machine runs everything. We have to move."

My tears seemed to spurt. I was very active, as I said, in women's groups, with consciousness raising, organizing cooperative babysitting, and always doing things for the kids. Plus I was playing with the occult, including receiving messages from the unseen. All of this was with some of the most wonderful women friends I have ever had — and all within walking distance in my neighborhood. I was emerging yet again.

"What do you want to do?" I asked, brushing my tears away.

"Union organizing. Union organizing could give me some power to make a difference. At least they are truthful. They try to help the people. This is just phony bullshit."

"Do we have to move?"

"The union offices are on the mainland." He shrugged his assumption that the move was essential.

"But...." My heart sank. Yet again, I was just beginning, launching new connections and new possibilities. Vancouver had a terrible vacancy rate at this point. But I flashed on an idea. "Hey, Bridget, our old Prince George friend must be almost done with her Masters! Maybe she is leaving her rental in Vancouver!" My intuition was right. She was! Bridget and her four children were heading back to Prince George, and we could take over her rental. Once again, we would be near our friends.

A few days later, we were sitting at a restaurant with several couples who were a part of our political family. Steven called Bridget's landlord to confirm our connection. The landlord hadn't raised the rent for a long, long time, so the rent he wanted was higher than our friend had paid. Steven flipped with cocky panache. Ever the political wizard, he was on his proverbial white horse, charging his steed through the political mire. "I can't, in consciousness, accept such a high rent rise."

The landlord said simply, "Fine with me." And we were without a place. I was on the search again. The Universe was a bit more obtuse then. It took me a long time...for some things. Within a few weeks, thanks to a dream I had, I saw that he was having an affair with one of the women who had been in our lunch group that day. It wasn't until after his passing, after our move to Fraser Valley and the loneliness of a new and isolated world, that I realized the truth of his "cocky panache" that day. He had to show her what he could do—the power and political integrity he had.

I was still identifying my success with being married as well as with Steven's dreams, even his political aspirations. Oh, I did my own organizing, philosophizing, mothering—gathering women around our needs, from our children to our politics—but I was defining myself and my success through him. I loved him. I saw myself married for life. I hadn't yet recognized myself, hadn't had my self-actualization yet, not to mention the awareness that I was a transformational being.

Our old, haunted house, Archie's house, sold immediately. The final weeks there were wonderful party weeks touting our move back across the great waters again. One of the celebrations was James Bay Days, a festival in the park with people drifting around selling goods such as art and jams, musicians playing, and people dancing, milling, picnicking, and just saying hello. The winds rustled through the trees. Trees and shadows seemed attuned to the rhythm of the fiddles. The day was sunny and wonderfully warm.

Steven came along with Naomi and me, a rare delight. Everywhere we walked, people came up to us to say how much they would miss Naomi and me. They thanked us and said how much they appreciated all I had done. I floated on a raft of recognition, enjoying hugs and laughter, story swaps, and the children running around.

Steven looked at me with curiosity. "How on earth do all these people know you?" He had no idea about our lives, he'd been so busy.

When I bought Archie's house, Steven was away. And when we sold it, he was away. Then when it was time to pack up, he was away again. For my last night there, a friend invited me to spend the night at her place. Naomi was doing an overnight with her girlfriend.

"No, thanks. I love this house so much and want to spend the last night here. Plus, the cat's fleas are a bit much. The flea fumigators will be here early—eight in the morning." Our bedroom was at the front of the house on the main floor. So I worked on sorting, packing, schlepping, sorting, packing, schlepping 'til finally, I fell into bed, exhausted.

That's when *it* started. Noises. Scratching on the walls. Sounds—crazy sounds. At first, I could ignore them, but soon, about midnight, I was losing my mental balance, becoming very frightened. What would happen next? Footsteps went up and down the stairs. The scratching grew louder and louder. I was used to Archie, but now...was I losing my mind?

I bolted my bedroom door as I began to panic. What a difference that would make! I laugh now. Then, as the racket built up, I frantically climbed out the bedroom window and, in my yellow nightgown, ran across the road and down a path to Marnie's, a numerological wizardess, the mother of Naomi's best friend, and one of mine.

We were both stunned by Archie's — we were sure it was Archie's — objections. The next morning, in time to let the deflea-ers in, I ran up the path between apartments again. The doors to the under-the-house parking, doors that took fierce muscle to open, were wide open. Lordy! Had we had a burglary? How could that happen? With trepidation, I skulked throughout the basement, then around the boxes and jumble upstairs, but it seemed that nothing had been touched. Even the fleas were still there! Later that day, I called the Victoria Psychic Society, and the woman explained, "Archie is distressed. You are moving some of his favorite furniture, old books, and other things that he had loved, plus taking away so much activity in his home. He doesn't want you to leave and is getting your attention any way he can. He means no harm. He just wants to stop this evacuation."

But I couldn't stop it. I was on a mission. First, let's get the fleas evacuated, followed by our family. If I knew then what I know now, I would've set up a ritual to help Archie go to the light, but I didn't have that knowledge yet.

As I mentioned, the Vancouver vacancy rate was very low. But it was my job to find a rental as Steven, with his typical magic, was indeed hired as a union organizer. After a lot of pounding the pavement, staying with friends, seeing dozens of places that couldn't work, finally, we found one about thirty-five minutes up the freeway from Vancouver, in idyllic Fort Langley. We moved just in time for Naomi to start a new school year.

We had some rollicking events there. Friends came from the city and stayed overnight as we sang and danced and partied. Those were the fun times, but our old friends were too far away for quick get-togethers. Steven, Naomi, and I gardened, biked, and toured around the countryside, but he was gone—a lot. When he was home, I was often edgy and defensive with him. My brain speed was still off the charts, which I didn't quite understand yet. And my old, nighttime friend insomnia was a frequent companion. I was aching in loneliness and the feeling of not being involved any longer—a familiar feeling to my inner self. Again, I was lost inside. Who was I? That gap ached in me and wouldn't go away no matter what the setting.

Naomi had had a rough time of it in Victoria. But she managed to find some of her own grounding in Fort Langley, attending the second grade, living more in nature, and joining a Brownie troop. She earned badges and had sleepovers with her new friends. I look back and see that that time was almost okay for her. I had an arrangement with her teacher for the times that she couldn't handle life. Periodically, I would receive a frantic calls from her teacher: "Mrs. Holtby, she is gone again." I would go over to the school to find her. One day, she was in a garbage can with the lid on. Another time, she was riding the free Albion Ferry, like a Huckleberry Finn act, all afternoon before we caught on. One day, she picked up her entire desk and hurled it across the room. The teacher admitted, "She terrifies me! I have nightmares about her."

When her pressure was too much for her, one successful response was that I would take her out of school, and we would ride our bikes ten miles or so to buy farm eggs or even just two miles to the supermarket. To inspire learning, I had her weigh and measure the bulk veggies and fruits. She planted seeds, grew carrots, pulled weeds, and cut flowers from the garden to decorate our house. I wanted her to learn as much as possible even outside of school. We both took piano lessons, which was a blessing—even scales were soothing. Naomi and I were growing, sometimes very close.

In retrospect, I see that I was angry with Steven, torn by my commitment to him and my search for myself. While the three of us as a family did have some great times together, the times with just Naomi and me were the dominant focus. I rued living my domestic role while Steven went on to a more exotic rapport with a full life as a union organizer. Naomi was difficult, but it was easing a bit. I was still writhing with self-judgments and anxieties about who I was, plus the challenge of handling a complicated and rebellious child alone. I was resentful and discouraged and emotionally unbalanced. But I did think it would get better. Steven didn't believe my reports about Naomi's disappearances: "You are just too dramatic!" He was so happy to have a native child, and he displayed her photos proudly. And I, always self-challenging, believed him—that somehow I was making up the problems, the disappearances. It was the old question, did I see what I thought I saw, did I experience what I thought I experienced? Those were questions I would have to answer soon enough.

Yet, there were ways in which Naomi was growing more and more stable, learning a great deal, doing well at school in spite of it all. Life seemed to be "coming together" for her...and for us.

In our idyllic location, Jackson the donkey was our closest neighbor. We loved feeding him each day. In those days, I also enjoyed looking after the lawns and garden, but my resentments burned some of the underpinnings of my relationship.

The Christmas of 'seventy-four was shared with my entire family. It was a lively, fun festival, judging from my tour of the photos some forty years later. Na and I played carols on the piano—maybe not as well as the family maestro, my sister, but play we did! Everyone sang. We were all loved and enjoyed by everyone that Christmas.

Steven noticed he had a lump in his testicle and would have it checked after the holidays. That was truly the death knell of the life of our family.

CHAPTER FIVE

Death Is a Birth Canal

The next sixteen months were earthquaking steps into Steven's passing. He underwent surgeries, chemo, craziness. I recognized his lover, intuitively, from my dream. She was a woman from my consciousness-raising group. It must've been payback from tryst I had made a few years back with a friend's husband! We'd played guitar and sung together while our spouses argued politics vehemently. That process ultimately did raise my consciousness, but it took emotional work to get there. I tried to steer my ship through these turbulent waters, but I was undone.

His treatments stretched into a very hot summer. My piano playing was a balm for me, even just those soothing scales. One of those hot nights when Steven was lying in bed, high-speed fans aimed carefully to cool his radiation burns, I was playing songs by John Denver. "I'd like to share my life with you / And show you things I've seen...." Suddenly, I knew that with all the "hold the hope in your heart" we were instructed to keep, all the efforts we were making, it was over. No matter how I had resented him, or was mad at him, I loved him. No matter how much I hoped and believed otherwise, I would lose him and my life — and really, the entire identity I had propped up on our marriage.

I dissolved in tears, sneaking out to the front stoop where I could let my pent-up tears flow. I wept and wept and wept. Steven came outside and gathered me up in his arms the way he used to. "I'm sorry. I am so sorry." His voice so soft. "I wouldn't do this to you. I love you and always will." We both rocked and cried as the tendrils of our shared world dissipated. They had to or we would have torn one another apart in all the heart-wrenching, unfolding drama.

My feet were hot and swollen that summer. I hadn't yet learned that that meant trouble with my adrenal glands and a need for pantothenic acid. That would come to me a couple of years later when I looked up hot feet in that amazing nutritional bible *Let's Eat Right to Keep Fit* by Adele Davis. But one night, I had a mystical healing experience with them, lying on our bright, red couch, feet perched up on its arm, pulsing in pain. I prayed, "Dear God, I can't bear this. Please help me!" Suddenly, the apparition of a woman, obviously from India, appeared. She was wearing an airy sari. With a motherly motion, she flapped a huge piece of cloth, like a thin bedspread, light blue with tiny white flowers on it, a kind of etheric Wedgewood cloth. As she waved it over my body, my feet cooled down and my entire being was soothed. I felt so lifted and loved. I popped my eyes open to see her, to hold on to her, but she disappeared, evanescent. Yet I knew something now: I was protected. I softened and felt grateful.

Our trips to the cancer clinic in Vancouver increased. Too often, we were on that freeway heading to the hospital for treatment. So we moved again to be closer, this time to a townhouse in East Vancouver. But then shortly after, more changes ground up our world. Steven's anger grew, and he moved out to be with a different woman. He pushed me away and wouldn't speak to me at all. He forbade the doctors to give me any information about his progress, results, anything. They complied. The patient was always right.

Steven was often irate. I swear that chemo, at least in those days, makes a lot of people violent. I continued to be there at the cancer clinic for his treatment times, sometimes sitting in the sun in the parking lot, working on my reports for the Government Task Force on Women in Engineering and Allied Trades. I was also reading *On Death and Dying* by Elisabeth Kübler-Ross, which had just come out. A friend had sent it to me, and it helped a great deal.

One day, two older ladies, sisters-in-law, quite fragile and sensitive, were awaiting their husband/brother. I have always attracted people who need to talk, and this was no different. One of them, tiny, softly wrinkled, and delicate, approached me. She started to weep. "I am so confused. We have been married for sixty-five years, and suddenly he beat me with his cane. He hit me! He has never hit me or anybody else!" She wept as her sister patted her arm.

I shared what I thought I was understanding at that point. "You know that the cancer treatments make them crazy. They aren't themselves. I think it's all the chemical stuff....I know he still loves you. He is literally out of his mind!" At that point, I myself had broken ribs.

My moments of sitting in the parking lot, strangely enough, were a rich source of support. Thank heaven it was warm in Vancouver that summer! As fall approached, I tried to keep Naomi's life balanced with Brownies and another new school, but it was hard. I was weighed down inside as if I had swallowed buckets of sand. I couldn't feel a balance. My whole life was falling like the autumn leaves, in a flurry of betrayals. As I said above, there are many, many spiritual benefits of betrayal that usher us into our spiritual awakenings. I would reap their rewards over the next ten years of my life. But back then it was too soon. I was quite crazy, vague, moving in and out of connection to life as it rolled by me.

Poor Naomi. I couldn't sleep, was anxious, couldn't be the strength she needed. She also became more and more spaced out. She roamed farther and farther. Several times, at eight and nine years old, the police brought her home late in the evening. "We found her hanging around at the 7-Eleven." I was panic stricken. When I called Steven about it, as usual he chided me for being dramatic. Again, I assumed he was right. I was pretty crazy. He was gone and cold. And I am, indeed, genetically predisposed to drama.

I took Na to Montreal for Christmas to be with friends and avoid the heart-wrenching normalcy of the festivities. When we returned, I was told by some of my close friends that Steven was in the hospital, with his chemotherapy treatments amped up. So no matter what the circumstances of his love life, or even my own, I swallowed my pride and went to visit him. My visits were either sitting through icy, staring silences or, at other times, very funny. He would be happy to see me, laughing and quipping with me in our old sparkling-repartee style as if we were old friends.

"Hi, Iggy," I said one day, entering his hospital room. Twig-like hairs were sticking out of his scalp, which had been thoroughly denuded by the treatments. It reminded me of Iggy in the old *Nancy* cartoon. We both laughed. I didn't talk about our domestic world.

When he heard I was dating, he wept. "I hear you are dating a really nice man." So should the "nice man" I was dating have wept. I look back and have such respect for him, humbled by knowing how kind he was as I put him through all this extreme drama.

Soon after Christmas, a friend told me that Steven was coming out of the hospital again, and currently was looking for a room to be near Naomi and me part of the time and near the woman he was dating in Victoria part of the time. Our good friends, Marianne and Cliff, were moving out of their sweet, little, cottagey, old house in Vancouver in the Dunbar area, my favorite. I was planning to take over their rental. The house was small, but had lots of windows, a fireplace, and best of all, one southern-facing bedroom— which could catch the most of that elusive sunshine in the often-gloomy climate.

I might be dramatic and sensitive, but I am also faithful and courageous. Off I went to the cancer clinic. "Steven, Naomi and I are moving. You are welcome there if you would like. There is a south-facing bedroom that you can have if you want to come home. But I can't handle you going back and forth to another woman. Take your time and think about it. I promise I won't touch you." Touching him had been an issue for him a few months back.

"I need time," he said, ironic for a man with little time. "A week. Okay?" His eyes were bright and thoughtful. I couldn't call him Iggy any more. His hair was growing back thick and curly and vibrant, and he looked handsome but scrawny. He had lost a tremendous amount of weight.

It was only a few days later when he called. "I want to come home. I want to be with you and Naomi. I want you to touch me. I want us all to be together again." Very often during this period, I just didn't know how to feel. It was a little late for us, but deep down I still loved him.

The move was easy thanks to friends, borrowed trucks, laughter, and antics. These people had known us since our days of "Jesus Loves Me" at the manse and throughout the mires of all our adventures. I was so grateful that we would now be near some of them.

That first night back, while Steven was ensconced in our upstairs bedroom as I packed up the townhouse, Naomi went missing again. I didn't want to tell him and start the old "You are just being dramatic!" I felt crazy enough in these experiences—like, "He must be right—what I saw wasn't there, what I experienced wasn't real." Interesting how much had I used external judgment and fear, other people's opinions, as a guide—a guide to suppress me, to keep myself away from my own knowing. I would learn, though, and eventually I would step through that fire, make my way in the world, seeing and hearing what isn't actually there in 3D. Meanwhile, the call of the Universe challenged me into being true to myself, and that included being dramatic.

Close to eleven that night, the phone rang. The police had found Naomi, who had just turned nine, hanging around the 7-Eleven again. They were bringing her home.

This time, Steven heard me on the phone. He called down from our bedroom. "It's true, isn't it? She has been running. I am so sorry. So sorry. Over the last year I've seen lots of different mothering styles." Almost as a benediction, he added, "You are a good mum."

Soon there were more hospital visits with long waits in the hallways on cold, metal chairs while he went through tests and chemo. He had given permission, so I was now privy to all the latest information as well as details of his body functions—it went from nothing to "too much information."

One day, as I was sitting in the hallway with a couple of friends, several white-coated doctors came rushing down the hallway. "Which one is Mrs. Holtby?"

I stood up. "Here I am."

"Follow his every whim. His chances have dropped to about two percent."

They turned on their heels and left me in their cold wind. I had no feelings at all. The drama, each chapter held in hope, had already been too much for me. I couldn't stay aware of my own feelings. I likened it to hitting my thumb with a hammer. First, the numbness. Then, the riot of pains. Too many, too much.

"Okay, thanks." I think I whispered my response, as they weren't going to hear me anyway. And what did it mean to follow his every whim? I thought back on his moving in and out of our home, flailing in his own way, being heroic at work in the union, going off with other women, or leading our political circles. What other whims can I follow? I thought of me showing up at the clinic, questioning what I should be doing, chasing Naomi down, smiling so people wouldn't reject me in their discomfort, trying to act happy, which in retrospect looks pretty loony. Actually, I was outright crazy and would be for years.

My own family had a hard time tolerating my life. One day Mum said, "All we have done for you, and you are going to be a thirty-two-year-old widow." She stormed away. My dad just avoided me. And of course I was still belaboring being "bad." But Steven's dad, Gordon, would come and sit on the couch with me, just holding my hands. He and I had some kind of special closeness, for which I remain grateful today. He actually died on my birthday some years later, which I took as an honor.

I also had some great support, and two of my most supportive connections were my dear friend Pat and her mother. Pat's mother was in AA. We could sit at her table and drink coffee and talk about anything, admit anything — light or dark, laugh, and simply be. I admired Mrs. Sturdy who had traversed a treacherous route through alcoholism and found a path that helped everyone around her heal. It was a balm to sit around, sip cups of coffee, and either laugh or cry, being real about our challenges. It was healing to sit among others who were experiencing their oddly wrapped gifts of experience, too.

We moved to the little cottage on the edge of Vancouver's Dunbar District. Close to longtime friends again, I briefly felt more at home for the first time since Victoria. My brother-in-law, Ernie, came to visit and convinced Steven that going to Maui would be good for him. I was horrified. I prayed he'd say no. And like a number of major turning points in my life — the job in the Cache, adoption, and so many others — my prayers weren't answered. I was so afraid he would die there, and then what? How would I handle that? But Steven, vaulting from our rucksacking mentality, ordered first-class tickets, and off we went. There we were, on Maui. Friends had set us up in a soft, rainy section, which was too familiar and dour for these Vancouverites. We moved down to the beach. Super skinny, with eyes beyond bright and wildly curly hair now, he spent the days with a flask constantly in hand, swigging Brompton cocktail, a brandy-based mixture of cocaine and morphine, for his pain.

We had some sweet times. He would reach for me — my long-held dream — but I recoiled at his emaciated body with its terrifying, pungent odors, especially from his colostomy bag. Two sensitive, mutable, and bright personalities ran through strange reactions: Anger. Sadness. Reaching for one another. Anger. Fear. Snapping at one another.

"I am not dying this minute, so don't get all enthusiastic."

I curled up inside. Would I think that way? Be brightly enthusiastic if he died?

"But if I do die, I want a party. Not a funeral. And no somber black. Tell our friends, too, to dress up and be bright." And on went the list of instructions. "And I want a feast. Dozens of grass cookies, wine and beer, great food, the Rolling Stones and Beatles music, Eric Clapton, Van Morrison...."

Then he'd playfully threaten me: "If you don't, you know I will be there...."

On Maui, I took two hours a day in our little rented car to roam and explore, to offer Naomi and him an opportunity to be together, and to give me a break. Also, Na could learn her math with her dad. Those times were often a wrangle. She fought him tooth and nail. I would return to both of them either sullen or angry, glaring at one another. Both easily agitated, his temper met Naomi's resistance.

Prowling for the freshest food I could find and some kind of balance inside, I then cooked and fed him healing vegetables and fruits. I kept a smile plastered to my face, which I'm sure looked manic. Actually, it was. But I was so worried that people would reel back from me and from Naomi. That smile cinched a kind of madness.

Then the nightmare: he ran out of Brompton cocktail, his elixir of pain relief. And here we were in a different country — a country that was world famous for its costly and privileged medical care. It took me two days of making connections and following referrals — questions, questions, Maui, Canada — as I asked for a refill for his potion of brandy, morphine, and cocaine. Finally and magically, the answer came from the Maui General Hospital. I met the second doctor in my life that was a Divine Intervention. He truly gifted me.

This doctor met me at the pharmacy and handed me my prescription. And like a true doctor/healer—or maybe an angel—he soothed and empowered me. Sitting together, on a bench under huge waving palms, he asked me for my story, heard my confusion and sadness, and told me about himself. He had had a large practice in New York. But, "Science has considered death as a failure. I couldn't handle it. So I chose to come here to Maui where they prepare for coming death as they prepare for a wedding. Songs. Food. Prayer. Dreams. It's natural—a natural evolutionary transition."

I felt seen, known, heard, inspired, and strengthened. I paid for the fiery potion, but the heartfelt words and hug of this wonderful, wonderful angel were worth millions. As I drove to our motel, I felt lifted over a threshold of consciousness.

Two nights later, in the middle of the night, Steven woke me. "It's time."

I rose, booked flights, and packed us up. Our flight was again first class for comfort. Our families met our plane, and soon he was relatively comfortable back in the little south-facing room, and I was functioning like an automaton.

Naomi went off to school again as we attempted to keep a bit of normalcy. Her times tables were less polished than we could have hoped. But, still, she went.

The time both dragged and sped. His needs, his volatile temperament, his physical discomforts were beyond me. What could I have known when, in the fervor of the moment, I promised him that he could die at home? But he wouldn't allow nurses at the house. So with the help of our best man and good friend Don, I called the ambulance when his pain and discomfort were beyond us both. Soon, I was sitting by his bed in the hospital, often staring out the window into the rain.

My life seemed to slide down the window pane like those raindrops — slowly swelling, bulging, then dissipating to slick the window. Time-scoping memory bites ran through my head. My aims and goals were losing form. I vaguely recalled dreams of speaking French, traveling the world, adopting children from many countries, and growing old with Steven. I remembered how I wanted to write and dream for a living and how I always wanted to contribute to a changing world....to help install a *love love love* light. Always self-deprecating and ashamed, I felt so lost about who I was. I had wrapped myself up in my identity as Steven's wife. Now did I even have a right to be here?

I still had my longing for God — who, as I've mentioned, obviously needed therapy Himself! — and my soul journey. It had been difficult for me to function in the world as "normal." I was better at being a dreamer, a philosophical wanderer, an explorer, one who couldn't seem to keep my attention on more normal things like a job and money.

Why was he dying? What will my life be? Why did it have to be so complicated with him rushing off with other women? Why did I have to be so volatile? I was looking for something to blame, and I was still always a good target. We were both angry by this time — he was angry at the world and the way it worked, at dying, and at me because I promised him he could die at home. Over and over, I replayed the vivid images of him as he readied himself for the ambulance: trembling as he painfully and meticulously dressed himself; choosing his socks, desert boots, good pants, and "backpacking your troubles away" T-shirt; then muttering to me as they strapped him onto the gurney, "Thanks a lot!" He glowered. "Thanks a lot!" as if I were turning him in.

Once there, he drifted in and out of sleep or trances, but when his folks, friends, even union brothers visited, he seemed fully awake. At his request, I ran interference, backing people out of the room for him. At times, he was desperate for quiet or couldn't emotionally handle certain visitors.

He set up a list in his mind and had me call in specific people. Doing this is apparently an interesting phase during the process of dying. So I called, for example, Ray and told him that Steven wanted to see him. It was quite the list, and as each one came to visit him, no matter how he was feeling, Steven would rally, laugh, exchange ideas, and sometimes give them something of his. It seemed intricately scripted. Then for another week or so, no more talk, just sporadic glares at me as I sat there for hours each day while he scrolled in and out of life.

As the relentless rain pattered its tune into my trance one day, Steven suddenly called out to me. "Hey, kid!" It was a nickname left over from our Africa days. "Thanks, kid. You did the right thing. I should be here. I always knew I could count on you," he said. What a relief! I was forgiven!

He fought death like a good revolutionary, living beyond any doctor's expectation. One Thursday, the doctor called me at home. "Don't come in today, Mrs. Holtby. He is still fighting hard." Ironically, that day I went shopping — shopping for a dress, a bright fuchsia dress, for his memorial. We were early on the emerging "celebration-of-life" trail. He passed that afternoon. I did think it strange that I was buying a dress for his passing as he decided to stop fighting.

By this time, Mum was staying with us to help with Naomi and the household. When the doctor called, Naomi was in the bath. I lifted her out of the tub, rubbed her down with a towel, and said, "Daddy just passed, Naomi. He is gone."

She burst into tears, lifted her head, and with her big, brown eyes sparking, she screamed, "Eight times eight is sixty-four! Eight times nine is seventy-two!"

Mum and I went to the hospital to see him at peace. As we pulled into the parking lot, the attendant said, "That'd be fifty cents, please." Mum and I cracked up, spontaneously hooting as it sounded like the money was for the viewing.

We set up the wake, full of Steven's favorites: the wine, Greek food from our favorite Greek restaurant, and his favorite music, the Rolling Stones, the Beatles, Led Zeppelin, and so many other rock treasures. Some of us sang, danced, and rocked, holding hands in a huge circle. Others were confused by our celebrative manner. But we followed his instructions to the T. Even my parents ate the cookies. They didn't feel a thing, but they were so surprised that the traffic lights en route home were so long. "They just went on and on," they commented. I chuckled, knowing that famous time-stretching effect of marijuana. I felt Steven's presence. So did others, and we knew he was pleased as we touted the journey of his soul. I felt oddly disconnected.

Life really fell apart then. I was in the birth canal, certifiably crazy, with a buzzing in my head and streams of sounds—

sometimes chords, sometimes just streams carrying one tone at a time. They didn't stop. Friendships that we had nested in for years and years were stricken with the drama of our betrayals, of the pain that Steven had gone through, loyalties that were torn through his leaving me and coming back home, of my dramatic reactions, of his other women. I realized two things as Naomi and I were ostracized. One is that people want to help a dying man recover, or heal, or whatever they perceive could happen. The other was that it seemed most of our friend connections were to him.

I didn't know who to believe in or who to trust. That theme of exploring trust was to carry me through my life and help me refine myself over and over again — kind of like sandpaper or, more eloquently, a lathe. The electricity of that intense time hotwired my attention to it. And to that I embraced my theme of transformation, or of always consciously forging the deepening truth of my identity.

I couldn't concentrate. I couldn't even read — me, a book hound. That went on for about five years. My paranoia hurt as I tried desperately to find some kind of safe haven. The fractures of my journey sent me within, reconnecting with the beloved velvet being inside whom I had known as a child, the me who had always lived and always would live, who was still a quiet and tremendous observer. My initiation continues. Maybe it does for one's entire life. But over a period of four to six years, I lived a demanding alignment, no matter what everyone else was doing, with discovering what was real for me, looking at it, exploring what I really felt, and learning what I really was. I looked pretty eccentric, but I had to do it. It opened me more and more to the ancient soul truth, a stream that has run through my lives — that of being an intuitive, a psychic. This gift inside could shine out into my world.

CHAPTER SIX

New Roots and Routes

Ronnnnnnnnnni! Ronnnnnnnnnnnnnnnnnnnnni!

I went out to the front stoop. No one was there. There was a banging on the roof, kind of insistent and staccato. I peered over the edge of the house. Nothing. I wandered around in a daze trying to attend to Naomi's school demands, cooking, cleaning—the usual routine—but I wasn't home inside myself. I was in a constant spaced-out, woozy feeling. I shook a lot.

My relationship with Naomi was strained as she, too, went through her grief response. I found her notebook with "Our father who art in heaven, can you see me?" and other heartbreaking pleas for the dad who "indopted" her. She missed him, and her fear of her dad, now that he was on the other side, was intense. She was deeply lost as the family that had tried to gather her had disintegrated. Writing this, I am more aware of how the loss seared her deep inner self and oft-abandoned soul.

Nor was I a great mother at this point. I just couldn't focus. I didn't know what I felt. I was hurt, angry, and irrational. I didn't trust anyone anymore. It was difficult to help me. Some tried. My visions were also crazy—snapping, sliding around.

One day, a jar fell off the fridge, which tweaked my memory. I got it...the deal Steven and I made under the rhododendrons. The lamp didn't fall over, but the tapping on the roof and the calling—now also *Naomi, Na-oooooooommmmmmi!*—became louder.

Naomi heard it, too; she kept coming in from playing outside. "Mum, are you calling me?"

"No, Na. What did you hear?"

My sister and a friend each consulted a psychic for themselves a month or so after Steven died. With a little chagrin, each reported messages from Steven to me. "I don't want to pay for readings that are all about you!" was the complaint. The messages were simple: that he was all right, that becoming a party girl wouldn't help, plus other short bits of advice. But with my buzzing mind and paranoia, it took a few weeks or maybe a month for me to remember our original deal to actually make contact to the other when one of us passed.

I went out with friends at night as often as I could. It was so hard to stay home—I felt like I would shoot through my skin or pop out of the top of my head. Voices or odd sounds ran through my mind. I could "see," inside my head, a chaotic tangle of multicolored thread-like wires, buzzing like the movies of electrons on the move, confused pathways. These days I might actually enjoy popping out of the top of my head as I feel freer, not being run by some mystery. Sometimes I partied, sometimes it was just going along with friends for a walk or to the pub.

There were times I went to Pender Island to camp with Naomi on the site my parents owned. We would go rowing, hiking, or myriad other activities. Wherever we went, it was easy to stay busy or find a group going somewhere and doing something. At night, we'd cook over the fire, and then Na would curl up in her sleeping bag and read with her lamp. I would sit in front of the campfire while sounds, like a haunted toning, just moved through me.

During one of those camping periods, I suddenly "saw" inside of people. It's as if an awareness just popped open in me. I could "see" chakras in people, whether the people were actually sitting with me or I was just thinking about them. Their chakra colors would brighten, and between the vibrant disks, I would see spirals of colors picking up speed and pulsing throughout their bodies, both their physical bodies and energy bodies. These glimpses would flash and disappear. Afterward, I would center and stabilize, with the clearing help of those unbidden tones. Then lights would again pick up their pulse through a person. I didn't tell anyone as, by then, I was sure I was crazy.

Also around that time, I began to see triangles — large, oddly shaped, almost living triangles — emerging in scenes or in people. They could be equilateral, or they could be like the sails on the omnipresent little boats in the Vancouver harbor, tipping, angling, with concave or convex sides, with strong points or weak, vague points. Fascinated, I "knew" what they meant. How? I don't know. My awareness told me that they spoke of body/mind/spirit balance and are a portal to other dimensions, a pathway through life's endless array of experiences.

More messages came through intuitives I visited, or who friends visited, from Steven: "She's not a party girl. She needs to calm herself and set up her life." I was rattled deeply by the loss of my trust in Steven, friends, and family. Like a geyser, my own unresolved childhood issues, time-released angers, reactions, abandonment, and fears burst upwardly in reactions. Everything stung. I reeled back, recoiling in fear from anyone who told me what to do. More friends pulled away. I was a pariah. I was deeply disturbed. The relentless zooming and buzzing continued inside. At times, I was fun and articulate, easily laughing and playing for wild snippets of time. At other times, in an effort to be open and honest, I would tell people exactly what I thought. "You aren't being honest." "That relationship is going to hurt you. "You are smiling, but I can see you are unhappy." "You missed that opportunity. But never mind. Life spirals. It will come back, and you will be at a new level."

Efforts to sort through all the weird feelings and thoughts that rose out of the file folders of my mind, in their own way, failed. "I just need to prioritize my emotions," I told myself as I felt the swill of impossibilities. But my emotions boiled up an inner fracas. I was scared especially of women, scared of the political world, scared of just being. That fear was expressed by my snapping nerves and spontaneous visions, bursts of sweat, unbalanced gait when I walked—that lack of balance I have noticed through the years with people who are mentally unbalanced—sudden tears, seeing everyone down that darned but familiar tunnel, which was now a long, gray tube of fog that would last several more years. I was angry and on edge, and I never felt well. I was like an electric fence. Nights when I stayed home, once Na was in bed, I sorted through Steven's seemingly infinite supply of papers. Burning old letters and bills in the fireplace, throwing out his things, sorting through my own things for what I would ever want again—it was a therapeutic but grueling task.

Inside my brain, I felt like the engine of a lawnmower or outboard motor. Someone had pulled the cord to start it. My brain raced and raced. I talked fast, walked fast, and just couldn't slow down, inside or out. That horrible, driving feeling of wanting to run went on and on for years.

Poor Naomi. She couldn't count on me for stability at that point. I kept her in school, made sure she was washed and dressed, and fed her, but my support for the holes in her soul was weak. I could barely deal with my own holes. We read and cooked, she played and played, and we did the basics. But we were both lost. She continued disappearing, but only for a few hours here and there.

I wanted to disappear as well, to run away, to live anywhere else, to live where memories and judgments wouldn't keep stinging. The "geographic cure" is not recommended, as I heard later. But I did it anyway. When the school holidays started, I took Naomi and headed for my dream of France, starting in England. My brother, a mainstay support for me at that time although he was only twenty-four, took over the little house on Sixteenth and the caretaking of Hoop Tac the cat.

Our tour started at the home of my dear friend Pat, who was in England with her husband Eddy. Pat was studying opera on a Canada Council Grant. Even though we had been friends for a long time and knew each other well, I know I presented a different self. As a widow now, I presented the me that came with the snapping words, snapping visions, strange feelings, dizziness, waves of tears, acting out. I was strange and over-reactive, as though held together by a gossamer fabric stretching out impossibly at times. She was a wonderful support.

Naomi and I took trips around England and Wales, visiting relatives in Sussex and Somerset whom I had met on my journey years back. Mum's cousin in Devon hosted us for a few days. One day, while Naomi stayed with Barbara and played in her yard, I walked the hills. Finally, as sunshine bathed me and the green, rolling hills, I started to cry. I needed the many, many miles between the drama and the present moment to let go. Like a tapped geyser, I burst; then I was on the ground, pounding my fists into the earth, sobs gushing.

On my walk back along the winding, village road, in my peripheral vision, I saw a discreet sign, Society for Spiritualism. Despite my dishevelment, I went in. An older woman was shelving books by a stained-glass window in the old, stone building. She turned and startled at my depleted self.

"Welcome, dear." With the ongoing synchronicity that continues to feed my journey, she began doing a spiritual reading for me—just what I needed, comfort and connection with benevolence from the beyond. "Talk to your Spirit companions, dear. Ask them to take away the veils you keep putting around yourself. You have so much help, but you don't seem to know it." I narrowed my eyes. *Trust trust trust.* Veils. That sounded soft. Before I heard her words, I'd felt more like I was wrapped up or held together by huge, uneven sheets of sticky paper. When I got back to the house, I felt refreshed. "What do you think about the psychic stuff? Or Spiritualism?" I asked Barbara.

"Shhhhhhhhh!" Her quieting sounds were loud. She peeked into the next room to make sure her husband hadn't heard me. "Don't let Bryan hear you. As a minister, he can't accept it. In our family, after meals the men used to go to the drawing room, the women to the kitchen to clean up. There we would read each other's cards. Men can't handle it. You must be quiet."

I chuckled. "The men can't handle it" was definitely a belief from my lineage. Mum always said that about Dad and emotions. "Don't talk to your dad about your feelings. He is sensitive. Men can't handle it."

A few days later, right after our return to Pat and Eddy's in Muswell Hill, London, nine-year-old Naomi disappeared.

Money was missing from their change jar. We called the police, but where on earth should we begin looking for Na? About fourteen hours later, she was found somewhere in the heart of London, just being herself, wandering. They brought her back sullen and unrepentant.

Pat and Eddy were kind and loving, even forgiving, about the money. I was sickly, tired, an insomniac. That huge, deadening hole in my solar plexus, a common imprint for widows or others in situations of intense loss, refused any food I ate. My digestion was on strike! I watched as Naomi's behavior became even more erratic and dangerous for her and others. I knew we simply had to go back to Vancouver and establish a home and some structure. We needed therapy—both of us.

I dreaded the humility of returning from my "I'm leaving" tantrum. I had said I would be gone forever, but I bit the bullet and we were home. What was home? We were forging that from the inside out. After a series of busses and taxis, I landed us at a restaurant on the waterfront in Vancouver. I was brooding, reentering the womb of all the drama. Naomi went off and phoned one of my closest friends at the time, Sally, who came to get us, clearly annoyed. Our University friends had been in and out of their own dramas, often staying at our UBC townhouse while they righted themselves. I thought this would be no different. It was. I was in an extreme passage, disconnected, all my beliefs and reactions whirling through me, making me scary and impossible to relate to.

Some friends did welcome us to stay, however, and I looked for a house to buy in the Dunbar area near the old West Sixteenth home. Finally, I chose a fine one with a view and in which we'd build a basement suite to rent out, on the advice of a good friend who was overlooking my legacy.

I set Naomi back up with school and Brownies, yet she was running away more and more. Memories race out of sequence in my mind, which, as I've said, was moving too fast and furious to make sense. My lifelong anxieties and questions kept an electric fertility in that inner gap that I've complained about, the distance between my inner being and my rapport with life. It was hard for Na. I did find a child therapist for her and a therapist for me. But nothing seemed to work. She just kept running farther and farther.

There was a good part of this fracturing time, too, however. Rising through the shambles, the broken trusts, the tattered identity, was my intuitive nature. It was breaking through the many membranes that, like the house of my mind, held my consciousness in definable layers. I was awakening. A truer me was birthing. But its labor was a torment.

Writings about grief were one of the only things I, once the ever-avid reader, could focus on. Otherwise, words just bounced and blurred before my eyes. I even found myself a grief group, a new concept in Vancouver in 1976.

Psychic material was another big focus. So many people in the throes of huge loss experience visions, flashing insights, and more. That was true for me as well. I started to go to readers, taking copious notes. My brain speed was still off the charts, still with the whirring and buzzing. I asked the various psychics for help with my visions or perspective over my life, or just expressed plain, ordinary curiosity about my visions and how they could be used.

Steven kept showing up, as well. He wanted to talk to me from his new etheric perspective. I wasn't sure. I thought two things at the time. The first was I wondered if calling in the departed and interacting with them would be hanging on to them, which might hold them back from the unfolding journey I knew we all could make. And two, I was mad at him. People stoked that fire in me by telling me more things he had done. I wish I didn't know so much. I didn't have strength or confidence to handle more emotional grit with my nerves snapping and my mind racing.

When I saw his smile and heard his "Hi!" instead of being charmed as he shone away there from his new dimensional reality, I would wave him away. "Go on. Go to the light. You have caused enough trouble!" I knew somehow that I could block his communications.

I laugh now at a memory. One psychic read, "Your husband is going to guide your relationships." I reeled. "No, no, no, no, no you don't! Mind your own damn business!" I stormed at his etheric presence.

Going through paperwork that I could barely focus on, however, trying to sort and file and build a financial foundation, periodically I would yell, "Steven! What am I going to do? You dragged me all over and now left me in a mess! I don't even know where to live, what to believe," I would howl at the ceiling.

But I also thanked him for leaving me with a legacy. He didn't believe in insurance, but just before we went to Maui, several of his political friends arrived and sat with him until he signed various papers for insurance. Thanks to the union and to Steven's friends, I was all right for a time. And today, although it took me a few years to truly feel this, I have so much to thank him for. He tore up my concepts of home and many old attachments that ruled me. I have had to sort through the insecurities and fears that tethered me. I often say to clients that when a relationship pulls apart, it can rip off your packaging, then out comes the stuffing, and you get an opportunity to sort through your own inner fears and anxieties.

With him and our lifestyle, there was very little of "This is the way you have to be." He, or our life together, made me think, learn, be flexible, and explore more of my own truth and not the designs of others. But he was critical on a personal level. Naomi added to that, too, with her roaming and the choices she made from her deep, unfathomable drives. There are times, perhaps the "grief spasms" I read about, which will happen throughout life, that I miss him. I mostly miss the humor and adventure we shared. And I think, "Hey, Steven. What happened? Where did you go?" In *Forrest Gump*, that inspiring movie, when Forrest says at the graveside of his love, "Ever since you died..." and on goes the quote, "life has been harder......." I wept then. After almost forty years since he passed, I still feel that inside of myself I am growing, changing, becoming, becoming, becoming...and wasn't our marriage a port in the storm in some ways? It was certainly a place to be funny, be challenging, and reach for the world-changing stars.

I spent more and more time either alone or with new friends I met, mostly out of fear of misinterpretations or even references made by old connections. Added to that, I was in a phase of precariously balancing hurt and emergence. Fragile on all levels, I couldn't count on myself even to stand without shaking or wobbling under scrutiny. Relentless inner voices contradicted one another, each with a kind of shooting electricity. My nerves shook, were twanged by...well, everything. Deep down, I always knew I would get through it and be something else. That is what kept me going through the days. But I also knew that if anyone knew what was going on in my brain, I would be locked up – at least for those first few years. They were hard.

I heard over the radio one day that when you are depressed, don't just lie in bed in the morning. Oh, darn! That's so tempting. I was very heavy inside. A friend said, "Aren't there days when you just want to lie under the bed?" Oh, yes.

"Always put your shoes on," I heard. "Announce to your body that you are ready for your day."

My sister called me many a morning. "Hello. How are you? You up?"

"I'm fine. Yes, I'm up," I lied as I put my shoes on. Then, after Naomi went off to school, I would often walk up and down the hills around the house, even down to the beach a few miles away – putting those shoes to use. Even to this day, first thing in my morning comes a walk, armed back then with a journal and nowadays a computer, saying mantras, affirmations, or prayers, heading out to a coffee place to *write write write write*. It still works magic for me.

One night, putting my paranoia in my back pocket, I summoned up the courage and went to a party, an annual event hosted by one of the couples in our old group. Sally, formerly my very close friend, was there. In my shame and my own inability to present a coherent self, I had basically been hiding from our old friends. But it was mutual. They were hiding from me, too, what with my bursts of non-stop talk alternating with frozen silences, trying to protect my heart that was writhing to express the pain we all shared. Or perhaps just because....

Obviously my isolations had hurt Sally's feelings. She misinterpreted them, the usual route to disagreements all around the world. Interpretations always come through the subjective mind with its forest of projections and assumptions. She was smoking marijuana and also drinking, but even given that, her approach was very strange.

"I knew you would come back," she hissed at me. I still remember a part of her speech: "You are doing everything wrong, and you will do what I say or you won't survive."

Then began one of my first horrendous psychic experiences, a personalized movie. Her face began to shift, her teeth pointing like a cat's. Blood ran through them. My stomach felt like it was being ripped, as if those teeth were digging in to it the whole time we were talking. I tried to talk to her, to explain what I was doing and learning. She couldn't hear me. We were in such different realities. I remember being terrified of her and sobbing and sobbing. People separated us. It was never discussed. Would I have told anyone what I "saw"? Probably not. I could never trust people or myself enough to share my visions.

Karmic experiences are those experiences that push and pull you or enfold you in a life-and-death feeling. They can trigger awakening or unplug old, emotion-filled energy patterns. We can feel pretty crazy as more and more facets of archived, old emotions/reactions of our immense journey pop up, seemingly to toss us randomly around in our drama.

For instance, there's my one acid trip, somewhere around 1969 or 1970, which I can still tap for multidimensional information, with all its swirling, vibrational imprints. And I now have added my own many portals. During that journey on LSD out in the wilds of Northern British Columbia, and the wilds of new dimensions, I opened to experience energy and energy fields. I even conducted the music of the universe, waving my arms to paint life with emotions in transcendent colors. Told to the wrong people, this could have knocked me right into a mental hospital—my old fear. Later I reexperienced, during a past-life regression to the end times of Atlantis, that I had taught that same orchestration of frequencies and sounds. That day, or was it a portal to time, I ran through fields of eyeglasses trying to find the right ones. Then I moved out into the universe on a cake walk, that old carnival path made of colored pieces that move in unpredictable directions, meeting people with whom I was involved, but finding that we were tied together with barbed wire. Panic rose in me as my barbed-wire-wrapped husband embraced me until I said, "Okay, if that is what he wants to wear, it's okay." And the threat evaporated. Then out I went into the universe on another cake walk, this one brilliantly radiant. As I raised my arms, I could orchestrate sound and color throughout the skies in glorious, transcendent beauty. "Shall I go back?" I felt like a butterfly, spreading its shimmering wings for the first time. The ecstasy of its beauty filled me. No, it *was* me. Tears flowed from every part of my body. Yet, softly, strongly, I knew I had to return. Nine or ten hours after we ingested the acid, I returned to my friends at the campsite. Sitting cross-legged, bare-breasted with only my bikini bottoms on, I beat my chest in a rhythm and chanted, "I AM I AM I AM...." Some of those experiences recorded themselves in my brain with all their attending sounds and feelings. Like other intense emotional memories, when four senses out of five line up with those settings, a person can reenter those experiences.

Hearing "I AM," even without the breast-beating, still evokes a transcendence in me. As I write, this sounds like the proliferating descriptions of near-death experiences in our world these days. But neither a grand angel nor Jesus sent me back—just a deep, inner knowing that I really should make that trek. Sitting by the campfire with the nine of us, the kettle burst into energy-field flames, with patterns of radiance that I still use these days to understand healing. With my hands on people's heads, feeling and smoothing, the radiances are like that kettle on the fire. I didn't recover. I changed. Therein lies the potential danger. Like my old outboard-motor or lawnmower metaphor, I was activated.

"Why didn't you tell me what acid's like? It was so far beyond anything I expected!" I asked my brother and a couple of other more experienced friends.

"We didn't know!" They were surprised I was gone for ten hours.

My changes keep going to this day. They can be restrained or resisted, slowed down, but they've never actually stopped. That ten-hour jaunt out of the 3D world launched something. It would take another few years before I would see these changes as wildly spiraling colors moving through the core of our beings, pulling light and information from the chakras, directed by our minds and hearts, dancing with the amazing universal frequencies of our times. That part of knowing the transformational dynamic of humanity took five to ten years of emergence, or the ripping of my fabric through loss and trauma, or initiation, to kick in. I chuckle at the "emergency of emergence." I took a while to be able to hold it all.

Sally and I were never able to rekindle our friendship. But this terrifying experience, like so many other aspects of my life, sparked awarenesses. In this case, it was about karmic contracts with their current impacts. Millie had been a soothsayer, a psychic Sally and I had visited some months earlier. She told us about us, a mother and daughter, tragically torn apart by shifting continents in an epic earth change. "One of you was the mother," Millie told us, "dominant, the leader, and still wants to be in charge. Kind of bitchy. The daughter must be pulled away to realize herself." It explains why the push-pull and deep love between us was so intense. It's the pull of soul mates. "So sayeth the soothsayer" goes the old cliché. When Sally said, "You'll do it my way," I heard her throughout my body mind. I hurt. Scared, I recoiled.

"I have never despised anyone more than I have despised you," she'd said. Now, so many years later, I contemplate in wonder how those projections and interpretations she made about me must have come from an unfathomable soul experience. Really, I was hiding from shame and shakiness, a fear of being unwelcome—not to hurt her or anyone else. Just hurting. But how we hide in fear can slice at someone else's safety, poking at their own losses and hurts. Her fierce feelings might still be active. I wonder if our soul contract is done yet.

It could have been simply an imprint of a mother-and-daughter connection floating out there in the collective. But such an intense emotional connection is usually demanding and irrational, its tumultuous push/pulls can be a warning. I try to acknowledge the deep feelings that rise with soul people, call them up, feel their resonance and where they live in me, and release them.

Over those bumpy decades, I learned more and more. "Oh, boy! I just know this person. We really know one another." When that happens now, when I feel that "Oh, I *know* that person" attraction, I just walk on by—especially when it affects my belly first, the good, old womb of the subconscious. I promise you. we don't have to live out every one of these soul tangles. Just recognize and feel them as evidence of unfinished dramas, asking your Higher Self for confirmation. Command total release of the pushing and pulling feelings and then sashay right on by.

"Okay," some of you might be asking, "what if it is a message that this is my twin flame, soul mate, or prince or princess charming?" "Seek and ye shall find." This famous biblical advice tells us to just ask, ask for confirmation. We needn't just walk away from what could be love gifts. No matter what, these connections, even if seconds long, can be transformational and teach us about love. We'll feel more love, receive more love, and give more of love as we unhook...and unhook...and unhook throughout our years.

Meanwhile, back in my wobbly home life, although I was trying, I still wasn't able to conduct the most responsible motherhood role. I was angry and frustrated—at life. I was abrupt in my speech, short with my temper.

Then came the completion of the basement apartment that I was having built. Lo and behold, the Universe was once again at the helm. My first tenant arrived. Would you believe it? She was, and still is, a psychic. "I owe you," she said. "We have karma, and I have to help you." Interesting how that works, especially given the challenges of my home life at that point.

Naomi continued running away. With amazing stealth, the stealth of an indigenous tracker, no matter how I watched, she would slip out the door—night after night. And, night after night, the police would bring her in. "We found this little girl downtown [or at the mall or at the train station or...somewhere], and she says she has nothing to eat," they would admonish me. "She says she is cold, and you won't give her a sweater." None of that was true. Then came more lecturing from the police, who wanted to support her. After a few of these episodes, instead of panicking and making wild calls for help, I would make the call to the police

and then curl my hair, vacuum, keep busy. I looked crazy —
because I was. My assumption was that it was all my fault,
that I could have helped her. I wasn't sure what was true
anymore. Was I really living in a reality that no one else was?
Was I really making everything up? My brain was still doing
its pulsing with colorful streams of energy with their
accompanying sounds.

One night in that house with the beautiful view, probably
about a year after Steven died, she was gone again. Slowly
and steadily, one at a time, women from my many
consciousness-raising experiences and from my various
phases of life as an activist started arriving at my home.
Finally, there were about twelve or thirteen. I really don't
know if it was organized or synchronistic. I will ask someone
soon if they remember so far back. Soon the police were at
the door once again with my errant daughter.

One friend, a principal at a school with a huge native
population, was there; twenty-five years later, she told me
that she met many, many Naomis. It would have been great
to know that then. She participated in so many wakes for
young people who had roamed, got caught on the streets,
and perished. That night, she pushed past me and shut the
door behind her as she talked to the policeman. Again,
Naomi had told her story. "This little girl says you won't let
her in...put a sweater on her...give her food...." I don't
remember all of the complaints any more. In retrospect, I
wish I'd known more about Na's tribal tendencies and her
early childhood abuses.

Naomi came in and was delighted to see all of these
women. "Hi, Aunt Maureen. How was Disneyland?" Her
cold lack of concern was the first actual evidence my sister
had had of Naomi's truer pathological behavior.

Sitting in a circle on the floor, the women passed her around. One at a time, they held her and asked her what she was doing. The answers weren't satisfying for anyone. She just didn't seem to know. "I'll stop," she assured us all. But that was for us in the moment. She couldn't remember her promises.

I sat beside my dear friend, now home from England, who instinctively rocked and rocked me, as I spun inside, somehow knowing that Naomi wasn't really present. I loved this girl with her big, brown eyes and cheeks as round as her eyes. I think of her so often with regret that I didn't have the inner balance and understanding, or even the awareness, of the abuses that we were dealing with—my own unhealed past and her pains aching to be found and nurtured. There was so much roaming in her lineage. My mind and heart needed a fuller healing to manage her. She had a deep, dark cloud in her belly when we adopted her at five and half. I used to see it or sense it and wonder if I could reach in and pull it out. When her challenges hit that program deep in her subconscious, she was impossible to contain. And I had my own version going on.

Maybe we did it just right for our souls. We shared the experiences that would fuel our growth. We laughed together. We loved, read, learned, shopped, fought. But I didn't know how to parent her.

Her final adoption with us was delayed by the government. The First Nations people were petitioning that their children should not be adopted by white people. I was so pleased when finally it went through. It was official: she was our daughter. But in retrospect, I understand their wisdom. We were placing these kids in an Anglo-Saxon framework. Their need to roam was hard for us. Their old tribal customs of extended families taking in kids who needed a break or expansion was unfamiliar to us. In my heart, I wanted to complete the adoption. Now I ask myself why. My dear friend Rose offered to take her on. Her life experience could help, but I couldn't accept. My friend Pat's mum, the AA wizard, suggested we find a farm in the North where Na could be raised. It was beyond me to let her go, to give up my daughter. But it would have been wiser to give her up in a way that would have expanded her world and reality. I just didn't know any better. I am so aware of how naïve I was. Steven, too. We thought we could accomplish everything with environment. Poor Naomi. Maybe adopting her was a version of that criminal way that native children were taken to residential schools so long ago.

Na and I both went for more therapy, for her a sand table and for me a powerful pull-you-apart kind of program for people in intense, unwieldy grief. That was me. That was Naomi, too. But grief studies were new then. I also worked on designing a Human Support System for the cancer clinic, one with a quiet room with soft chairs for meditation, classes, or groups to help guide families and their friends through this shattering experience. The old, metal chairs were cold and excruciating. Yet people who are very ill need the support of their closest people, people who themselves may be unbalanced in the face of the whims and moods and ups and downs of their loved ones on medication and in fear. The project helped me learn about my own craziness and felt productive. I was even featured in a television spot on grief. Eventually, I slipped away from the politics and pain of the cancer clinic and my project. A beautiful, white-haired older woman put an arm around me one day and said, "Why don't you go and make a new life for yourself? It isn't good for you to be here so much, dear." She was so kind and motherly that I wept as I packed up my volunteer's uniform and left.

Generally, however, I was at my wit's end with Naomi. I actually thought—with the hews and cries, the constant judgments, my own whirring, fractured mind—that I just might give up and die. But my thoughts went back to reincarnation and all the explorations and healings I wanted to do inside; leaving so many traits and faults undone in myself, I just couldn't. But the thought rose often. I just wasn't able to be a success.

I began to call Social Services and demand Naomi's early childhood records. "Not allowed," they said. "We don't want to jeopardize her success."

"I don't have the right information!" I just kept pushing and yelling at them. "I need help." Finally, from Victoria came the secret information about Na's earliest years. She had been in the system since she was six months old. Born to a fifteen-year-old drug addict and alcoholic, she had been left alone in a cabin in the woods. They claimed that she was a marvel—she could actually scale walls to feed herself. I am not sure about that as a fact, but the intensity of it, yes, is true.

I tried something else. I flew her up to Hazelton to the receiving home where we had first met her in 1972. She had been living there off and on since she was a year old, with time out for life in a foster family for two and a half years, but suddenly, inexplicably, we were told, she was sent back to the receiving home. "This child is a well-adjusted, happy, smart, little girl," they had told us. It was their marketing style. To be fair, they were trying not to prejudice her future by giving us negative information. Those were the days of intense and hopeful discussions about environment versus heritage. Environment hadn't been top of her line, we know. But many of her issues were deep. My further investigation—and I remind you and me both that the investigation I did was actually against the law — revealed that she had run away as soon as she could walk.

I left her in her receiving home for three weeks and another time with my sister and her boys for another three weeks in a desperate attempt to collect my wits and right myself. I brought her back home after I was assured she was really all right. But then came even more in-depth details of her history of abuse, neglect, and fetal alcohol syndrome, things I hadn't yet understood. I would have her visit other children's homes on overnighters thinking that their parents were better and maybe it would help. That didn't work.

During her times away, she was usually in a honeymoon period, and people thought I was wrong about her. It was just whatever I was doing. She told people I left her alone, and they believed her. Normally, she had a babysitter. One night I did leave her to go out for dinner with a friend. She convinced me, "Go, Mum. I'm ten. I'll call the restaurant if I need you." Okay, I thought. I would be just down the street. As soon as I left, she called Don, Steven's best man, who brought his work over and sat with her. He was angry. One subsequent attack was from a family member who, to this day probably, believes that Naomi told her the truth — that she was all alone in the house. On that night she was concerned about, there was a sitter there. They believed Na, who had more street smarts and guile than I will ever have.

Rifts as broad as the Rift Valley in my beloved Africa were fostered by judgments and ignorance between family members and me. In some cases, even though I healed and grew, our separations never healed. As with many karmic connections, an activation of many seeds of reaction had happened. I continued to be more and more "different"...as my intuitive nature grew.

123

Social Services worked out a plan with me. Two of the workers set up a twenty-four-hour call system. "Call as soon you find her gone. We'll be right there with you."

She disappeared that very night. I called and called and called, then carried on with our police/child merry-go-round for the three more days it took for them to respond. "You had better come over here," I threatened. Two workers came. "I am giving her back to you. I can't do this."

"What?" They sounded incredulous.

"Take her. You said you would help, but no one was there. You lied to me. I am so fragile. I am crazy. I am not going to live through this."

Naomi screamed. "You said you would be my mum forever!"

"You said you would stop running!"

A day later, they came for her and all the toys and the clothes she said she didn't have.

When she was dying thirty-five years later, I learned even more from her relatives who joined us around her hospital bed. Her mother would take her to a bar, set her up near a heater, and give her a bottle with wine in it. She was loved *and* neglected. I often think back, wondering if it could've been different if I'd understood more about the syndromes we were dealing with. I will be her mum forever as our souls are bonded, but not in 3D.

More hew and cry rose. "Who gives up a child?" "A poor little native girl!" "What kind of person are you?" and so on. Actually, I am a broken, crazy, terrified, overwhelmed, lost, lonely woman. What kind of person are you?

My counselor, an ex-Franciscan priest, was one encouraging voice. "Let her go. She has more ability to be in that system than you do. You did your best. You developed a core for her." His litany of support, plus more from a couple of strong friends, kept me at least bobbing up to the surface of my oceanic pool.

"Look, Steven is dead. It's all over now." "Get your life together." "Get a job." "You just want to have fun." "You are so irresponsible....." And more. Like a guitar string, I was plucked and plucked. And like a strained guitar string, I was losing any pleasant resonances.

A close friend said, "I don't know how to deal with you. One day you are happy, then I think you are going to kill yourself. Get a job. Any kind of job." I didn't explain that I couldn't kill myself because of reincarnation, although I probably could have told her. She has stuck with me. At the time, though, I just went blank as that feeling of "gotta be careful" took charge.

I did have small jobs. The Government Task Force was done. Thanks to a fraternity brother of Steven's, I worked over Christmas at a downtown liquor store. There, among my workmates, was an unusual friend for me—a tough-looking biker. He immediately "saw" my fragility and befriended me. He was funny and tough. He never hustled me, just protected me at times. People knew Chuck as gnarly, yet he was kind and perceptive at work. He regaled us with wonderful biking stories about freedom, far outside my own life experiences. At times, I substituted for the manager in a little dress shop, visiting with an assortment of people who came in to talk. I learned from one fellow about the amazing world of the Sufis. I reeled back from him, afraid it was all madness. Funny, huh? Madness is still such a subjective word.

But I needed a real job. I was so unbalanced, darting away from people I knew. My nerves and ability to relate were a long way inside of me, oddly floating. I couldn't bring my social self forward past the humming and thrumming of the streams of colored wire that whirred through my brain. I was paranoid and skitterish, which just amped up the slew of judgments, both inside and out. I saw Naomi in her foster home on an irregular basis. She was in her honeymoon period, which usually lasted about three months, and we enjoyed short visits.

Big changes came. Jobs were scarce in Vancouver at that point. Adding my own need, in my fear and paranoia, to hide from people, I announced to the few who cared, "I'm going to the Prairies to get work." I had to get away. It reminded me of the times ten years earlier when the psychotherapist said, "You have to get over your reactions to your mother, or move yourself at least three thousand miles away." I had to move.

"What?" "You can't do that." "Really?"

I wasn't sure I could stay. It seemed easier to put miles under me.

My mother, who had seemed to be the cause of my trauma, if I didn't believe in the possibilities of karma, was supportive. She was becoming able to hear at least a part of me.

I drove up through Prince George to visit her and my dad on the way to Alberta, my little, red Honda loaded to the gunnels, the rest to follow in a moving truck when I found a new home. My speedy exit from Vancouver was punctuated by the spinning red cherry on top of the Mounty's highway patrol car and a few sliding whines from his siren! Maybe it was a warning — slow down on all levels. Caught speeding, I had a hearty ticket.

After visiting Mum and Dad, I stopped off in Calgary to visit my aunt and uncle. They were so kind. My aunt, a nurse who had also studied psychology, was able to handle me and could talk easily about some of my feelings, even some of the snippets of perception I had. I applied for a couple of community-development jobs there in Calgary but to no avail. So I headed four hours north to Edmonton where I landed a position as the administrative assistant for a number of agencies for the disabled. Back to Vancouver I flew to assemble myself and load up the moving van, ready to ground my new life.

CHAPTER SEVEN

The Pivotal Life in Edmonton

I was starting anew, but I was still doing things wrong. My energy was crazy. My brain speeds were so fast that I could barely focus. I collapsed easily, panicked frequently, and drove myself and others crazy with my hyperactivity. I was amazed that although my job was with a nonprofit meant to help guide the disabled, it was strangely fraught with politics and power issues. The "hidden agenda" was still hidden to me. Although I developed friends, my heart hung heavily with loneliness. I couldn't concentrate on much.

I took on a boyfriend, a dead-of-the-night lover. Today we'd call it a booty call. Whatever the term, the activity was highly questionable for friends who knew about it. I had announced to God, "No more intelligent men!" Somehow that made sense. And he wasn't. He was tough, a man of few words. But he and I provided something for one another. To me it was a safe closeness while risking so little. I didn't offer him much.

Yet I also developed some new friends, played racquetball, worked, partied, and danced. Again, new friends in transition stayed at my house, and some have remained friends.

In the meantime, back in Vancouver, my tenant, the psychic, moved from downstairs to upstairs, and I rented out the basement suite. About six months after I left, we made national news. The police bashed in the door of my house, busting my new renter for dealing heroine. Woo-hoo — we were famous! Immediately, I put the house on the hill in Dunbar, the preferred area of Vancouver, on the market and, when it sold, I was relieved. Had I waited, I could have made a small fortune. But the complications with all the strings from my past holding on to my becoming were beyond me at that point. I needed to invest closer to home, in Edmonton. I found a charming, little log house and settled in.

At that point, I just needed family. I felt that I had grown a lot and even done some healing. I missed Naomi and parts of our life together. So I called Social Services and asked for another opportunity to raise her. My Calgary aunt heard that I was going to try to work it out with Naomi again, and she came to visit me. My little house, with the sun shining through the many wooden-framed windows, our pot of tea, and steam rising from pretty china cups, was so homey. We visited. Gently and carefully, she cautioned me. She seemed to be the only relative at the time who truly understood how broken I was. "Ronni, you don't have to do this. You don't have to try again with Naomi." Her earnest and kind focus reached into me. I was deeply touched. Her wisdom, filled with her knowledge of human dynamics, helped me ground.

But still, I simply had to do it. I was incomplete with Naomi. I loved her and felt I had failed her. I was unsteady inside still, but I knew I had to try again.

A few weeks later, I picked Naomi up at the airport. Her brown eyes were bright, and both of us were so happy to be together again. We loved our cozy log cabin, and together we set up her little bedroom. We started off with enthusiasm and real love. I lined up her new school as well as therapy for each of us. And...soon I was on antidepressants.

The complexities of being a single mum mounted. I was afraid of leaving her unattended in after-school hours. The job was making less and less sense to me. The challenges of our life, homework, my own work, the house, finances — all the attributes of life — triggered leftover reactions from each of our traumatic memories. My own grief and abuse issues were still unhealed. We both had a kind of PTSD from childhood and the ragged endings of family life with Steven. The antidepressants sat like a cement lid over the boiling pots of my mind. My mind still writhed, but on the outside I was quieter and simply couldn't express. It kept me emotionally tidier but internally messier.

Naomi had learned a lot in the foster system since we had parted. I tried to be strict and keep the lines of expectation clear and strong, leaving after-school notes for her. She would be home while I was at work. We were given a caregiver for after-school by the social service, for support. Now here was the Law of Attraction at work! It would be funny if it didn't hurt so much. Remember, I was quite crazy. Diana, the caregiver, was also quite odd. She sent in a complaint that I was unfair. My notes were somehow too much. "Hi. There is a snack on the counter. Do your homework, feed the cat, and play outside. I'll be home at five. Love, Mum." Or some such. The notes were collected as "evidence." The investigation took time. I was reeling. What am I doing wrong? I was trying to correct my mothering, be firm, consistent, and steady — qualities I hadn't mastered before. Yet home was still falling apart! After extensive investigation, I was exonerated, the evidence dismissed. Our caregiver was found to be emotionally unstable (join the club!), even schizophrenic, they said. Wow, what a reflection! At that point, my teeth were grinding, my mind was racing, and my body was shaking deep inside all the time. I was whirling inside, thinking of what destruction I kept bringing to me. To us. Judgments, my own and others', abounded.

"You are dictatorial!" said one of my friends, who stayed with Naomi when I was away at a conference for a weekend. She was a young counselor for the disabled and was quite a fun and free thinker. I was trying too hard to keep boundaries and expectations clarified—probably desperately, terrified that I was a terrible mother, that I would lose control over Naomi.

When my friend was through helping Naomi feel free of all my stern expectations, Na became wild again, doing whatever she wanted and acting up at school. Then she was expelled. I was never clear on what actually happened. I believe to this day that the real messages were my soul lessons coming up in spades. I was riding the ship of my jerry-rigged identity to its lowest point, to literally shatter it. The counseling and the faithful presence of the social worker were kind, but they just weren't working. Naomi started stealing, then roaming again. I was drowning, scared, defensive, collapsing under pressure, unable to focus or keep things running smoothly. The honeymoon period was over. I was not what she needed. Judgments and projections from friends filled my world again. But they didn't know, really. What I was learning was that I wasn't an able mum. I sat with that and wept.

Interestingly, one of her young playmates in the neighborhood had two parents who were deaf. Their daughter was hearing, very sweet, and well behaved. The mother, perceptive, wrote a supportive note. "Try not to worry. I have known several children like this. They turned out all right once they grew up." I could feel her heart.

Our social worker continued to visit us regularly to see how things were going. But there were reports from the school, the truancies that lead to her being expelled, my fears and anxieties, Naomi's resistance to rules, and a huge anger between us that probably started years ago, but was escalating with her hormones. One day, the social worker said, "You know, Ronni, we are going to have to apprehend Naomi again. She is eleven now and her problems are mounting. You can't handle her." I died with my dream.

I have no idea what I did between that day and the courtroom drama, which I believe was a few weeks later. It seems that I stumbled around inside myself. I called my mum and asked her to come, which she did. She tried to be there for us. Setting Naomi up to handle the rejection again was heart wrenching, as well. Next, like someone on daytime television, I was standing in a courtroom beside my social worker while the judge read a description of Naomi's life. Her early records were brought out of Victoria again. After the judge read the records, she said, "It is time for you to begin your life. This little one has been damaged from her birth onward. Add the loss of her adopted father. And for you, it's only been a few years since your husband passed. Get on with your life, my dear. Naomi is now to be a permanent ward of the province." The gavel banged. My mind and heart felt sentenced forever.

A few days later, they picked up my eleven-year-old with her assorted bags. "I'll never forget you, Mum," she waved, smiling as she left, our dream of home and family with her.

Life, with me at the helm, was not working. I was aware that if this was *my* life, it would work. But what was *my* life? A nine-to-five mind-numbing job and a house to be tended?

That sure wasn't making any sense to me. With no more mother responsibilities, by then I was employed by a second nonprofit organization, again working with the disabled. This office ironically was even more poisoned with politics, even withholding services if clients spoke their mind. I quit that insane job.

I stopped paying bills, put my little log house on the market, and began to do yoga from a book, *The ABC's of Yoga*. I'd count my breaths and hold the postures exactly according to the instructions. "A specific and definite angle, reach, hold for thirty-five breaths, while focusing straight ahead...." I did it. Normally too impatient to follow instructions, I was impeccable. I felt that the rules were sacred. If they had been that particular for thousands of years, it must be for a reason. For three hours a day, I lived and moved with my ABC's of yoga, followed by a new Iyengar book from my next Divine Intervention connection.

People came and went in my house just as they had at UBC. In between relationships or jobs or both, friends would stay there. One day, in the middle of my practice there in front of my fireplace, one of the women who used to move in and out of my house during her changes, walked in. She knew I had resigned from my job and stopped paying my mortgage. In fact, I'd quit everything I had set up to have a "normal" life. She also knew that in three days, the bank was going to foreclose on my house. But there I was, doing alternate nostril breathing.

"Are you crazy?"

"Actually, I might be, but I am going to learn all about it."

Another synchronistic event opened a new chapter for me. That night, I was immediately attracted to a presentation by the rather well-known Richard Sutphen, the reincarnation guru. No one wanted to join me, so off I went by myself. Sitting in the second row, I saw in front of me a woman I hadn't seen for many years. I tapped her on the shoulder.

"Christine, is that you?"

"Oh, Ronni. Oh, Heavens! It's you! Where is Steven?"

"I am sorry, Christine. He passed away a few years ago."

"Lordy. Lordy! Let's talk...."

We did, after a highly relevant journey with Mr. Sutphen who regressed some people right there on the spot. He also explained how past lives often bring us together with knots and tangles, and how old feelings and patterns can be unhooked through awareness. He was mesmerizing.

Afterward, we had tea and tales from her life and mine. I told her about my rebellion, including the alternate-nostril breathing craziness and the foreclosure due in three days.

"My husband is in finances. We'll talk to him. He might help."

And help he did. He co-signed my loan. The heat was off, thanks to my old friends Christine, Richard, and Divine Intervention. And add more Divinity: on the very day of the pending foreclosure, a huge tree that spanned the width of my log house frothed with white blossoms. The house seemed charmed and three offers were brought in that afternoon.

The sale would close in six weeks. Now it was time. I had to head back to the West Coast and figure out if I could handle it now. I had missed the ocean, the ferries and seagulls, the mountains, and some of the people. I knew that with all my drama, I had challenged their lives. I knew that I had run away and needed to go back and not be in self-imposed exile. And yet, I had trepidation, my nerves were still snapping at times, and I was afraid, in the sting of my memories. I still had trouble concentrating and reading much. But I was getting better. Handing Naomi off to the system again had zeroed out my confidence one more time and broken my heart even more. My physical presentation was unreal. People thought I just didn't care. But I had to go back.

In Beulah, my cheeky, bright red Honda Civic, her sunroof wide open, I headed down through the magnificent trench of the Rockies from Jasper to Banff, 'round Lake Louise and the Slocan Valley, through the Okanagan. The spectacular scenery met, challenged, and soothed the choppy feelings in me. My little, red Honda ashram was a rich vessel of transformation, a crucible.

I sang, chanted, spoke affirmations, and flipped shakily through highly charged memories of loss and failure, of my unmanageable brain, with dollops of paranoia laced by a little triumph. I knew I was stronger—strong enough to explore my homeland again, the land I had been afraid of. "You can never go back," flashed in my mind, and I was lifted.

By then, I was coloring my hair redder and redder. I was still pursuing psychics, and the latest one told me, "You are taking on more and more of your Spanish heritage."

I laughed. "Right! We don't have Spanish heritage!"

"You might be surprised," she said.

"Ha ha!" I chuckled my glib retort. I was sure she was wrong.

Back in Vancouver, my mum was visiting my sister. As I joined them on the patio, Mum said, "Oh, you look more and more like your Spanish great-grandmother."

"I do? We have a Spanish great-grandmother?"

Mum explained that this ancestor had married an Irish man, and together they had created a special type of grapefruit known as the Shaddock grapefruit. Interesting. Also, I have always been frustrated with my square feet. Other than Roald Dahl saying that witches have square feet in his book *The Big Friendly Giant*, I have had no real appreciation for them. So one day around that time, in an international shoe store, a fellow was trying to fit me.

"I have such difficult feet. They are square."

He looked at them and said, "Ask for Spanish shoes. They'll fit you. This is a Spanish kind of foot!" So my heritage, a weaving that is common for Canadians and Americans, even Brits, was showing some of its streaks.

On went my tour. For six weeks, self-conscious and insecure, I reconnected with a few friends and family, especially old friends who shared my yen for spiritual centering and community. But then, as I threaded my way north on the twisting mountain highways of Vancouver Island, one decision began to make itself. Lolling around all night with my friend from Victoria days, we discussed a shared interest in herbs and foods, healing, and some of the colorful tools of self-exploration, fantasizing about the ideal. We dreamed of different settings for a natural-stuff general store. My friend wanted hers in a rural community. I didn't know what I wanted, or where. I knew I was fascinated by the world of alternative healing, but was not sure which focus I would choose.

I did know that there was a health-food store in Nanaimo owned by people connected to Steven's and my community-development days. I found them listed in that pre-Google icon, the phone book. Traveling back down the island, I stopped and introduced myself to the Baich family in their store. I hadn't felt well—probably all my life, but most particularly recently. They responded to many of my questions with information on the effects of different foods on the body and then recommended products that could help me. My fascination grew.

"You could be just what we are looking for," Vic Baich said. "Terry, my nephew, wants someone to work in his shop in Burnaby. Why don't you call him up?"

I did.

CHAPTER EIGHT

Nurturing My Turn-Around

There on Kingsway, a highway that stretches east from Vancouver to Burnaby, I met Terry, a man with a round, flat, bowling-ball hairdo with matching but smaller bowling-ball eyes. He looked ageless. I found out he was only a year older than I was.

"I have been 'putting it out there' that someone would come in," he said. "But it's been awhile. You might be just what I need."

We settled on minimum wage with supplements at cost, a type of paid education.

"When do you want me?"

"Whenever you want to come."

"Hmmmm…." I smiled. No one had ever given me that kind of leeway before. "I have to return to Edmonton to pack up the house I just sold, then I will be back."

"Okay. If it is meant to be…I look forward to it."

Later, he told me how he'd taken one look at me, then thirty-five, and thought, "Lordy, Lordy—I have to get this girl well. She is a mess!"

Back in Vancouver, before going off to sort and pack my Edmonton life, I pulled up in front of the home of my friend Marianne, always so soft, kind, and strong. There I was, in debilitating shame, skulking behind my wheel. Life was still at the other end of a tunnel for me. Marianne, who was an icon in the women's movement, whose little cottage we had rented for Steven's final weeks, who had hosted the grand wake we had for Steven, who had stood behind me as I prepared to leave for Edmonton, measured her sauntering up to my car.

I started to cry as I looked at her big, brown eyes. "I'm back. Said I wouldn't be, but here I am. Going to work in health foods."

"Let's have a cup of tea. I'm happy to see you," she welcomed me warmly while peering at me. She—and I in my more settled times—was committed to helping women out of the traditions that kept us small. I feel it so much as I write this all these years later. Soon she invited me to live in her basement when I returned and while I reestablished myself, another great gift.

Off I went back to Edmonton to close out the house, gather my things, and say good-bye to the friends I had made there—that is, the ones who weren't angry with me over my releasing Naomi again. Edmonton was a challenging interlude, but with some help I packed things quite quickly. Then I was retroactively fired because I'd sent out a bulletin telling exactly what was going on. Oh, naïveté at the helm again! I thought everyone wanted to know the truth. The Board members were angry as hidden agendas, which I didn't understand, were illuminated. Some of the Board quit. It was little like throwing a huge, vengeful grenade, a reactive and defensive response. They were glad to be rid of me, I am sure.

It was a lot to deal with, and I remember how exhausted I felt with the entire scenario of loss and failure. But I was now so relieved to be done with arranging an identity in order to look normal and secure, where I could be legitimate in the eyes of my past. How would I replace it? What was true for me?

Back to my burgeoning life in Burnaby, Terry and I agreed on the specifics of the position where I could learn by clerking and studying. Walking through the long, narrow store with its myriad tiny bottles lining the shelves, however, I was defiant. "Never!" I was so sure. "I am not going learn about all those!" I pointed to the supplements with a grand sweep of my arm.

He, in his coercive fashion of conscious manipulation, agreed with me. "Okay!" But he knew better. Like a good mentor, he always remained undaunted by my resistances. He knew my curiosity and success with customers would woo me...and how! I read and read — morning, noon, and night. I tested products on myself, monitoring the results. I felt better. I looked better. I studied healing through foods and learned muscle testing before I helped customers try things out on themselves and in their lives and develop their own programs, but mostly I was seeing and experiencing results. I learned quickly. The cause and effect was profound.

In health foods, there was an answer to a deeper calling. And like most of the steps I have taken into my authentic nature, this was a portal to other portals. The portal of Burnaby Health Foods became an infinite aperture to studying nutrition via books, my own body's response, as well as the effects in the many, many customers I worked with. We'd refer to literature to look up their problems, find suggested solutions, and saw so many amazing results. It was incredibly rewarding. I also studied business at the community college and answered ads for apartments. I needed a view, but again the Vancouver vacancy rate was very, very low.

My affirmation was, "I have a wonderful apartment with a view" — I said it over and over and over again. One day, about three months after I moved into Marianne's basement, finally, there was an ad in the paper: an apartment at Sixteenth and Dunbar. I had to go see it fast, but I was almost an hour away, and I had only one free hour between closing the shop and class.

I called my hostess, whom I lovingly called Merry Old Annie. "Is there any way you can check into this ad for me? I have class tonight in Burnaby and I am going to miss out."

"Sure, kiddo. I will."

Thanks again to Marianne, the apartment was mine. There was a long waitlist; when the owners called the people ahead of me, however, no one answered. But my friend Marianne was right there — the latest Divine Intervention disguise! Its northern exposure gave the apartment diffused light and a place where my inner turmoil could rest as I gazed at the mountains, the peaks called the Lions, and the inlets of the ocean that shone in front of my bedroom and living room.

The move was chaotic, but finally, after moving my stuff in, worn out but pleased, I closed the door. I knew this was a beginning. I would change everything about myself that I could. The sounds in my head were still whirring. I was achingly lonely, but conscious that my loneliness was a point of entry for something. I remember reading in *Initiation* by Elisabeth Haich that loneliness was a calling to one's path. I began looking at life around me as if I were in another dimension. But I could handle that now. I was accustomed to it.

I had a checklist:

1. Find out how I worked, using foods as the major mining and reconstruction tool. Re-creation, too. Resources were many.

2. Find out if I am truly crazy, or what does my being different really mean?
3. Repair all the things I have done wrong that made people so angry with me.
4. Find out why visions rise unbidden and how to stop them.
5. Follow my truth, my intuitive guidance.
6. Be in truth with myself, know who I really am, and improve myself before I mate again.
7. Meditate.
8. Be more loving. [And here I wrangled daily with terrible pain about Naomi and about my relationship with Steven and others. Was I so quick to react, to judge? Did I destroy them?]
9. Fix and heal all of my past. What did I bring to relationship? What can I bring now?
10. Discover why my brain is moving in a hectic, electric way. Keep working on slowing it down so I can focus.

Lordy! I was always hectic inside, even more so now that I was driven to re-create myself. I was very, very wary of any authority, almost paranoid, so I tested everything on myself, listening to nothing that didn't "work." Operation Health was a sleuthing process.

As I closed the Edmonton door behind my last helper, I also closed it against my old way of attracting a houseful of characters, usually in transition. Now I would establish a life that was orderly, in which every appliance would work, and where there would be no mess. In my own pristine space, I could figure out who I was, how crazy I was, why I was "different," and why my head buzzed, whirred, thrummed, and kept me in a reality that was emotionally separated from this one. Where did my visions come from? What food should I eat to be really me and which foods create negative reactions? How could I move into the real flow of Veronica Marie Holtby?

Affirmations work just fine, although that one about avoiding a house full of characters wasn't quite arranged consciously. But no one came. It was magic! My message had gone "out there." The phone hardly rang. I had no more company. The fun and frolics with the motley crews I often attracted had kept my personality distracted. But the real me was under it all — trying to please, be busy, and be popular. I said to myself, "There will be no more of that." I pressed my back against my already closed door and looked the length of the narrow apartment to the long windows, then out to the mountains and sea through the latticing poles and wires. The familiar loneliness drooped deeply inside of me into an aching kind of hole, a dark hole, but it was mine and beckoned me to start the work.

Daily I drove to the health-food store, and for a while I loved it and learned a great deal. One morning, I was standing at the front desk. The store was empty. The long and narrow pill-lined shelves with their strange herbal smells yawned in a formidable array. Creak! Bang! The back door was pushed open. Heather, a young customer in her housecoat, was carrying her laundry. I hurried to help her as bottles of vinegar, molasses, and antler-horn tonic teetered, threatening her and her cottony tornado. She was steaming mad and glared at me with a blotchy red face.

"You okay?" I asked warily.

"Look at me! Just look! You and your niacin!" Right there in the shop, clutching her laundry, her blue eyes popping under blonde curls, she pointed as her skin reddened right before my eyes. I got the giggles.

"What is happening?" She dumped her laundry — T-shirts, bras, sweat pants, underpants — unceremoniously on the shop floor. She tore off her kimono, bared her itchy, reddening arms and legs, and jigged about. I couldn't help myself and burst into uncontrollable laughter. "Thanks a lot," she muttered.

"Just wait! Give it another ten minutes," I promised her as I tried to collect my wits.

We bagged her laundry while the niacin rushed through her brain, softening her mood. That is the way it works. Fresh blood and oxygen calmed her tensions and freshened her skin.

"Remember," I told her, "you are exercising lazy capillaries to your brain, organs, skin — wherever you have any."

The first time I took niacin, I took my clothes off and stood in front of a full-length mirror and watched as the flush moved through my entire body. Fascinating, even amusing. Of course there is a little itch. And with the flush, my depressions or sadnesses lifted. Wonderful!

Heather actually continued with the niacin, handling its diminishing flush and learned additional ways to benefit herself. If they hadn't already been chronicled by wizardesses like Adele Davis or even earlier health teachers, a lot of the experiences would have been called miracles. As people studied and experimented, eye bags and allergies shifted, moods changed, relationships got better, children became more even-tempered, people's energy improved. I remember one woman who always looked sleepy and droopy eyed with dark circles. Her simple choice was garlic-oil capsules and, except for the ignoble scent of that potent bulb, she looked very different, was sleeping better, and her skin and eyes looked much brighter. Some talked in covert terms about their sex life finally standing up for itself.

"Gloria, those garlic pills made such a difference with you. You look like a new woman."

"Sure," Gloria quipped cynically, sounding a lot like I had a few months earlier. "Sure. Good sales pitch! How do I know?"

"Here, look in the mirror. Look at your eyes — remember your bags?" I asked, something I repeated over the next twenty-five years. "Get yourself a little pocket mirror and check it regularly before and after. You can see for yourself. Know how you feel." Half of the deal with supplements is breaking into your own code. As Terry used to say, "There is no reason to be an ugly older person."

Henna was hilarious. I would explain to people how to mix it like a pie filling and then plop it on their heads. If they didn't get it, I explained that for it to work it has to look like horse poo; so then several of the older ladies came in with friends, nudging each other as I said it again. "Horse poo — hahaha." They didn't forget. Then there was chamomile, rosemary, mint, many herbs — that is, before the weevils that liked to find homes in unsprayed herbs, nuts, and seeds caught up with them. "You can eat it, drink it, and bathe in it," I'd tell them. "Even wear it in your hair."

Terry taught me well. As soon as someone walked into that store, he knew exactly what he or she needed, by his or her skin, eyes, walk, all the messages of the whole person. I followed right in his footsteps. The lore and wonders of the tiny bottles spoke to me in that little health-food store. I also read and read and read. It was an advantage to be an insomniac in those days. Lying awake at night, or during quiet times at the shop, I devoured books and tried the nutritional supplements.

My intuitive education was amping up. I was learning to read people's faces and, without realizing it, their energy fields. Customers would come in the door, and I would watch them; before they reached the front counter, I knew what their deficiencies were: *B6, Zinc, Vitamin D, needs a ton of vitamin C.* Trust of my intuitive nature grew and grew as my knowledge grew and grew. B1 for fear, B15 for better use of oxygen—made some people run faster, but, interestingly, made me sleep better. B-Complex just for metabolic balance..."Brains, beauty, and booze," Under the heading of "booze," we put any kind of blood-sugar interruptions like coffee, tea, sugars of any kind.

Terry was a would-be actor. And me? I wanted to be a writer. My family was always performing, and my siblings and I regularly set up plays as kids. Some years, I set up mini Christmas plays that we would all perform for my folks on Christmas Day. In the health-food store days, I put that practice to good use: "Hey, Terry, let's perform miraculous healings with supplements!"

We both smoked in those days. Smoke from our cigarettes curled out the back of the health-food store as our performance started. One of us would hobble in, barely ambulatory.

"Hi, there," the other would say to the pretend customer.

"Hi. I am seventy-five years old," one would say, nearly inaudible.

The other would exaggerate with rolled eyes. "So? Here, take this vitamin C, B-complex, and now this antler-horn tonic from China." The aging crisis of our seventy-five-year-old would unravel bit by bit, and our old person would rise, stand straighter, become more ebullient. We could barely stand up amidst our laughter, then we would swig out of antler-horn tonic bottles—we were always testing new potions for their promised hit of energy. Customers who stumbled in on us would join in the fun.

When someone said, "You look good," the best response was, "Yes, I am seventy-five years old, but I take vitamins." Hahaha.

During those days, everywhere I went, I hauled a huge plastic grocery bag of supplements around. At the first inner sign of a drop of a nutrient in my system, a pain, a pulse, low-blood sugar, increased tension, I would rummage in that bag for the appropriate micronutrients, minerals, or vitamins. I was my laboratory. To me it was fascinating. Some friends pulled away — as usual. "Take a number," I thought. Some worried that I had truly lost my narrow grip on sanity. I was more concerned with finding it.

"That's dangerous!" "Are you crazy?" "Don't you think you are a little out of control?"

"Maybe, but I am going to figure out how I work!"

"Go to the doctor." "Settle down!" "Find yourself a good man!" "Get a real job!"

Well, I couldn't and I didn't.

One night, some old friends and I were on a deck overlooking a spectacular Vancouver sunset, indulging in some wine and cheese. Marianne was there. I loved her. She seemed to understand that underneath my quirks and craziness, there was a valuable me. We laughed a lot at the hilarious plots for animations we would create for "out there" in the mythical realms of "someday." But my bag rustling and pill popping of micronutrients was a little too much even for her.

"You are getting carried away! Couldn't that be dangerous?"

We went through my lists of references. The greatest of those was *me*, my own research lab. I had been very uneven, close to off-the-rails crazy. And Marianne had known me throughout those times. She was also very sensitive and had been hospitalized for a mental and emotional crisis years earlier. She wasn't afraid of my madness. "Okay, I can see you look better and seem more yourself," she finally said.

Then, I wobbled. Although Terry was letting me buy supplements at cost, I started to worry that I was being sucked in, that he was getting me hooked on them.

I decided one day, "I am looking and feeling good. Oh, well. I am all better now." And I stopped taking anything.

Less than a week later, brown eyes flashing, Terry challenged me. "You have stopped taking your supplements, haven't you?" He could tell just by looking at me that I was slipping.

"Yes." I cocked my hip and my attitude in defense. "I don't want to be stuck, hooked, always indebted to you, Terry." In fact, I will always owe him for all the teaching, the encouragement, the fun support...I am joyfully indebted to him.

Somehow, in his subtle style, he got in step with me, and I started my program again. How did he do that? I don't know. I should have realized he would be able to see that I had begun to slide back into my old ways of feeling, seeing, thinking. I was not okay. But he subtly turned some kind of crank, and very shortly I was back "up."

A lifelong dependency on nutrition? Well, of course! But I was refining it and was also learning how to use nutrition as therapy. I was witnessing the health of so many others around me — and in me, too — with supplements, those rows and rows of tiny bottles that I had announced I would *never* learn. Funny. I often think of how many *nevers* I have had to eat. What a banquet!

Terry and I became wonderful friends. One day, as we were stocking and sorting shelves, he looked at me pointedly. "You know, Mrs. Holtby, you and I were almost through. When you stopped your supplements, I wanted to fire you. I came so close. But you caught on fast enough. You are hard work, my friend." He shook his head and his finger at me. Under his eagle eye, he could watch my rebalancing click in again.

Just a note to you: Supplements are a little different nowadays. You really need to ensure that your sources are pure and free of GMOs.

One night, I arrived home to my little apartment to some dire news. Naomi had disappeared again from her foster situation. Even though I had given her up more than a year before, I was reeling, hurt, confused, and very broken up. "What could I have done differently? Who am I? A pariah of failure. What is going to happen to her?" Staring at myself in my bathroom mirror, tweezers set to pluck my bushy brows, lo and behold, I discovered that I had a moustache! A dark, bristly moustache! I was horrified. My story-telling mind scripted, "At thirty-five, she popped a swarthy moustache, but continued soul searching anyway."

My younger sister, camping with me between husbands, came home to the little apartment. There I was, sitting in my bed, drinking wine, and, that terrible taboo, smoking cigarettes in bed — something I never did.

"Hi!" She peered into my room "Hello. Everything okay?" she asked warily.

"Naomi is gone again."

"Oh, I'm sorry." She hugged me warmly and soothingly as she added, "Ronni, you may never totally get over her."

"There's something else. I have a moustache!" I wailed. She fell onto my bed, pummeling and tickling me as if we were kids again, giggling hysterically.

"You always had to try the next thing. And now you have a moustache!" We laughed as tears ran down our faces.

She was right about Naomi. I have never totally recovered from my failure as her mum, even though the years offer more and more information on the hurdles we were dealing with — both mine and hers. Besides, with grief we never recover. We become. We develop. Our time together and our losses stretched my boundaries on all levels. Her soul journey needed her to come through some deep and difficult traps of addiction, abuse, and dominations from darker entities. And, I believe, by the time she passed at forty-five, she had made it. Although she was still addicted, she had a bright light and was helping other street people spiritually. She had turned herself into a contributor.

Nor would I recover from the moustache sprout. Instead it launched some painful and often hilarious moustache-ripping events, on a par with Shirley MacLean's incident in the old movie *Steel Magnolias*, that continue to this day. There's testosterone in Chinese herbs!

A few days later, Terry was at the front end of the store answering a woman's questions. "Does it matter which of these Chinese remedies women should take? Royal Jelly or ginseng?" she asked.

"Oh, no," he assured her.

"Ahem, ahem," I coughed down the aisle toward them. I was scratching my upper lip, meaningfully cocking my head. He could barely contain himself, choking back his laughter as my antics jogged his memory. There was testosterone in the ginseng. Oh, yes, it charged us up, but...I learned a lot.

Somewhere during that time, Steven's dad Gordon, in one of his visits to me, saw that I was still deeply locked inside. As a minister, he could "see" some of the emotional traps. He came with me to my storage locker, crammed with detritus from our travels, our marriage, our life together in the Cache and Victoria. He suggested we dredge it for old letters, my wedding dress, photos of Steven and me — a vault full of memory. He was concerned that I was clinging to it all. I was. I thought I was working things out, but I was really still clinging. Together we assembled a grand boxful, and together we ceremoniously dumped it all. I am often flooded with gratitude for how he stood by me.

As far as finding myself a good man, though, obviously I wasn't ready yet. I was in a thorough reconstruction process. At times, I was still enshrouded by shame, filled with self-doubt. Then love. When I finally did fall in love, post-Steven, I could run like the wind. But my illusions were profound. Peering through their curtain, I realized that the new lover I had attracted, even after all my growing and changing, was an alcoholic. I was devastated. All my knowledge and all the supplements in the world just couldn't help him — or me, in fact. Since we see the self in everyone we meet, he reflected back to me the heritage of alcoholism, all in harmony with the frequencies of my self-deprecation. I liked my wine, and my family always visited around wine, sometimes home-made and sometimes bought. The good part was that this man was intrinsically a good man. And I was pushed into learning about alcoholism as a terrible trap. It took a while, months, in fact, for me to realize how impossible the situation was...and longer to learn that it was a bid to reach spiritual heights, confounding the same center of the brain — the addiction and the quest for transcendence physiologically are apparently lodged in the same section of the brain.

Otherwise, I was growing. The clicks and licks I felt in my body or mind and my emotional whirls called more and more subtly to me. Answering all their calls from my plastic shopping bag, I could soon feel how I was tuning up my own body's chemistry. So many feelings were balanced out by any of the Bs, or by sorting out digestion problems, or by detoxifying my body. I boosted my energy with C-complex balanced with bioflavenoids, the cell-building aspect of oranges and grapefruits. I learned from "the codfather," Dale Alexander, about healing my immune system with cod-liver oil. And *so* much more. I became very different to people who had known me most of my life: fewer dark circles, calmer, fewer emotional fluctuations or reactions. My skin was stunning and radiant with all the flax and good oils.

I was still only able to concentrate on books if they were about grief and nutrition. Spirituality was soon added. Greats like Yogananda, writing about his own awakenings in *Autobiography of a Yogi*, actually filled in some of my great intuitive gaps. Then I became attracted to gatherings of the Emissaries of Light as they emerged in the Vancouver scene. Their goal was to awaken us to the rising consciousness of our species. None too early! We learned to meditate together and to honor our intuitive wisdom, promptings from our higher selves.

The defeats of the Sixties weren't total. It was a welcome relief to know that there was still a movement toward peace and love, but now, "It has to start within each of you," said Dorothy McLean of the famed Findhorn Community in Northern Scotland. She spoke of the magic of working with intuition and guides with Peter and Eileen Caddy: "All our instructions come from the fairies, land devas, and our own intuition, and they are in intentional harmony with one another. The cabbages we grew in the sand and harsh weather were huge beyond belief." She taught us meditative techniques to access our own guidance.

Some of it was funny or bizarre. "Follow your desires. Resistance blocks your path." A couple of the Emissaries would drink their brains out, "following their desires." I wondered about that, knowing the danger. But resistances can be a huge block to our evolution. I understand that....balance. Always balance. Our gatherings always started off with a meditation. It felt different there, new to me, to be in a society with what I now know as a coherent, positive field, a society that was open and honest. It was entrancing.

I felt possible — still shaky...but more possible.

CHAPTER NINE

Deepening

At this point, I found myself longing for a total immersion experience—a kind of a womb where I could eat and sleep, dream and evolve into my true nature, work with healing, and retune my body and my psyche. I wanted a true holistic experience. Through one of my new Emissary friends who was cataloguing the emerging "wholistic" options, I found one, a healing center on Orcas Island. Dr. Randolph Stone and his team of practitioners used a system of energy release, vegan diet, physical activity, hot tubs, and lectures. It was a huge plunge for me! Even though it was a little scary, I was ready for it.

Each day we rose at six to exercise. Actually, it was more like exorcize! The day started out seriously. We worked hard, rolling our muscles back and forth against strong pole constructions, making sounds all the while. We had to press hard, like wiping peanut butter off a knife. I felt a kind of anguish as the emotional pains, which were locked in my thighs, were released. Though it hurt physically while we rolled, it wasn't long before we could feel the changes in ourselves. Dr. Stone taught us that the higher parts of our thighs and the joints where they connect to the hips hold vengeance, anguish, and suspicion. We learned how to apply pressure to key points in one another's bodies to facilitate letting go of angers, hatreds, resistances, and so many more.

It wasn't only physical. My attitude needed work, too, and this was the place. Going to the admitting desk, I complained about my accommodations. I wanted more privacy.

"I hear you," the person at the desk kindly acknowledged me.

Hmmm, how odd. My contrary, argumentative nature was just being loved. The predominant attitude there, the ambiance among the staff and actually most of the people like me who had come for healing, was loving.

We checked in from various towns and realities—no aliens that I know of—a minister, a senator, a cocaine addict, a young artist, a woman who had been raped and was looking for peace, some women with young children, people who wanted to study Dr. Stone's magic. There was a bit of a cultish attitude as well, speaking about the higher roles of the male and female. I rolled my eyes as the children arrived, but interestingly, they, too, were calming and accepting. They had obviously learned that. Or maybe they just knew it.

At times, each one of us flared up in anger or became a little belligerent. Remember, we were all there to sort through challenges and old patterns. "I can't stand this!" was met with recognition and agreement, even from the little children. We would find ourselves backing up inside and our defiance just seemed to disperse. It was amazing. The tone of the place was relentlessly peaceful no matter what our issues were that brought us to Doe Bay. Parts of it reminded me of Terry and how he had, over and over again, put me back on track with no adversity. I was being unhooked from some of my deeper resistances and mistrusts. Oh, I resisted at first, wanting to cling to the familiar. Resistance, they say, is one of the greatest stumbling blocks to enlightenment. Oh, how I resisted knowing that! We took turns standing in front of the group. The way we stood, the way we were built, our jaw line, all of our amazing personal features were used to discuss our soul's presentation, or our karma. What was said about me? "This jaw line shows that you are determined" — it wasn't the set of my jaw, but its intrinsic line. The reading included my posture as a defensive stance, the build of a body showing inherited or tribal ways of moving and grooving. Apparently, I am a meso-morph, a warrior.

As soon as I'd walked onto the Doe Bay Resort Land, I started crying. During that wombing week, a cork popped deep inside of me as if I were a sparkling drink that had been shaken. My tears effervesced. I couldn't stop them. It was as if who I really am had been tamped down inside, crouched underneath so many influences. Just being seen and accepted took that cork out. Visions wobbled in and out of my days, sometimes frightening me as people wafted through my sight. During the intense classes there — spiritual, meditative, trancing — we learned how we were all reflecting aspects of one another. I felt more uncharted releases, and then I would cry and cry again. Others there were as unbalanced as I was. Even the senator and his wife had the courage to work on their own inner demons, like the dance of fame, power, and promiscuity. The cocaine addict was hilarious as he grieved for cocaine, a stand-up-comedy act, but he was determined to get beyond it. Evenings in the hot tubs were a social time when we entertained one another with tales of personal madnesses. Humor ripened and as we teased each other, old self-doubts seemed to be tweezed out of us in the ambiance. The week was life-changing.

Meanwhile, interspersed through Burnaby Health Foods, Doe Bay, and *learning learning learning*, I was still exploring my visions and learning to stop them, as well as studying how to empower myself through my experiences. Wanting to help me through my "life's lessons" were my friend Phil, the writer with the shoe hanging from his ceiling, and his mother, Mrs. Surguy, who invited me to every little tea-leaf-reading gathering she had at her house. Their imagery and her love lifted my spirits. Her humble and sweet living room, filled with photos and flowers, was a little like the Victoria Psychic Society where we had "Tea and a Reading" for seventy-five cents. But instead of seventy-five cents, these teacup readings were paid for by little gifts for Mrs. Surguy, one of the most giving women I have ever met. The high end of Pisces, she loved and lived to give and give and give some more to lift people. Years later, when I was living in the East, I heard she had passed. Apparently she was very excited to go, even carrying her favorite pillow to the hospital, her final destination. Her faith was strong and contagious.

At one tea gathering, a couple of the older women were chatting. They seemed older to me then, being in my thirties. They'd be more like my world now.

"You know, Mrs. Surguy," one said. "I was in the bathroom this morning applying makeup" — I had marveled at her rosy-apple cheeks — "when I saw a woman standing there, and the scent of roses filled the room. She was lovely."

Wouldn't that be wonderful if I could ever get there, I thought. Would I ever be as sure as they are now that spirit beings were so available?

"I smell lilacs whenever my mother is near," the other woman mentioned.

"The day my husband died, I was visiting back East," said Mrs. Surguy. "A large picture slid down the wall to the floor. I knew. I just stood up and caught the nearest plane home. My son knew and met the plane." No doubts. No questions.

I would understand, too—but a little later. I hadn't yet learned to live in the altered states of America. When I heard of a psychic in Edmonton, or even earlier in Vancouver, off I would go for a reading, taking copious, copious notes. At first I didn't know why, but as I studied those notes, what emerged was a lot like the qualities of literature, and I knew more and more which levels they read from. Over the years, it became more and more obvious—maybe without consciously knowing it—that I was learning about levels of dimension, spiritual intelligence, and vibrations, both from my insides and my external world. I was shy and certainly still besieged by my agitated brain, but I was emerging.

Once some friends and I even did a cable shoot at a psychic fair, where I went from reader to reader and had a little read on me, looking for the golden chord between them all, looking for a common streak of wisdom. We did six shoots over the years and they were always followed by fun screening parties, but in this case people were uncomfortable and left early. I have to laugh in retrospect. The subject, between my seeming self-obsession and the craziness of the psychic world, was way too much. What I wanted to discover were ways of entering the deeper identity of myself or of anyone in my audience, an identity more personal than those projected on one another. I knew by then that we project upon everyone and often all we know is the reflection back, not the real person. And most of us don't even know our own real self! The friends who came to share the first run of this little show perhaps found this shoot a little too much about me, too personal—not universal enough. I laugh. Maybe that was true, although my intention was to reveal a lot of layers of beingness that we all have and the ways and means of breaking into it using such a broad selection of doorways—like vibrations, eyes, soul journey, seeing/ feeling/knowing…and I think it did show that. It just made people uncomfortable.

CHAPTER TEN

Windows and Bridges

My college, the tiny but deep transformative college of Burnaby Health Foods on Kingsway in Burnaby, British Columbia, was a successful, seven-month pivot for me. Short but thorough. I turned my own health around as well as gained energy — and even beauty — I didn't know I had. I still, however, lived with the determination of a jackhammer to keep moving past the relentless thrumming in my head, the hole in my heart, and the insanity of my restlessness. My apartment was an isolation tank, so much of my time was spent there alone or, as I mused, "a loan," aware that I was very much "en route," with space for my daily yoga, my piles of books and papers, and my plastic bag of supplements, all attuned to the trusty clackety clack of the old, portable typewriter I had inherited from our CYC days. Nighttimes there, I would write my way out of my inner tangles. Oddly, I felt a deep panic when anything was moved — even a little bit for cleaning. Somewhere in all my trauma, I was trying to make and keep life reliable.

At work, desperate for expansion, I writhed inside. Now what? I was learning. The information was reliable. It worked. But Terry was rarely there at this point. Our lively "blue smoke" plays, called that because of the blue smoke wafting upward from our cigarettes, were done. His teachings were no longer my lifeblood. He was out having fun and looking for his own expression and ways to expand his world. The walls of the tiny shop were closing in on me.

I watched a sweet local psychic come to the counter one day, carrying her herbs and supplements, brown rice, and molasses. She smiled at me and said, as if in response to a question, "My goodness, dear, it doesn't matter what you do. Just help others." Then she burst out laughing. "You want to get out of here, don't you? Your aura is pointed as if it is trying to poke a hole in the ceiling!" She burst out laughing as she waddled away.

She was one of the many psychics who Terry marveled at: heavy and ate a lot of sugar. He used to make cracks about how our blood-sugar fluctuations, sudden drops and rises, give us visions. I needed to know all that to monitor my own unbidden visions. But the ones induced by blood-sugar fluctuations are much less reliable. "How many psychics are real and how many just have hypoglycemia?" His eyes twinkled and sparkled with his cynical humor at life.

I was on the trail of releasing myself from the disturbance of my unbidden visions, the possibility of being crazy. I wasn't, at least not yet, really aiming to become a psychic. "Terry, I have to leave. I need to expand—desperately."

"Okay, okay," he hissed, annoyed, obviously let down. "But you could buy the shop. Buy it. You are good here. You'll have a good living for yourself."

"No, Terry. It's too small. I don't know how, but I need to expand."

A few days later, I addressed another psychic, a regular customer who was buying her potions. "Hello, Mrs. Jenson. Can you answer one question for me, please?"

"Sure, dear."

"I am working so hard to turn myself around. How am I doing?"

After quietly rolling her eyes up to the side and taking a little breath, she shrugged. "You are about a fifth of the way there."

Oh, my Lord! I crashed. I had been dredging my inner self, turning myself inside out like a sock that has uncomfortable knots inside, eating, supplementing, thinking, dreaming, reading, praying, *deepening deepening deepening* to the truth of myself....Lordy! Only a fifth of the way. I wanted to throw myself down on the floor and howl and pound my fists. I didn't. I had nothing to do but keep going.

Onward! My next research focus was nutrition and mental health. The money from the sale of my Edmonton house finally came, so with a little of the money, off I went, kind of unsure again about the possibility of quackery, to attend a schizophrenia and nutrition conference in Toronto. Lo and behold, there were hundreds of people who, exploring the effects of nutrition in their families, counseling practices, ministries, or even schools and hospitals, spouted miracle after miracle and turnaround incident after turnaround incident. One of the social workers I met was from the inner city of Chicago, who worked with kids who were in trouble. "Once you get them off Coca-Cola, even for a week or two, you can't pay them to drink the stuff. They basically don't want to be in trouble. They don't want to be 'bad.'" They became totally different kids without that familiar drink.

Testimonials were startling; some of the most memorable came from parents who had run through mazes of professionals to find help for their children. The opposition they encountered as they ran against the currents of marketed medication and therapy is a familiar story. They were shunned. People turned away, just like in that older movie, *Close Encounters of the Third Kind*—when the hero pursued his vision in spite of the normal responsibilities that defined him, the world shunned him, too. But he found his dream, his dream that illuminated so many.

The light was powerful there. Discussions and testimonials and real-life experiences pulled the lid off situation after situation. So many people there had turned a child, partner, client, or friend around with nutritional therapies.

Abram Hoffer, the pioneer Canadian psychiatrist, spoke of his successes treating schizophrenia with niacin, or B3, the capillary flusher that helps supply fresh blood for the brain, and there was a lot of burble about his clinics. The material throughout the conference was exciting and empowering. I had been enrapt by studying Hoffer and a few others who were teaching about the mind and nutrition; I was certainly delighted to learn even more about niacin along with other supplements to straighten out my mind, my blood sugar, and my insomnia.

We learned about the history of pellagra, a dreadful disease that involves the breakdown of skin and mind. There were even institutions for those with this disease. It was discovered in the 1800s that pellagra developed via a deficiency of B3 in badly stored corn, which couldn't hold its nutritional balance. But the market didn't want to relinquish its profits—does that sound familiar?—so the corn would still be sent to prison, mental institutions, and orphanges and fed to the various clumps of society they housed. Interesting that corn today has been so GMO'd that in its many forms, even in the making of Vitamin C, it is dangerous for many…a reemergence of the problem with tainted foods and stronger markets. Back then, people suffered from this terminal illness of skin lesions and mental deterioration, which all could have been changed. A few more efforts were tried, but in the 'thirties Dr. Hoffer followed the lead of a few other doctors who knew about this blight. The toxic corn, with its missing nutrient of B3 (also known as niacin), was taken off the market. Interestingly enough, the disease suddenly disappeared a few hundred years after the deficiencies that created it had been discovered. Dr. Hoffer became famous for his trials with B3, along with its flushing that people complain about, but which brings fresh blood through what were lazy or dormant capillaries to the skin, the organs, or the brain—a very helpful process. I still love the flush.

At the conference, I also heard of another miracle: B6 for people who don't remember dreams. Take it and dream!

"Hot diggity!" I said to myself. When I arrived back in my little hotel room, I popped several B6 tablets, and not only did I not dream, I didn't sleep at all. Yes, they can also give you energy. It reminded me of the time of dealing with the terrible restlessness that overtook me after Steven died. I couldn't focus. I couldn't stay still—apparently like a mongoose that loses its mate, I read. Looking through my Adele Davis bible, *Let's Eat Right to Keep Fit*, I learned that I needed magnesium. Okay! I took magnesium, all right, a whole tablespoonful. And my restlessness gave way to a desperate diarrhea, which sat me on the toilet for hours on end. I pushed my concentration to read a little farther along!

There was so much more. Greats like Lendon Smith, who was quite the comedian, talked about cravings and allergies—like when you want coffee so much that you literally pick up the pot and drink it straight from the coffee pot, get away from coffee! You know by that craving, it is an allergen. Bernard Jensen, with his information on tissue cleansing and digestive health, was another. I was riveted by these great purveyors of possibility.

I wanted so much to bring this information forward — the entire thing...not just the hilarious piece on gastrointestinal eruptions brought to you by magnesium. I wanted to share more and more about being able to change life by changing our biochemistry using foods and supplements, thus changing our entire possibility. I wanted to share it all. This information was like a window on the computer lurking in the background and needing to be brought forward. Who wouldn't want to know all this? These are accessible tools for health! I was evidence. I wasn't quite crazy anymore — oh, yes, very fragile, but my mind was working better than ever. People who knew me continued to remark that I had changed and opened, even seemed younger and less fraught. I was moving past that immaturity that comes from a frozen true self. And I had the evidence of so many customers from Burnaby Health Foods as they studied themselves and found routes through so many health difficulties.

Yet the marketing factions of society didn't want that. One day when I was at the shop, in came a representative of the Canadian Federal Government armed with thick rolls of masking tape. Fiercely, he ripped tape off a huge roll to create great crisscrosses of the sticky stuff across the shelves, to prevent the sale of these "dangerous" supplements. Huge landslides of letters of protest loaded the health-department mails. The tape came off, and we carried on for a time. Cause and effect, self-empowerment, testimonial realities were our checks and balances. I was still naïve in spite of our Sixties experiences — still a Pollyanna. If these simple nutritional supports worked, who wouldn't want to know? Of course the world wants us all to be healthy. Oh, really?

Maybe I could do a television show. What it would take? I drove back out to Burnaby Health Foods. "Terry, I want to do a television show."

He was already on the same page. "Let's! Or we could start easier, with radio." And off we went. Next thing I knew, we were practicing night after night at my apartment or at the beach.

"Good evening, Ronni. This is Terry Presber, and you have tuned in to *It's Your Health*." I remember how nervous I was, even though it was just the two of us. I was still easily shattered, falling apart under the least provocation, shaking and crying when someone challenged me. Terry would, in his sweet, gay way, hand me a B vitamin and some lecithin or skullcap or other wondrous soothing agents to heal the sheaths around my nerves. We became stronger and better and actually began to perform.

As far as entering the world professionally, I was still at the end of that long corridor, disconnected. When I was feeling empowered, though, was when I was connected to how people work or how we feel—connected in service. In retrospect, I marvel at how grief, the death of my old self, and nutrition lit up a construction pathway for me through the tatters of my mind and nerves. Please God, never, ever again do I want to reenter that inner space of singing wires, shaking nerves and body, and fear of people—a real paranoia. A perceptual stew of electrical colors seemed chaotically matted in my head, each with its own sounds and feelings. It often seemed like my circuits blew and the wires exploded, spewing tangled strings of many colors.

Especially as the years go along, I recognized why people stayed away from me. We fear the reflection of our own vulnerability! Attacks were vicious and relentless, reflecting my own experience with authority in life. I knew that they couldn't care about who I really was—it was all about how my madness touched their inner fear, their judgments, their protection. I have known since my early years, when I sat in my favorite ditch remembering who I was, that I had gone on forever, that there were people out there somewhere who knew me, that God was pretty screwed up here. "Why?" I used to ask Him. Again that was before I recognized that God as we know Him/It is a creation from the mind of man.

For years, I was terrified of people and social times. I felt skewered by their judgments, not yet aware that my terror had to attract people who would attack. I would sit at rare social gatherings, deeply inside of myself, unable to find a way to connect for many years. I call it "essential narcissism"—the feeling that we can't look around until we climb a little farther out of the hole created by the loss of our identity and the need to reconstruct our own being.

My expansion with Terry was really pushing me to my limits. For a couple of months, we practiced, wrote out formats, called stations, and tried to get connected. It was a slow search until we arrived at West End Cable and began a series of cable-television shows, docudramas featuring alternative health. We started with massage at the home of a new friend, one of the Emissaries, and it was powerful. But during the third show, Terry's haughtiness collided with my defiant determination. Our row was loud. I don't remember what it was about, but I think it was simply him telling me, in what felt to me at the time was his pissy gay boss voice hissing at me, "Get this done now!" And, of course, I was skitterish. My inner self was still charging around wildly at the hint of danger. We both stormed off in different directions.

At the next meeting at the studio, there was no Terry. I called him a number of times at the store as well as at home. He wouldn't answer. "Come on, Boss," I would say into his answering machine. "Come on, Terry. We have a show to do." He didn't return my calls. I carried on with our project, gathering a different crew and learning to edit the old laborious way cutting and splicing pieces of film. With cable volunteers, I did six shows that were pretty rough as I was a slow, hard-to-focus kind of woman then, what with ADD and/or PTSD. I did it, I really did it. But I missed him so much. The transformative time in which we had known one another was rich. I missed his drama, his sensitivity, and his perceptions. I missed laughing riotously over the skits we performed in the back of the little health-food store. We always joked about it. Added were tales of our love life or our woes plus the directionals around diet and supplementing, and they were warm, happy times.

For the last few months of our planning and writing, I had been using his electric typewriter, which made my nightly writes easier. It was still on my table. I figured that it would eventually draw him back in. It did, but it took two years.

CHAPTER ELEVEN

It's All About Me, You Know —
And You, Too!

Those were the days — full of learning and expressing. I would get up naturally around seven AM, pop over to the local café that was kitty-cornered from my house for breakfast with the artists in the neighborhood. Then I would be off, rain or shine, on my six-mile walk along Spanish Banks, one of Vancouver's stunning beaches, while inside I would be inwardly looking at each vertebrae, untying energy knots, perceiving blocks, and then smoothing them. My inner sight was growing, and information was rising in me, guiding my self-unraveling from the cocoon of reactions I had spun around my true nature.

By this time, I was aware of my chakras and colored them, running the colors through my body until I could feel them and see them. I walked fast, building my speed, until I could feel my endorphins kick in, and then I would say my affirmations. No one stopped to chat. I was a woman on a mission, intense and determined! I would find out who I was, unearth what was true about myself and what my talents were, become more authentic, and use my visions for my art or service.

We each can be "different," I thought. We can make it our truth — but be different to exercise our unique creative nature.

I would stride past the herons, maybe six or seven of them standing majestically like a balanced air sign along the ocean. "Good morning, fellows!" I would call out to them. Their power of self-reflection and balance mesmerized me. They seemed to have what I sought: depth of self, purpose, healing, and transformation.

I was healing and becoming stronger. I was discovering myself...self-absorbed you might say, but how can you find self-realization without intense self-study? I was conscious of feeling that I was climbing out of a deep, deep pit, and until I scrambled out of it, my peripheral vision was limited.

I was also missing my periods. I thought that perhaps that was from just too much stress. One day, I ran into a woman I hadn't seen since my UBC days. Our chat toured nutrition, emotions, and our own histories that were so full of changes deepening inside and out—marriages, heartbreaks, blessings As we talked, we also swapped tales about alternative-health styles. I mentioned, "I haven't had a period for several months. I'm not pregnant. Nothing I take seems to work to bring it on."

"You ought to see my chiropractor."

"Yeah, right!" my old, cynical self reacted. With rapid thoughts and testy words, my defenses clicked into place. I even felt squeamish, my tummy rolling. Maybe it was a trick! I always wished I had been a sweet, gentle feminine spirit, able to wear pink and call myself May. But here I was, still in consciousness kindergarten wrangling my attitude. Still, I calmed down and listened and headed off to see her chiropractor, Dr. Bryan Hale from New Zealand. I read how chiropractic had begun with D.D. Palmer seeing his deaf workman's crooked neck. He straightened out his neck and voilà! Almost like magic, his friend could hear. So, actually, the art of chiropractic seemed less witchery and actually practical after all.

What an amazing man! Bryan was also one who looked at me, who looked into my eyes. He seemed to see me. I could even hint at my visions and strange perceptual flips. A few sessions with him, and my cycle revved up again. That was only a part of my distressed system. I went to him three times a week at least, while he retrained my nerve flows and my structure, and bit by bit I was feeling more powerful. Sometimes, however, I would find myself weeping uncontrollably. "Bryan, I come in feeling great," I complained. "You do your magic, and I cry for a couple of days! Last time I cried all weekend."

"Great! I love to make you cry!" he quipped cheekily. "You're just releasing stored-up tears!"

I feel a wry smile inside as I remember what I was like back then: uncomfortable, yet getting more and more comfortable. I would stride into his waiting room, but couldn't sit still. I needed to move or the energy in me would be out of control, pushing and pulling me. So I would go outside and walk in the fresh air. I could not be trapped. People, feeling my urgency, automatically gave me a wide berth.

Well, maybe I was still crazy, but I was getting better at managing myself. I was still seeing the world through a long tunnel. How long will this go on—this never quite being here? My strange disquiet filled a room. I still had visions, although the more I stabilized my blood sugar, the clearer they became. They would begin uncomfortably while talking with someone. A gray mask would emerge and take over a "normal" face. This mask had slipped out of some hidden closet, probably my etheric belly, which is a repository for my karma. It would pull on people's faces and slide on a new face, one with wrinkles, aged by perhaps a thousand years. Eyes became someone else's eyes. I rarely followed it all the way through. Instead, nervously, I would avert my focus and be uneasy, keep my eyes moving. Shifty, you might say.

This had been going off and on since high school and was happening more and more often. In my determination to figure out how I worked, I was also determined to figure out what all these slipping faces meant.

Bryan was working successfully on a number of mental-health cases, even schizophrenia, by sorting out cross-circuits of energy flows and the brain. Maybe he could help me. I sure wasn't going to fully admit to him yet what my mind was doing, though...just in case. I did send him a number of great clients—as usual, I was attracting into my life people with problems, and in attraction to my own search, they tended to be having unusual mental-health trials. The Law of Attraction was going strong! He loved it.

I wanted to know how it all worked. "I don't stop and explain to anyone," he grumbled, but then he would explain to me anyway, in great detail, the workings of the body. He answered my broad spectrum of questions during sessions. I was fascinated. "You should go back to school and become a chiropractor," he stated. I couldn't handle it then, but he might have been right as my focus on the body/mind connection has remained vital for many years now.

Seeing how keen I was, Bryan offered me a job as an office assistant. I tried, but being tethered to a chair and trying to enter numbers for insurance forms, set appointments, answer phone calls, and tend to people's requirements was simply beyond me. I couldn't sit still there. My head pounded. My heart pounded. I was afraid all the time and trembled in fear of people. The job itself was technically easy, but I wasn't. I couldn't bear the tight, externally designed construction at that point in my recovery.

I lasted almost two weeks, but even though I left the job, I didn't leave Bryan. In fact, while Terry was still working with me, we did a cable-television interview with him on the magic of chiropractic. It was the second in our series of six docudramas exploring alternative healing tools. Bryan's explorations and wizardry were getting him in trouble with the Canadian Medical Association, though. His work on schizophrenics and cancer patients — all kinds of difficult cases we weren't allowed to talk about — threatened the CMA. Years later, I heard he finally had to leave his practice in Canada. He was too much of a challenge for the marketplace, for the system. Yet I am so grateful to him, as are many, many others. He is another angelic medicine man who remains pivotal in my legend, turning my hormones, my brain, my life around. He accelerated my physical and emotional healing, opening a world of true healing.

Cable television also launched a dream of mine that is still very much alive. I'd interview innovative people coming from "the edge," or the frontiers, of personal consciousness. Some of them were traditional, like the acupuncturists from China and Ayurvedic practitioners from India. I interviewed nutritional wizards, artists who literally moved people from within their body or minds, always receiving a demon-stration of their gift. My lifelong fantasy to be a writer was charged up even more. In fact, inside my mind, I was always concocting stories or writing entertaining material to present in my mind, always on stage in my fantasy. My self-doubts and restlessness and, truthfully, shyness made it hard. But maybe, just maybe, I would bring the natural-healing information forward. The world is dying for it—literally! There is a big world beyond the marketplace. Pollyanna strikes again, you say?

I added audio interviews to the ones I was doing at cable TV. With my handy dandy little tape recorder, I went from Bryan and his humble office on Fraser Street to meet an acupuncturist in a most sumptuous office on Broadway near Granville in Vancouver. His was by far the only elegant office I would visit among the broad array of alternative healers lighting up my horizon. An immigrant from China with an MD from Cambridge University, Dr. Chan Gunn was annoyed at the assumption that a Chinese person would be expected to do acupuncture instead of Western medicine, so he set out to prove, scientifically, that acupuncture doesn't work. Lo and behold, his control group of chronic back patients all got well and retrieved their heretofore simmering lives. He, of course, continued his Eastern medical studies, and by the time I met him he had set up his practice. His rates were high.

That regal office was much different than the offices of most of the traditional Asian practitioners, with their plumes of smoke from exotic, cigar-like moxie bustions (whose smoke and heat prepared sites for the healing of congested energy centers on the body), or other strange-looking non-technical instruments. Each of them gave me a generous taste of his or her art out of little rooms in honeycombs in the lower-rent areas of Vancouver. Or I would wander around the West End or the university district of Vancouver, which my brother referred to as "granola country." That was where the alternative people and health-food nuts shone in little stores before their wares were incorporated into the larger chains.

The day I visited Dr. Gunn, he noted that the small amount of rash on my hands was due to a block in a meridian, a specific site. "Oh," I said. "My chiropractor often adjusts that vertebrae and it does help. It's great how things work together."

His rebuttal was quick. "Chiropractic is very, very dangerous" he cautioned me. "After a number of sessions, you will find your spine is loose, and you will not be able to be upright."

I returned his comment to Bryan who, with a robust guffaw, said, "Go back and tell Dr. Gunn that when you stick needles in people, all their blood falls on the floor!" I laughed, but I didn't carry that message back.

On my search, I experienced some of everything I learned. A part of me was stirring. That little, inner, brown-and-black velvet me that was so ancient and distant from my other me's began to awaken that part of me that knew that my outer was a skin, a performance.

My mum actually tried to be supportive through this time. My father was just gone — there was little or no contact. But Mum did try. She would refer weakly to my "nervous breakdown" and look away quickly, embarrassed. But one day, she wrote in a letter from her home in Prince George, "What exactly are you doing?"

I answered her clearly: "Living on the insurance money from Steven's death and learning how I work. I am exploring nutrition to figure out why I have always felt bad, adding explorations of body structure, acupuncture, past-life regressions, color therapy, and music. I want to figure out the body/mind connection. I'd like to be a writer, Mum. I'd like to present all these fascinating alternatives that bring the body, mind, emotions, and spiritual life into balance. But I have to do it for myself first." I hadn't yet learned to say that little truth I keep thinking about these days, "It's all about me, you know. And you, too!"

She was embarrassed, but perhaps a little inspired. After she died, we found notebooks she had stashed that were full of story beginnings she wrote years ago. She knew the writer's heart. In our family, though, we didn't say what was true. We just looked away. In my seeking, my expressions and my changing made my siblings, as well as their spouses, angry at me. It took years for me to truly feel compassion for them and to understand that I was ripping and tearing at the very fabric of our family life, disturbing those tacit agreements that are held so dearly in families.

As I'd mentioned in my letter to my mum, around that time, in and around my explorations, I went into past-life regressions. The first was strange and made my healer angry. I wouldn't go farther than becoming a blue light, a beautiful blue light. And I wouldn't, or couldn't, talk. I was ecstatic. Now I think that that was my Arcturian self whom, later, my guides I have grown to love began to speak of. As a blue light, I had only being—and being was a loving, peaceful feeling. I would love to stay there, like when I was on the colored cake walk and then universal skies of my acid trip. It was beautiful, loving peace through and through. And I came out of that first regression with my healer saying, a little piqued, "Come on. Come on. Oh, well, if you won't respond...." He was apparently new to all this, too.

But then, soon after that, I had a spontaneous past-life experience in which I saw myself as a man named John—not tall, more like my average frame now, with longish hair. I was the successful captain of a beautiful, wooden, tall-masted trading boat. It was huge with a great, long, pointing bow at the front. I kept looking at my wife sitting at a huge, wooden table in our home in this scenario. She was lovely, and I knew her. I could recognize something in her eyes. "Oh, my Lord, it's Mum." Her name then was Mary.

"Please don't go. Please don't go. I am afraid for your health. Don't go!" she begged as she wept and reached for me.

I scoffed. "Stop it. You are just crazy! Stop it now!" I pushed her away as I donned a fancy hat and exited our rather elegant home in northern Europe.

The scenario changed to a battle on the ship, a mutiny, I think. I could "see" in my visions several large men I knew, one a huge friend of my later husband Glenn, a friend with whom I battled periodically. In this battle, the ship was rammed and began a descent into the deep waters of the Atlantic. As I went down, I felt a huge bang on my head from a timber beam that had broken off the ship. As I slipped out of life, I remembered Mary's warning. I had broken her heart. She loved me. I left her, denying her warning and saying she was wrong, but she had been right. My ship went down amidst turmoil. Maybe this explained, at least partially, why she was so angry with me when I was a young child!

Back to my transformational tour of myself in this life....During those intervals, I had to be still and was unable to make choices that suited me, or any choices at all. But more and more, my journey was steered by my inner light and my intuition. I rarely made decisions based on earning money. Mostly, it was to grow, to become whole, to find out who I was so I could take it into the world be helpful — but not yet.

As you well know by now, I am like Pollyanna. At that point, it didn't occur to me to be embarrassed at myself as I trudged, driven by an inner urge, pulled this way and that by the sludge of my past—the trust issues and flinching of a battered child, the distortions of and by the socially created God design, freezing at road blocks. I was always trying to figure out what (not necessarily who) I was, how this body/mind/spirit works, and what attitudes I still had. Too much stimulation or any challenge and I fell apart, crying uncontrollably for maybe a day or two. My gossamer façade was new and fragile.

Delving into my own craziness, unraveling the mysteries of self, and exploring its gateways was a fulltime job. Then there was grappling with my innate love of my therapy-needing God. I meditated, ate perfectly, and was very, very impatient with my rapid-fire brain, although I was practicing to be nonreactive. But I was still too far inside myself to share much. I often thought I was like someone who'd been dropped deep into a narrow hole. As I've mentioned, scrabbling out, there is no peripheral vision. I would have to get to the top to see across the land. In my work with thousands of clients now and as I noted above, I call that phase "the essential narcissism." It truly has to be all about you and your rebirth.

At that point, in the middle of conversations, I was conscious of my frozen sense of self. Then, as if on a catapult, I experienced a bizarre need to leave the room, an agitation about who I was and who was there, and a fuse about a quarter of an inch long. I found it almost impossible to be with anyone, but I needed grounding. Finally, through my breakfasts with the local artists at the café across the street, I found a lover. Finally, I had some snuggling. But...he was the alcoholic I told you about earlier. I loved him, but it was exhausting. I was being grounded, but more deeply than was practical. First I had that dire isolation at the end of a tunnel, then a time of being dragged by someone who was not reliable, who was not there. My apartment didn't feel like mine anymore. It felt full—of the man who wasn't there. It was a strange reflection of my expectations, as in a fun-house mirror. Perhaps it was more of a completion of old woundings.

But universal abundance was at the helm. During that time, my soul was fed by a new flurry of metaphysical friends and the atmosphere of possibility that formed around me. They were stepping—or, as I had been, spilled—out of jobs and other more normal packets of life. We were all hearing the same wake-up call and began to gather for pot-lucks, meditations, and classes with various teachers of metaphysics. Our little tape library was a terrific stream of wisdom and words to comfort and teach. I learned so much during this time of my illusion of a love. He was a place-holder of sorts.

Whenever my Emissary friends gathered, we sat for half an hour in silent meditation. It was wonderfully deepening. We shared dreams. "Let's open a healing center." Or, "Let's travel to Findhorn and intuit the rising energies in ourselves." Or we'd see movies we could discuss, such as *Resurrection* with Ellen Burstyn and *My Dinner with Andre*. Today, it would be *What the Bleep Do We Know?* or *The Secret* or *I AM*. Our philosophy was to follow our intuition, create dreams, and follow our own truth, rather than trying to please something or someone outside of us. We aimed to become one with our own vibrational reality and not that of the socially constructed world. Like tops, we were sent spinning by our higher selves into the same space, some wobbling this way, some that. Our differences were celebrated and enjoyed.

179

In addition to the hypnotic regression into past lives, I explored experiences with rebirthing — an intense breathing technique for flushing old reactions out of the body. I also discovered sound/music healings, vibrations and how they work, and more amazing colorful portals into our unlimited possibilities.

One weekend, one of our Emissaries, Margaret Kruger, cook extraordinaire, was hosting a special event: a crystal healer was coming to town to teach about crystals. My intuitive sense said, "Do not attend this workshop." My legacy was dwindling and I just didn't feel drawn.

"Oh, come on. Come with us."

I still wanted to belong so, next thing I knew, I was involved. First, I was to drive our illustrious healer around Vancouver in Beulah, my little, red Honda, named for the "peel me a grape" fame, with the sunroof open. Touring the town before his workshop was fun. He gave me a reading, and we shared our processes of self-realization, meditation, diet, supplements, walking, yoga, dance workout, stillness, and following the flow.

"But," he asked me, "why aren't you in a relationship?" I wasn't admitting to my alcoholic man who wasn't there. "Of all the people I know, you seem the least likely to stay single."

"Oh, I have a checklist," I said earnestly. "It's rather long, but inch by inch I am working my way out of how I've been and into becoming true to myself."

He laughed and laughed and laughed and laughed, and laughed some more, lolling around in my front seat. I scratched my head. His vibration was high and lively. He was coming on to me like mad, which, in my crazy brain, I took as some kind of judgment.

With a big, green handkerchief, he wiped his eyes and told me, "Relationships are crucial. Get that reflection — close up and personal. You'll grow much better in a relationship than outside of one. I promise you." His chuckles filled my tiny car ashram again.

I attended his workshop the next day. It seemed weak and contrived. My inner self coiled and recoiled, and I exploded. Eighty dollars for this? I'd even known better. I not only wasted my time and money but, much more, I had betrayed my own emerging self-trust.

A few hours in, I couldn't sit still another minute. Writhing, I stormed to the back of the room and lit up a cigarette. Can you believe not only that was I still smoking but also that it was allowed in a healing class? I paced and paced and puffed and puffed like a powerful magic dragon. I had a lifelong fantasy of being a gentle, sweet soul. Remember my desire to wear pink and call myself May? Hardly! I look sickly in pink. May is too sweet and delicate a name for a dragon! I barely kept myself together until the day was over. My brazen pacing dance among plumes of smoke rose from my inner fire.

I went home and started crying and crying and crying. Once again, my sobs seemed unstoppable.

As the sun swung into nighttime, I was still wild, pacing and circling 'round and 'round my little apartment. I couldn't seem to break up with my unreliable lover. I was lonely. I was trying so hard to grow and change and, yet, here I was, so deeply alone. On that level, the crystal teacher might've been right. I took out my creation journal and began designing affirmations for a mate.

I, Ronni, have a wonderful man in my life. We love each other, and we love sharing experiences and learning together.

Ronni, you have a wonderful man in your life. You love each other, and you love sharing experiences and learning together.

Ronni has a wonderful man in her life. She and he love one another, and they love sharing experiences and learning together.

I, Ronni, and my husband are growing, we travel the world, and we have a family and lots of money.

Ronni, you and your husband are growing, you travel the world, and you have a family and lots of money.

Ronni and her husband are growing, they travel the world, and they have a family and lots of money.

The descriptions grew and flourished. Details started to include growing love, harmony, consciousness, friends, and the years. I put twenty-three of them on a tape that I played behind everything I did so my subconscious would be imprinted.

The next day, I poured my tears into the day, still wild and frustrated. I walked, performed yoga breathing, and did my dance workout, but couldn't go to the workshop. Yet the healer's gifts to me emerged. So even though my intuition had told me not to attend the workshop, my high self knew I was to go. I went, but not for the workshop itself. My old affirmation routine was reinvigorated, plus I found a new friend at that crystal workshop. Or, really, he found me. François. François was a sparkly, little Swiss man, elegant and compassionate, with bright eyes and curly gray hair — his signature. We'd met the first day of the workshop, then he asked a friend for my number. That second day at break, he phoned. "Ronni, where are you?"

"I can't do it. I am out of alignment with my purpose, and he is screwy! I sold myself out — too easily." I still didn't trust the integrity of many teachers. I began to weep again.

"Would you like company after the workshop?" His Swiss accent was lyrical.

"Yes, please." He came over and sat patiently as I wailed about deception; about the grueling relationship I had been in with the alcoholic and how I couldn't seem to get free; about how much I longed for home and family but didn't even have *me* to begin with. And our wonderful, transformative, treasured friendship began.

This sweet man was full of spirit and longing for more. He did two things well. He taught flying. And he waited tables at a very elegant restaurant in Vancouver. As I wrote every night without fail—streams of consciousness or the beginnings of stories or scripts—it was easy to add François to my routine, popping down to his restaurant to sit at a table in a quiet section. He would fill my wine glass and give me sample foods from the kitchen as I wrote feverishly. He mythologized my fervor, telling diners that I worked for the Canadian Broadcast Company or some other famous information source. We would visit when the restaurant was empty, chatting and swapping tales of our growth, spiritual yearnings, readings we had, and perceptions of one another.

We spent many an hour together, giggling and even arguing over metaphysics. "Keep yourself light!" he often said. We went to University Beach with its huge rocks. "Run," he coached. Then, holding hands, we would run along the tops of rocks, toes barely touching the great rocks, one after the other, playing like little kids. Lithe. Graceful. At first, it was scary, but soon delightful. It made me strong... very strong...after the initial terror that I would fall or turn my ankle or some such. I treasure those moments with Fran-çois. Could I ever do such a thing today? Probably not. But my mind has learned to hop over experiences—sometimes, anyway—with more grace.

183

Those affirmations were effective. The very next weekend, a friend from that same group invited me to a different gathering for an intuitive healer from Australia named Lionel Fifield. I was very drawn to this one. Lionel had been an accountant—a Scorpio accountant—and was very handsome. His intuition had started kicking in, rattling his perceptions and awarenesses, demanding his attention. He released his secure job. He attuned himself to his intuitive guidance; then, adding meditations, affirmations, goal setting, and centering, he opened a facility in Brisbane, Australia. He guided us to move toward our own center and to live intuitively.

"Be grateful for *everything* that happens. For every experience," he said. "Even if you don't like it." As if scripted, Beulah, her nose high under the hook of a city tow truck, rolled by our window. Amidst cheers and howling laughter, I rolled my eyes, and growled, "Thank you. Thank you." We were learning, or trying to anyway, that the Universe blesses and expands—not contracts—us.

Lionel was magical. He scheduled his international seminars, planned his travels, and booked his plane tickets before he had the money, in sync with his guidance. Then, as he prepared to leave Australia, the money always came. He always received enough, and the first thing he did with his income was tithe to a spiritually inspiring source. He taught us that we are essentially creative beings. We are programmed, but are able to create far beyond our programming. For instance, when designing and calling for a relationship, we might not be sent one that follows our usual templates of body type or personality. We might find ourselves drawn to someone who is different, someone we would have walked by in the past. But still we are attracted. Maybe that person needs healing. Well, go ahead, take the chance — put the cart before the horse and trust that the Universe is supplying whatever we need. The pattern breaking and the healing begins.

Lionel had lost his son Simon, who had died at two years old. It was the first time I heard anyone talk about attuning with the soul, in this case Simon's soul. Lionel meditated on him for months until eventually, he could experience the joy in the heartbreak of his loss.

Something happened inside of me. My inner being hurtled forward to take a stronger place in my life with his teachings.

On that magic carpet rode Glenn Entwistle, the tall, dark British stranger who came along with my friends Molly and Tony. He was, I could see immediately, in terrible emotional pain. I remember feeling it as I looked at him. His large, beautiful, round, brown eyes seemed to be cracked, and the hurt lurked in each of the pieces. I reeled back and recognized that I could put the cart before the horse. I truly wanted a relationship. François was the first and Glenn was the second of four men whom I met the weekend I began my regular petitions for companionship — four potentials almost immediately.

Glenn talked about his internal journey, tantra, foods, and more. Soon we shared dreams of traveling around the world and exploring all types of healing modes. We quickly bonded.

One early morning after my walk along the Spanish Banks, I flicked on my car radio to hear one of the two-minute radio blurbs by Earl Nightingale. I loved his format with little snippets of inspiring information. This one was about an Israeli psoriasis clinic using the mineral brine of the Dead Sea for healing. People traveled from all over the world to benefit from its magic. "Okay, I'm ready. I'd like to go to Israel," I said to my radio, also known as the Universe.

That evening Glenn called. "I'm taking a job with Israeli Aircraft. Want to come to Israel?"

"Yes," I said on my outbreath. I felt such promise in his words, and within four months, he was leaving to work in Tel Aviv. I was packing up my little apartment womb and planning to meet him there and, of course, check out the psoriasis clinic and the ancient and modern healing sites. We were on our way.

He kept me a secret. "Don't tell anyone you're with me," he cautioned as we prepared for the farewell party I threw for him. The people coming knew him as married and knew his wife. He couldn't handle it. I ignored that reflection in me — after all, I didn't actually honor me either.

My friends celebrated with me that I was throwing in the towel on my wombing, my bizarre self-explorations, my plastic bag of supplements, and my little north-facing apartment, which they sometimes borrowed for their own illicit affairs. But I had been nosing around the CBC and my friends who worked there, thinking I would like a job with that organization. Some of my CBC friends saw Israel differently.

"You would drop efforts to go into the CBC for a man?" they growled. And I did, as I would at that time.

As I've said, there had been little connection with my parents, although a little more with Mum, during the post-Steven-and-Naomi time. They were uncomfortable with my emotional pain and fluctuating moods. My siblings pulled away. "You have been a pain in the ass ever since Steven died!"

When I ran into family friends, they would glare at me and say they knew all about my life. What did they know? Retelling, reflections, projections of who I was and what I was doing were bent through their minds. To them, the rules of life seemed more tried and true, honored by convention.

Not to me. I was busily and determinedly tearing up old traditions and belief structures. I hunted for my behavioral patterns or saw them repeat in my world and tore them up. That must have been hard for my family. It was hard enough for me, but for them there was no port in the storm, especially if they felt they had to help make me "safe." My hearing voices and seeing things was becoming a mining expedition. What did they mean? Back in the Sixties, I, who actually love fashion, had dumped consumerism for deepening quality of life, although back then I did make my own clothes copied from pictures in *Vogue* and sewed ties for the guys in psychedelic fabrics! Now I only wore clothes in fabrics and colors that were soothing against my edgy skin, no matter how odd they looked. I was committed to discovering what was within me. I thought that I would eventually just integrate, and then I would worry about the outside. Also, that confusing discomfort of speeding energy firing through my brain all the time was hard to manage. But I was trying to calm it with supplements and breathing techniques. I was very strange and, for my family, as I looked lost and aimless on the outside, probably scary.

But I chuckle now or even am embarrassed at how they must have felt in my parade of peculiarities. Could I have put them at ease with, "Oh, gee, I am going to be a psychic"? Probably not. I didn't actually know it yet either. One brother-in-law wouldn't allow me in their house, even at Christmastime, because I was doing my grief journey wrong, he deemed.

187

In my family, heart-ripping outbursts punctuated every self-actualizing step I took. During one episode I said, "I understand your anger." I explained what I had learned in a spontaneous past-life memory. "Apparently in another life we were fighting hand to hand with great sticks. You were very tall. I was very short. Yet I killed you."

That brought on fury. "Nobody talks like that!"

"I do. Just trying to work things out, you know, to understand and take responsibility!"

No matter what my next step was, usually because of an explosion of inspiration—whether it was my Israel trip, or opening to channel, perhaps moving to Pennsylvania, marrying Glenn, leaving Glenn, choosing a move between Bellingham, Washington, or Tucson, Arizona—every one of those turning points caused outrage. But in some ways, those reactions mothered my steps, propelled me away farther, to follow my inner prompts. There was no safe home here. I was homesteading my inner self. And as far as I could understand, we had chosen to come together to neutralize old, karmic soul patterns. I often see families as hot-air balloons, their strings in a bunch, the balloons wafting with little mobility. Releasing soul attachments and reactions made me similar to a balloon getting free—drifting, drifting. I fought it for years, as I still wanted loyalty and understanding. But that wasn't the contract among my family members this time. I had to keep flowing freely enough to not pull their strings as I mined my inner self for my truer nature. That could ultimately bring freedom and harmony. The souls, more than the people, knew.

My farewell party was at Marianne's, my stalwart supporter. We all sang with my brother, whom I adored. My sisters sat and stared at me, no words. As you well know by now, my family doesn't talk about what's real. Several women asked me, "Who are those women?" One said, "They don't like you."

Nowadays, instead of lurching with hurt, I could say, "I don't blame them. I am shredding our shared beliefs. I am ripping the family fabric." But at that time, I ached in the veils of silences and rejection they dropped. But breaking out is a crazy, chaotic, process. Once they had decided that I was "crazy" or "unreliable" or "self-centered" or "dishonest," everything I did fueled their judgments. Cautiously, at times, I tried to forestall the judgment: "Is this all right for you?" Again, they were infuriated by my annoying checking-things-out behavior.

One year, a teacup reader said, "It's hard to be with you. You don't keep things light. Tell them about something pretty you saw...or...or...."

I worked at it. One sister responded as I talked about a lovely china teapot I had seen, "You don't need to tell anyone about stuff like that. You are single now." That Christmas, I went to my sister's and sang carols outside her front door while the rest of the family and friends were reveling inside. Someone let me in the front door, but no one greeted me. No one looked at me. I smiled and said, "Hi! Merry Christmas!" Finally, a friend of the family glared at them all, came over, and said, "Merry Christmas. Come on in." He hugged me.

My craziness and acting out, my eccentric focus about everything I did, ate, thought, and moved thoroughly cleaved me from my family of origin. Grief, self-exploration, deep pain, searching, searching, always searching had led me to a rocketing away and acting from a newfound center of truth. If we feel something, we must be true about it. So I cried when I wanted to, laughed when I wanted to, and tried to be with what was real. I guess I was impossible to be with. But I recognize in so many of us on the path that the essential

breaking away from the family of origin's beliefs and structures has to happen. The soul's knife was too hot. The butter
couldn't stick.

For years, I assumed that if I got better and better at who
I really am, if I cleared old beliefs and healed the limitations
of my fears and resistances to the deepening of my intuitive
flow, they would embrace me back in the family. I simply
loved them (and still do). So I trucked on, learning about
what I do and how it is reflected back to me from others,
what my dreams are, my body and mind health, fueling my
soul's expression into my body and mind, my astrological
drives, my Four Enneagram design. And then, of course,
came more goal setting, deepening motivations through
intuition, and so on...and on...and on....After all this self-
exploration and self-improvement, they would accept me. I
would be welcome.

Not so. Completely separating from the beliefs and
substructures of family of origin is essential for claiming
one's self and becoming the actress, not the reactress. But it
doesn't work as a healing tool in the family. Okay, John
Bradshaw of the family dynamics fame became a noble
model: the scapegoat becomes the healer. When will that
happen, Mr. Bradshaw?

Onward. I cried a lot—volcanic eruptions along my
evolutionary trail. My illusion that people would
understand when I explained my truth wasn't working.
Judgments abounded. My fears of people mounted. I still
wanted to belong, although I did everything I could to be
incompatible with convention! Hahaha. I chuckle here, once
again, at my naiveté. Resistances hold back our evolution, I
realized. I had learned to let feelings flow freely through me,
unbridled, to catalyze wisdom. "Icky," said a friend who was
avoiding me by then

But I was dedicated to sorting things out "right now" — in the minute, that very minute. I laugh as I write this. I would talk about my abuse issues, insomnia, explorations into the psyche, nutrition, philosophy. I wanted to be up front and honest with my feelings so that people wouldn't be conflicted in themselves by confusion, the kind I had felt as an empathetic child in the dangerous pressure cooker of leaking, unclaimed emotions or my misinterpretations of unclaimed, leaking rage. If I explained everything, how I felt, how whoever I was talking to, friends or family, felt then, all would be well. What a trial for those with hidden agendas or even introverts! Later, in a hypnotherapy class I took at age fifty, I learned that half of humanity goes into a trance when we are direct. Oh, goodness! I burst out laughing at my years of misspent efforts at being so direct. Disruptive — that's what it was, as I wavered between being deeply inward, or absolutely straightforward, written off as someone who was emotionally wrecked. I wasn't hiding it or leaking it. I was it!

Anyway, my wombing years in my little, north-facing apartment ended with an apartment sale, reducing my possessions radically. I watched my hat rack being carried out, as well as the many hats I had collected and hung on it, perched now on the heads of friends leaving my sale.

"Always leave a place better than you found it." I left my alcoholic lover by vacuuming his whole house while harmonizing loudly to Hoyt Axton singing, "Let's go out in a blaze of glory." I felt a new beginning, taking my health-food learning, the philosophical wonders of myriad books and tapes, meditations, my inner searches on my beach walks, and my daily writings. The investigations I had made into the blossoming fields of healing arts, television shows, and radio scripts became a new foundation. My past two years there had filled me, ironically, with emptying, evolving, creating, and expanding. I was blooming with layers of the growth of a deeper knowing and connection with spirit — my own and the Creator Being.

The final afternoon there, Marianne and another friend, Fran, and I cleaned out my apartment. The view of the mountains was all fuzzy as fog clung to them like a hairdo. Reflections of the sinking sun warmed the blue. We chatted as we scrubbed this site of our social gatherings, our writing and presenting, the post-video parties where we danced and wore hats with great feathers and celebrated amazing changes in all our lives that we reflected back and forth to one another.

"Hey, mail-order bride," Marianne teased, "come on and stay at our house again 'til you head across to Israel." Once again, like the traveling sister, I bunked in with Marianne and Cliff in their Dunbar home.

In the midst of that final rush to leave Vancouver for Israel, a month before I was actually to leave, there on my message machine was a precious call from Terry Presber, my old health-food mentor. I was thrilled. He called just in time to be at Glenn's farewell party and to sport my favorite hat, its long grouse feathers cocking the side of its brim. Our separation had gone for on a year and a half, my few calls on his voicemail keeping us connected, but it was clear that he'd refused to connect. I had missed him so much.

"Ronni." My heart leapt as his voice — sweet, sibilant, and sensitive — filled me. "This is the boss. It has been too long, and I think we should get back together. Besides, you have my typewriter."

I called him back at the shop immediately. "Burnaby Health Foods."

"Hi, Terry."

"Hi." I felt our joy surge. "I am s-s-s-so glad to hear your voice."

Distances and charged disagreements can fuel terrific growth. It was certainly true for us. Separately, since that spitting row outside of the West End Cable, we had both grown so much. Who was responsible? How did it happen? Who cares?

"Hi, boss." My heart warmed.

We met on the Spanish Banks, near the herons, and walked for hours, holding hands. The smells of the ocean wafted on the soft breezes, mingling with fries and vinegar, coffee, and each other. Those herons seemed to know about life, with their still legs, knees strong against the wind. There was only a month left to play before Israel. I told him about the alcoholic, then about meeting Glenn and getting ready about to leave for Israel. He had me laughing and weeping over his abortive attempts to find his own special soul mate. He found men with broken wings and, oh, how they needed healing. He had not found The One. Maybe I had? Terry was the mother figure, the Adele Davis of his limping crowd. This was in 1981.

He told me that his mum had suggested to him that he and I marry. We were so close and both so wanting home and relationship. "I wouldn't do that to you," he said. We laughed, knowing our love was deep.

I told him that our shows were actually running on cable television.

"You really stuck to it! You really did it! I am so proud of you!" His eyes watered with pleasure and his loss. "I just couldn't call. I am weak and didn't have the courage."

I loved him for talking with me about what was real, whether it was about a hidden fear, or a great dream, even a flaccid penis. But I didn't tell him about my recent mini radio scripts. We had both by then been warned to be careful as someone could scoop our ideas. This was big news in the media world. Then I wasn't sure if he would steal mine, but he never would have. Later, I sent him my sample tape and he loved it. Again, "You did it! You really did it. I am so proud of you. You stuck to your dreams!"

A couple of years later, Glenn and I returned from Israel, set up our new home in Kingston, Ontario, for a while, then moved to Montreal. We visited Terry from there where he met my beautiful surprise-child Bridget when she was seven months old. Then off my new little family went to Pennsylvania, so Glenn could work with the United States aircraft technology, and I began the my final phase of my degree at Goddard College in Vermont.

I heard from Terry that he wasn't very well. "I just can't seem to get over this. I look like I just came out of Treblinka," he wrote. "Even with all the best supplements, I just kept being slammed by some kind of a virus!" Finally it became TB.

In March 1986, I received a note from his mother, Kay, who was also my friend. Terry had always been very close to her. As I held that envelope, I knew. "Terry passed away last week. He had your tape right beside him and played it a lot. He was so proud of you. He kept getting pneumonia, and we couldn't figure out what was wrong. I will miss him so much, Ronni. I don't know what I will do without him. But he was so sick."

My grief lay still and deep. For his mum. For myself. My funny friend, my mentor is still within me. We didn't know much about AIDS at that time, but he was one of the first gay men in Vancouver to die from it.

CHAPTER TWELVE

I Have a New Job—My Awakening!

Glenn brought me huge gifts: a tape of Van Morrison's *Wavelength*, my first experience with the nurturing male, and two amazing daughters. Synchronistically, at that point I was also fascinated by the mysteries of wavelengths and, as I would say now, how they carry light and information, the building blocks to creating our reality. I added Van Morrison to my regular singing, dancing, and energy-clearing routine—the daily routine that now combines meditation, action, breathing, visualization, and the connecting of the halves of my brain to create a holistic comprehension of life.

Using his lyrics to add to my programming manifestations with words, I let Van take me forward and deeply inward. "This is a song about my wavelength / And your wavelength, baby." I start up, stretching in all directions, breathing deeply, limbering up. And as the tempo builds, I start to dance wildly, conscious of moving all my limbs and joints, twisting my hips—have to keep a waist, you know. I call in light; I like to see it as a spiraling bottle washer style, moving through the top of my head, down through the body, and into the floor.

Then I move that light with my mind into one chakra at a time, using it as a kind of scrub, chakra by chakra, 'til the red chakra is bright and I can feel it tingling. Then I move up to the orange and on up through the yellow, green, blue, indigo, and violet. I also sing along with the song, or apply a chant, chakra by chakra, adding to the vitality of it. I was conscious to only use words that are uplifting, so that I didn't drill in words of songs of heartache into my psyche. To this day, the routine still carries me beyond. I started adding words of several of songs, some lines of which are "then I'd talk to my angels"..."writing a song"..."hungry for your love" (I'd direct that plea to myself and Spirit) and onward to lost dreams and found dreams in America. I end it with a vital strutting because by then my singing has so invigorated me.

"I'm going to walk down the street until I see my shining light," I remember saying to Glenn while we still lived in Canada and laughing at my strutting image. Today, though, I expect to *be* that light!

But before I saw that light clearly, I lost the dream of our marriage and I left Glenn. I had been so relieved to be in a relationship. I worked hard to feed our body/minds with my best nutritional awareness, plus to improve my ability to relate, which needed perking up after my collapse and inner journey. I had such dedication to my deepening awakening to truth of myself, I could not forfeit it, even for a relationship. Glenn was nurturing—in fact, as I said, he was the first nurturing man I had ever experienced. At least it started that way, as he was freshly out of his marriage and still hurting. We did lots of healing with and for one another. At first, intuitively, he would perceive, even from work, when I was dropping into places of self-judgment or self-loss. He would phone, ask me what's happening, and then talk to me.

Our ten months in Israel were amazing: trips to the ancient cradles of Islam, Christianity, and Judaism, plus the headiness of Jerusalem. We experienced stunning awarenesses of years crusted on one another. One weekend, we wandered down the Via Dolorosa, where Jesus had supposedly carried the cross two thousand years earlier. What an experience! We sat for a break drinking a Heineken beer—a good Dutch beer—served by Arabs, Africans all around, the booming tones of the Rolling Stones filling the air, punctuated with the sounds of the Muslim calls to prayer. We laughed at Jerusalem's heady, strange weaving of time, layers of civilizations woven throughout and inside in our own soul's journeys, one on top of the other, a dynamic yet sensual parfait. It was intoxicating to body and mind!

The Dead Sea is a bizarre phenomenon—a brine more than a lake, on which you can actually float. Little fresh-water taps have been placed all around the sea to quickly rinse off splashes that can burn your eyes. Several times when my eyes threatened, I would rush to the taps and soothe them.

As we entered the Dead Sea region, I read to Glenn from the guidebook. "The minerals in suspension hold a high level of magnesium, which can put people to sleep." At that very moment, the guidebook slid to the floor as I, the old insomniac, fell asleep in mid-sentence.

The mists that rise off the Dead Sea hold those minerals in suspension, and combined with the heavy atmospheric pressure there at the lowest part of the earth, its pearlized presence can literally relax you enough to drop you off to sleep in a heartbeat. Yet, if prompted, you can rise right out of sleep to run like the wind—the dense combination of the high levels of oxygen in the etheric mineral scramble gives you tremendous energy.

The Dead Sea was otherworldly, edged with healing clinics. And there, right in its midst was the very psoriasis clinic I had heard about that fortuitous day in Vancouver sitting in my car listening to Earle Nightingale, that very day that Glenn called to invite me to join him in Israel. Interesting characters, young and old, travel to the Dead Sea annually, from all around the world, many from the U.S. The combination of the atmosphere straining the sun's rays and the minerals of the region apparently releases some people from their psoriasis for long periods of time.

Another atmospheric wonder rises off of Lake Tiberius. Its mineral-laden haze makes you fall in love. Seriously. Starry eyed, we floated around in our new romance that delightful weekend. Talk about coherent fields, or empathy with the atmosphere!

Back in Tel Aviv, while Glenn spent long days at work, I met people of all kinds — merchants, neighbors in the square or in the Super Sol (like our super grocery stores), or the different coffee places I walked to write. There was a library up the road that was almost a daily destination and was where I watched mesmerizing videos on alternative healing from around the world by a young Bill Moyers, who is still a hero to me.

The folks in Tel Aviv required a little adjusting to. They were very assertive, almost frightening. I often rode busses around the city, and it wasn't unusual to get on a packed bus, lurch to a seat or a stanchion, and sit right beside a machine gun propped against the seat by my neighboring passenger. What a challenge for me from protected Canada. Scary, but real.

That was the time of the Lebanese Massacre, and although we didn't experience any action or see any guns except for the ones on the busses, our neighborhood was clearly in pain. Soldiers, both men and women, disappeared from our area, some never to return. One day, I watched two older women sitting together on a bench on our street. One was Arab, one was Jewish. They were hugging each other, rocking and crying, "It must stop. The killing must stop." I wept as I watched them. That vivid snapshot still vibrates in my memory as other wars go on.

Learning the behaviors accepted by the Israeli culture was challenging until I learned their ways. First of all, I was told by a couple of young women who coached me, "We have a right to refusal. In your culture, you don't."

"Here in Israel, you can just say no to a sweet, little old lady who is pushing you in line. Or even push back!"

In Canada, that would be unheard of. You just don't push little old ladies! But there, when I did hold my own, when I pushed back, those sweet, little old ladies (hey, I'm one now!) liked me better, even admired me more. I experienced kind hearts inside many of their brusque or sharp appearances. Glenn hated it. They were always pushing into his confined social space — so very British. He was depressed.

And then Lucy arrived. Here I was, in my mind anyway, having an adventure in an exotic country. Glenn's daughter Lucy was thirteen, very short, redheaded, and fair, with a number of health concerns. Her folks decided, without asking me or even wondering if it would infringe on this potentially "romantic" scene with my new lover, who worked five AM to six PM, that she would come for a month. "Who is going to look after her?" I asked the walls. Soon, there she was. I found other children for her, but she would have none of it. She wanted to perform, or write, or adventure — at anything. She wanted to hang out with me.

"Glenn, she needs to play." He didn't say anything. So I got over myself. Each morning, Lucy and I would go to one of the coffee shops on the corner, shops with the clanking of the chai sellers and the Turkish coffees bubbling in exotic pots. Right there at the corner of Dizengoff and Alozeroff, our corner, Lucy and I wrote grand poetry, arguing about our words and metaphors, whales, or whether animals are better than people.

Our apartment was above the Super Sol, and our balcony hung over its flat roof. One day, Lucy directed a play. Of course, I was her only possible "star" besides herself. I played a huge, buxom woman, with the help of my friend's nursing bra stuffed with socks, and Short Stuff played the man; the music was by Queen. She sent out invitations to our neighbors, British job shoppers and fellow Israeli Aircraft folks, who peered over their balconies to watch our play. I felt like an ass, but we performed anyway and our audience laughed hard.

Touring in the tremendous heat was a challenge to Lucy, but appearing like an albino Bedouin, with a huge, wet towel around her neck and head, she made it through our explorations of the truly ancient history. Back at the Dead Sea, we slathered our bodies with black mud. We climbed to the top of Mount Tabor, from which Jesus was to have ascended and now was the domain of a Franciscan Monastery. There I was in awe of so many there to honor the ascension. Peering out of her wet-towel wrap, big blue eyes, red curls peeking round her face, Lucy broke the silence. "Ronni," she asked, "did Jesus have to poop?" Good question. I don't think we have ever been told that. We collapsed laughing.

Weekends with Glenn were rich, exploring other great ruins. One was a huge, ancient, deserted amphitheater where we performed on the partially crumbled stages to the ancient spirits of audiences from times past, still sitting on the rock benches. When Lucy left that summer, after my full month as her nanny, I cried and cried. Glenn and I stayed for another four months or so. I was beginning to think I could live there, but it had become unbearable for Glenn. Back we went to Canada.

Glenn found a job in Kingston, Ontario. He hated that job. I thought of leaving him and moving on, as his frustrations were weighty. But lo and behold, I was pregnant! Soon we had our delightful surprise child. I returned to health foods, taking my wee one with me. Often Bridget was asleep in her Snugli as I filled bulk bins or spoke with customers. I planned television shows, but was quite shy about my approaches, and instead taught mini classes in the health-food store.

Then Glenn took a job he preferred in Montreal. After a few months, Bridget and I joined him. I loved Montreal. I was getting stronger, and there were people we knew there, including relatives and some old friends. Life was alive and well. I had the opportunity to be involved in a learning program, doing some video planning through the National Film Board Studio G. I dreamed of speaking French and having my own shows. Glenn was at Pratt and Whitney. Coincidentally, after all that time in Israel, our new home was in Snowdon, with its predominantly Jewish influence.

One of my wonderful nephews was exploring life after being a student, doing his own adventure from the inside out, and living in Montreal. He'd come by, often sharing stages of his own growth. Added were some interesting cousins from my mum's side of the family. We loved this new familyness; I felt more nested than I had for years and, once again, was beginning to emerge. I believe that the NFB video training helped me begin to find my soul journey again. I loved the chic, cosmopolitan verve of my new life.

Then, one day, it came. "I have a great opportunity to work in the U.S."

"What? Really? Where?"

201

"Pennsylvania. It's a Boeing plant just outside of Philadelphia. We'll have to go soon."

I shattered. Life was dissembling again, and it had been
a life I was growing into. I couldn't sleep, and I stopped
learning French. My overwhelm was reinvigorated. As we
left Montreal, I felt a new anger and loss.

We landed in Philadelphia just as Christie McAuliffe
blew up in the Challenger. The television replayed the scene
over and over again—an image of some of my dreams being
blown up? I wonder as I write about it now if maybe it was
a reflection of my attachment to Glenn's dreams. I didn't
think of it that way then, as my own dreams of having home
and family were also core.

Glenn hated Boeing Vertol. We both found Pennsylvania
to be closed off to newcomers. Pennsylvanians seem to know
their ancestry from their arrival in America and how many
generations ago that was. They weren't eager to include new,
transitory friends. But he had some of his old job-shopping
friends, some from the UK, to add familiarity. Glenn and I
both worked hard on our true selves and spiritual presence
for a while. His love for beauty, poetry, music, photography,
and us was strong. But then suddenly he stopped. "I just
don't want to!" He was depressed, cynical, and negative.

I still loved him and loved being in family. But I was
becoming more and more weighed down plus feeling old at
forty-five, unable, and useless. We were always broke. My
little Bridget was thriving at her Catholic college preschool,
and she often ran around with towels on her head saying,
"I'm Mother Teresa!" Lucy, my creative stepdaughter, now
in her mid-teens and who usually came for a month or so in
the summer, finally moved in with us permanently, sliding
into the family in the nick of time to qualify for her green
card. She was unraveling her own adolescent depression.

She joined drama groups and studied drama therapy. Wobbly but determined, she was steering her ship in interesting waters.

Once a week, Bridget, Lucy, and I broke out of the house and played. We were only shopping for weekly supplies, but it was such fun. We would shake free of the house with its overloaded schedules and money problems and head out to the Amish Market. There we would shop, laugh, play with carts, share hotdogs and sandwiches, giggle, and be silly. The three of us developed a lively family world.

Or Bridget and I would go downtown when Lucy was performing. One of the performances was the children's musical play, *The Fir Tree*. As it ended with the fir tree being burned (I think), the theater burst with children dancing in the aisles, Lucy and her cohorts dancing wildly on the stage, and I wept—so touched by the free nature of the joyful performance and at Lucy's amazing expression. At pre-school, when Bridget was singing loudly in the tiny children's Christmas chorus, again I wept and wept, deeply touched by their performances.

Though money was tight, I couldn't work during the interminable wait for our green cards or we would lose our place in the lineup. Glenn couldn't even accept a raise, so I decided, in for a dime, in for a dollar. I would finish off my almost degree through one of the pioneering mentoring colleges. My earning potential would increase when the green cards finally came. Goddard College in Vermont seemed perfect. Every six months, I would go to the campus for ten days of lectures, presentations, and classes, as well as setting up contracts with mentors. Then I'd go home to fulfill them.

I did three radio internships, lots of writing, and—my pièce de résistance—a hand-edited reel of interviews I did with women entrepreneurs talking about what it takes to be a successful female entrepreneur in our society. This inspired me. Traveling to Goddard was also a treat. In my berth on the overnight train, I would curl up and listen, sometimes shaking in fear, to Ramtha tapes on consciousness (Ramtha is an enlightened entity being channeled through JZ Knight) and how to survive the up-and-coming challenging times. Once in Vermont, I'd tuck myself in my little college room. At least during the first term, in my single space and shyness, I spent a lot of time in meditation. But then I began to join several new friends there, women from New York. And I was taught to "hang," to "hang out," a new concept to me. There were intriguing people throughout the college who were mentoring numerous activities, including gatherings, presentations of plays written by students, or therapies created by others, all of which were sometimes odd and sometimes truly inspiring. I was stiff and inhibited, words and concepts kind of stuck inside my mind. At times it felt like I needed to pry myself out of some kind of bedrock. Still, I gained.

The three terms were full and demanding. I set up three internships in real radio stations, one in downtown Philadelphia and two in Wilmington, Delaware. And I documented for my mentors at college all the work I did.

By that time, I also had developed a wonderful meditation routine in the basement of our townhouse in our little 'burb just southwest of Philadelphia. Usually when Bridget napped, I would descend into my treasured spiritual haven amongst my student-office stuff—an old green couch, a desk, mounds of paperwork, a typewriter, tape players, microphones, incense holders, hairy sage sticks, candles, holy pictures, the laundry, and the rafters with electrical wiring strung through the huge spikes on them. Van Morrison, always a click away from my beck and call, would begin. I would wind up, arms stretching in all directions, legs bending and squatting, then move into a dance movement. "This is a song about my wavelength / And your wavelength......"

Oh, if you saw me you wouldn't suggest that I enter *So You Think You Can Dance*. But I would call in light until I could feel it move through my head. As I mentioned, I would direct it through my body to the base chakra and whirl it and whirl it 'til it turned bright, bright red. It was a job! At times, there was little vibrancy there, or I could "see" lumps and bumps and dark patches. The work was clear. I was literally cleaning out the basement. Then I'd move on to the belly area, the orange chakra. Same thing—I'd work with the lights in my mind 'til it cleared up and was bright. All the way through each chakra I would go, singing loudly, scouring the chakras, directing the frequencies of my voice until they resonated through my body. The words of "Wavelength" became so familiar to me that I don't even consciously remember them today. They just flowed through me carrying vibrations to chakras as I moved.

I would dance faster and faster until I could literally "see" old frequencies drop off my limbs. More and more, my body would brighten up. Emotions would ether release or become happier. At the end of the chakra coloring, as I did back in Canada, I would call in a light from the universe, a light like a great spiral, corkscrew, or bottle washer, and run it through me into the earth. My favorite part was, after all that purification and frequency lighting, I would begin to "see" things: answers to questions I had asked at the beginning of my trance dance, or simply beings and Guides. I truly loved it.

I'd start out asking a question: How is my mother? Is Steven still around? Who is this person or that in my soul's history? What is the name of my Guide? I would drop my question once it was asked, move, work with my inner lights, and the answers would emerge. Visons and voices came, telling me about myself, my journey, even past lives.

One time was a challenge. I was told to "go up this path." I say it was challenge because each step needed me to push through something. It felt like a kind of gel. It took me several meditations over several days until the entire scene unfolded. There I was—I could see myself from another lifetime, a young man dressed in knickers and a whitish, puffed-sleeve shirt, hair bobbed. I wandered up the path with a stick and a piece of cloth, tied like a bag containing possessions, laid on my shoulder. I walked past a row of what looked like brownstones. An earlier version of today's townhomes, these were built with stone, semi-connected, and stood alongside my winding dirt pathway. I was directed to enter one of them.

There I saw myself as a woman. I was a writer in the little village, my editorials on politics and other opinions causing a ruckus or evoking dissension, you might say. I had asked my Guides the day before this scene began to unfold what Glenn Entwistle and I were doing together. He was always ready to help me with radio, television ideas, even my nutritional explorations on his well-being. As I walked up the lumpy, stone pathway and turned into the brownstone, I saw the firelit kitchen; various pots full of potions bubbled on the wood stove and a large, wooden table was laid out with pewter bowls. I saw myself, buxom, in my late thirties, curly hair awry, eccentric, worn. My son, about sixteen, came in flashing rage and disgust at me.

"What you been doing out there? You crazy woman, writing that shit." My iconoclastic words were prodding people to look at issues of power that were containing them. "People are pissed!"

"But they need to know...."

"Fuckin' 'ell they do! You are making us a laughing stock!"

I reached to restrain him and he pushed back—with a butcher knife that he plunged into my stomach. As I crumpled, I looked across the room to my husband, his dad, and there I saw my dad, looking more like Henry the Eighth, with leggings and puffy shorts, a braided jacket, very portly. I begged for help, but he just stood there looking at me, his eyes devoid of response. The scene was done, but not inside of me as I began to understand and even release some of the dissonances and angers between various members of my family and me.

Another day, I was just turning on "Wavelength" when Bridget, age two, came downstairs. She joined me and we danced and leapt together, singing. My heart was huge. I simply loved, and still love, this child so much. I asked to be shown who she is on my soul's journey. There she was, in my vision, emerging as a Sister Superior. That was Bridget. And I was a novice. She was stroking my hair, shaking her head, saying, "You'll eventually get it right. You have so much trouble sticking to it all...eventually it'll be alright." I could almost hear her sigh. I was weeping with my own frustration. Later, when she wanted to be in charge, hands on her little hips, I would say, "Hey, you are not the Sister Superior right now. I am...."

Our days with college and the radio internships as well as all the household demands and Glenn's Boeing job went on and on and on. But there in the basement, I found such joy playing in the dimensions, in the fields of answers, in the discoveries of the self.

One winter, Glenn and I were invited to a party with many of the engineering folks. There in the basement where I often was basking in radiant fields, I plopped on my broken couch, sad. I thought of the engineering wives and their diamonds and gold. I would have a rather paltry assortment of cheap adornments, one outfit I could wear that was a little worn. I started to weep. What kind of woman is forty-five and doesn't have anything? How can I go to this party with Glenn? As quickly as I thought that, there in my meditation den the fields parted and I "saw" my grandfather, my mum's dad. Granddad had been a wonderful and amazing man. Even though he was educated in England, he never quite "made it" in Canada. His boss, it was rumored, went down on the Titanic, and the job Granddad left the U.K. for never quite manifested after that. After a series of accounting jobs and owning some small corner stores, later in life he became a night watchman, walking the streets of the seamier parts of Vancouver. But everyone loved this tall Brit, with cigarette stubs under his moustache and a voice booming in a grand box at the horse races, "Two dollars to show!" with no concept of the distortions of status and wealth. Granddad truly loved all the folks, including the "rubbies," as he called the drunks, and the prostitutes. Nightly he toured their world making sure everything was safe and locked down. They all loved him. He also cajoled all the animals, named all the flowers and plants, strode with long, long legs and an overgrown hairdo through any social milieu he encountered. Our granddad—a real hero.

He came to the basement that day and said, "It will take a lot more than trinkets to make you happy! My life was very important to me. It was very rich. But I had no money." I felt his caring as he evaporated. I, of course, pulled myself together after his little tutorial. The party that night was just fine.

As I called forth my energy connections, I could see them more and more clearly as they expanded and grew. One day as I rounded the corners of the basement, pyramids appeared over me, growing far beyond the rafters and laundry of this townhouse basement. They even extended like tetrahedrons forward and back; I'd say they filled the space, but in the etheric the space never gets filled. It truly moves into realm after realm.

One workout day, the unfolding began a new level of spectacular. I was deeply in trance, moving to the music, singing those vibrations throughout my energy body. The geometrics vaulted, and with them the fields vibrated higher and higher. I loved it. Lo and behold, there was Steven, my vibrational husband. He was dancing with me, our teeth reflecting great, big grins as he matched and mocked my movements. I giggled. I have missed his humor since he passed.

"Stop, Steven. I only have a little time before Bridget wakes up. I want to follow the visions." He turned and looked and danced forward as I did. There were new Guides, including one named Joseph whom I grew to love. He was the closest to being human. The others seemed more like angels at that point. At the back of the basement were vortices shining and whirling, and in their center, I saw the Buddha. Again I wept. En route through this experience were different beings at different levels, and I was understanding more of existence in different vibrational levels, as frequency by frequency, layer by layer they emerged.

There that day, I saw that Steven and I shared some of the same Guides. Amazing. We cavorted in harmony, gazing ahead at the beings. But then the moment of change came when he turned and danced away up a different path. "Steven," I called after him with my mind. "Where are you going?" He just grinned back at me as he danced away. I turned to my own spiritual scenario again, engrossed by the rising beings and the changing emanations, alternately weeping and thinking. Somehow I knew more than I expected about the differences in paths. I was so grateful.

That basement sounds and feels amazing in retrospect. Another being, not one of my Guides, at least not in the normal sense of guides, kept showing up at different times. He was odd, maybe threatening looking. He had interesting cheek lines, and his facial skin was leathery like a goat's, almost black. He had curling horns like certain mountain goats. Now I had read enough and studied enough to know that we don't need to have uncomfortable visitations with beings from the dark. So as I encountered this one, I worked at erasing him from my fields. "Go to the Light! Go to the Light!" I waved him away.

He was carrying a portable recording/editing system. This was in 'eighty-seven, back when technology was bulky. I actually envied his. He held it, showing me that it could do a ton of things: receiving, editing, replicating with minimal labor, like what would become possible for us twenty years later.

Again I waved him away, not wanting to be wooed by stuff. "Enough of Greeks bearing gifts."

"What is the matter?" he asked.

"You are scaring me. You look so strange."

"You don't look so hot to me, either!"

I laughed, but kept shooing him away. I thought I should for spiritual integrity or protection or fear of the potentially dark.

"I just want to see how you are doing radio," he said.

I still laugh about it these days. After a few exchanges about a planet he lived on—I think he called it an approximation of WRooarh—he disappeared. In time I was a bit sad as I became aware that I would love to visit with him again. Maybe it'll happen yet. Maybe he'll come between time and space and we can start all over. I have more to show him now!

Back at college, second term, three of us bunked in together and were the "hang-out room." All kinds of students from different states, even different countries would gather in our space to talk and share, and I loved feeling alive again.

Three terms later, I had my BA in Education and Communication. So pleased, I booked my family into a cute, little cottage for the final celebratory weekend. All of us, my new friends and I, joined several hundred graduates, each of us giving our own final speech, a performance that stretched through several days. I was so proud of myself, not just for the degree, but for the emergence I could feel. I wanted my family to be proud, but Glenn got sick while we were there. Back and forth I ran to the cabin to tend to him and three-year-old Bridget, and I missed my call to speak. I was tacked onto the end—the very last person on the three-day roster of speeches. I was apparently pretty funny because my friends and mentors were all hooting and laughing as I bowed, enjoying the feedback.

Amid the cheers, the strong voice of my three-year-old broke the trance: "Gotta go poopie, Mummy." The aura of

211

the three-day ceremony blew open with more laughter as I ran offstage to my daughter.

After all of my work, I was so disappointed that Glenn couldn't share my success with me. It seemed to work that way with him. My stepping forward became more and more threatening. My energy was "down." People commented on how old I looked. I didn't know yet how to work with empathy to create. Instead, I was weighed down farther and farther. Intuitively, I "saw" Glenn and me as spirals, spirals that would alternatively flow together and then wildly pull apart. Then back together they would flow again. But then I saw intuitively that they wouldn't be coming to wind together anymore. It was a sad and hard lesson.

During our time together, Glenn had hated living in Israel; then he hated living in Kingston, Ontario. Montreal wasn't as bad for him, but then his dream moved onward to Philadelphia, where he would finally get into U.S. Aircraft. He hated it there. I said one day, "Two more moves and I am done." I couldn't get any traction or direction for myself in the working world, although I always notched my resume as we went. For years, I wanted to help people help themselves — a drive that took me through health foods, hypnosis, meditation, video planning, exploring, learning. But my plans were probably too nebulous to an engineer.

I wanted home and family, and I was still afraid of the world. But I was stepping out, or at least poking my toe out, of my self-limiting ways. Glenn helped me a lot, especially at first, encouraging me, noticing when I was hiding. Once we gained green-card status, I wanted to be able to work, to fly on my own path. If he was still discouraged about wherever we were, I knew that eventually I would have to leave the encumbering aura of his depression. With my own issues of healing and self-esteem, I found myself more and more unable to function in simple ways. But as I said, I had to learn more about being empathic. We absorb and resonate in family in ways that literally create a fabric that holds us all and can be dangerously limiting. My life was all about learning that; ultimately I could then teach about it.

I wasn't sure where I was headed, as I was also still edgy in my sensitive, skitterish reality. In a healing center called the Revitalization Center in Media, run by Judith Truthstone Brigham, a courageous, powerful leader, I met people who inspired me. It was energizing. Also it was the time of the Harmonic Convergence. I didn't take part much except through my inner awakening processes. Each one of them was also emerging; we shared processes and the precariousness of our steps out of our socialization. We talked about humanity evolving, awakening. I wanted so much to be healed and healing, to be significant, helpful, and who knows what else.

"Oh, wow! There's a channeling workshop in the Poconos! I'm going to take it! Then I'll really have a skill. I'll be useful—I'll be able to lift and heal people. Now I know what I'll do. I'll take Bridget and Glenn with me into the pine forests and the mountains." Glenn loved the mountains, and Bridget always felt better in nature; they could keep one another company.

I scheduled it, the Poconos for a whole weekend for all three of us—and spirits—in the beautiful woods. It was exciting for me. I felt like it was a brilliant threshold to my grand service in the world.

As we drove there, Bridget, then three, was in the back seat talking to herself. "Pretty, pretty girl." I turned around to admire her. With gum, she had created little curls in her hair across her forehead.

We pulled into the ashram and at the entrance desk we spoke to a very thin, very pale young man. To me he looked like a classic vegetarian meditator. They bulk up more these days, but that was my first thought.

"Do you have scissors?" Glenn asked him bluntly.

"Sorry. No."

"Never mind," Glenn said gruffly as he brought a hunting knife out. He then proceeded to saw the "curls" off the front of Bridget's hair as the man gasped. I gulped back hysterical laughter at the strange scenario and our pale concierge's horror.

The month before, I had gone to the ashram for a personal channeling. In the vaulted silence, my channeler brought through his etheric mentor. "Your marriage contract is ending." That truly shook me. I wouldn't accept his words, but their vibrations moved through me as if they were a laser sword. Deep down, I knew that the gap between Glenn and me and between aircraft and healing was widening.

The workshop started off with hours and hours of toning any sounds we chose, moving them through our bodies. It was an amped-up version of the sounds I had made spontaneously around the fire on Pender Island ten years earlier. Our sounding filled the room; the colorful frequencies we generated encircled the room, connecting us all. I watched them speed up, pulse — different streams of color being fed and shaped by our voices surging with their own spontaneous sounds. Sometimes we'd move into harmony, sometimes we'd stay rather cacophonous but melding in sparkling color and sound as the day moved along. Our heads and bodies were electric.

The rest of the weekend was a disaster. Glenn's depress-sion deepened. My little one was hyper, needing a lot of TLC. And she just wanted Mummy. I hadn't brought the milk I used to calm her at night. And here in this no-animal-product reality, there were no calming proteins for her, nor for him! Another factor was what with the charging up from the frequencies we were building in the channeling studies, I simply couldn't sleep.

The second day, the hallways were full of fellow students enthusiastically talking with spirits. I ached to reach farther into my perceptions, with all their buzzing promises. I needed to explore the gifts that were pushing at me. Yet I tended to the needs of my little family.

That Sunday morning, I left to join the early-morning yoga class. I stretched and rolled, pushing my bottom up mightily, but my downward dog collapsed into sobs. I sobbed and sobbed and sobbed. I couldn't pull myself together. Striding out of the half-done class, back to our room, tearstained, I announced, "We're going home. And you are never coming with me again. Never again!"

I stuffed clothes and toys in our bags when, once again, serendipity or Divine Intervention knocked. A friend had told our teacher that I was leaving. "Laura wants to speak with you before you leave," my friend said. I was weeping in frustration as I went to talk to the teacher.

"You have more of the channeling energy than anyone here," Laura said. "Stay for a couple of hours. Just 'til the first morning break."

"I will. Thanks."

Although I was exhausted, I stayed. And voilà — a break-through! The circling frequencies and trances broke me out of a membrane-like energy form that was confining my mind and a lot of my body. Our bodies also are intuitive and can

215

hold us within our identity. My tears also washed out old fears and feelings that were blocking my access. I could actually see and hear etheric beings knocking on the door, wanting to come through. Laura's suggestion had worked. I was at a new level of my multidimensional experience!

For the next few months, whenever Glenn came home from Boeing Vertol, where he was working on the Osprey, I would hold his hand (that was my way of making connection in the early days) and I would channel for ten minutes or so. I described the helicopter. He said nothing. I reported all kinds of personal issues. He said nothing. Then one day during my internship at WILM radio in Wilmington, Delaware, my boss and I went to cover news. Lo and behold, there it was — the very vehicle that was emerging every day, more and more, in my visions! My mentor said, pointing to a model in the middle of City Hall, "This is what your husband is working on. Top secret." In my daily visions I had the wrong color, but indeed the right picture. I was validated. I was studying radio...and became a radio.

Magically, readings began. Friends, especially our dear friend Pat, whose children were friends of Lucy, sent their friends. What a tremendous leg-up for me. I am so grateful to them to this day. And, as I was still pre-green card, I was legal, as I was working in the subject of my student visa: communications.

CHAPTER THIRTEEN

Oh, No—I'm Going to Have to Leave Again!

Entrancing drama ensued. I would call in the higher frequencies, scour the space with their light and beauty, surround us, and hold the person's hand. Then the frequencies of the Guides would come through carrying light, love, and words. My clients would weep and often I would, too. Issues lit up. One of my first clients asked about her sister who had committed suicide fifteen years earlier. I could "see" the sister rolling around in gray cloud-like fields, still unconscious. The Guides bid us to talk to her, to wake her up, and pray. We could actually feel the surges of healing energy flowing through her—from us! This client and I met weekly several more times, and each time her sister appeared more awake, learning that she had a choice to awaken and shake off her trance. She could feel the beings of light that surrounded her. Those were days of awakening for me as well as for clients as instruction poured through. The thirty dollars I received each time also mattered.

I chuckled. Each step in my journey was suddenly meaningful; every one of my experiences gave a little or a lot to everyone who came for sessions. My growing number of new clients searched for healing among their weeds of experience, or looked for who they really are. The sessions were profoundly touching. How do we get out of the weeds? How do we find those flows of empowerment innate in each of us, bogged down among old programs? How do we even recognize the programs? Through intentions and the highly charged counsel of loving, transcended beings, people felt healed or at least unfolding.

One evening the doorbell rang. Bridget ran to answer it, her little fountain hairdo with its bouncing red bow popping back and forth as she hopped. "Hi," she greeted the two women in the doorway. "You want a reading with my mum?"

"Yes, dear."

"I'm better than she is."

"I'll bet you are!"

We all laughed. I am still expecting her emergence.

I started creating new programs for my inner self like mad at this point—affirmations of prosperity and a move to the Southwest. It would be warm there, and my intuitive self said the lay of the land would be electric. The first thing that happened was the Canadian Government reinstated the widows' pension for those of us who had remarried. Wow! My affirmations have changed a whole country! Woo-hoo— California, here I come!

Sudden surprise changes often direct our lives. John Lennon said that famous line, "Life is what happens while you're busy making other plans." Or, in my case, are my life's changes orchestrated by my transformative Uranus in the eighth house? Change often happens quickly in my world.

One day in June 1987, Glenn came home from work in the middle of his workday with an excruciating headache. Ho lay upstairs in pain for four days. We did the usual aspirin, even extra strength, but it just became more dire. At four one morning, I took him to the ER.

"It's a migraine," said the resident. "A shot of Demerol, and he'll be fine."

Glenn briefly enjoyed the Demerol. But a few days later, he was still lying upstairs in pain, and now there was an odd smell around him. It was a strange smell, sour, sweet, and a little putrid, but almost familiar. Something was terribly wrong. Off we went to the hospital again in the middle of the night, where I had to leave him for testing. A few hours later, we got the news over the phone, and it was shockingly bleak. It brought me back to the metal chairs episode in the Vancouver cancer clinic's hallway.

"Mrs. Entwistle, your husband has had a very large brain hemorrhage, a 'bleed' — so large we are not sure that he will recover."

How can this be? I ran around inside myself. My questions tumbled with random thoughts from the edges of my mind — my edgy mind. "I am still recovering from and discovering myself after Steven's death and the loss of Naomi. Is it my cooking?" Remember, I had an out-of-control power that I feared. My stepdaughter Lucy and I clung to each other in the tiny kitchen of our townhouse. What to do? Oddly, I felt tremendous guilt. I had alienated my family of origin with my grief reactions. How could I tell them that I would cause them trouble again? Even writing this today, I feel the sad waste of all that insane guilt.

"Call his folks," the doctor said. "He may only have a few short days."

The words echoed Steven's doctors back in Vancouver flurrying to get away as they announced, "Follow his every whim. His chances have dropped."

The wires hummed across the Atlantic to Scotland and England and to the Canadian West Coast all that evening. Within three or four days, his mum, stepdad, and sister were flying in from the United Kingdom.

Daily, I drove the thirty-five miles to the hospital where Glenn lay in a coma. I would sit there and pray and channel his higher self. Often, it looked as though he were sitting on a throne. Hmmmmm....what was that? Images of his being in charge? Twenty-five years later, I was at a five-day silent retreat of Divine Openings. One of the exercises was for each of us to deepen, then experience ourselves sitting on the throne at the head of our own soul's journey. Aha! I smiled. Glenn's higher self knew the scoop way back then. I didn't yet.

I wept all the way to the massive hospital, prettied up, then followed the route I planned carefully to get to his room. "Are you going to live, Glenn?" I would ask his higher self on its throne.

"Haven't decided," he told me repeatedly. "I don't know yet."

I would weep again all the way home, thirty-five miles back down the freeway, and, just before going into the house, pretty up again for Lucy, then nineteen, and Bridget, three. Lucy was running the household for us. This all happened around his birthday, June 29, and his folks were scheduled to arrive on July 4.

Always, even in dire circumstances, there can be comic relief. We needed to laugh. We had been having car and financial troubles so we had a hired a clunky rent-a-wreck for a week. It was sitting outside the townhouse. Right after Glenn was transported to the Philadelphia hospital, Lucy said, "We had better get that rented car back. It'll really cost!"

"Oh, right!" We grabbed the keys and went out to the car. It was full of fishing gear and half-empty coffee cups in the cup holders. We looked at each other as the light dawned. This isn't the rent-a-wreck!

"Dad stole the car!" Lucy's blue eyes were huge. "My dad stole a car!" The keys we had didn't work of course. More pondering....

Lucy dug through the glove compartment for identification and called the man who owned the car and reported the incident to the police, who quickly came over. The scene was bizarre as most of the main characters assembled in our tiny kitchen.

"I came out of work, and I couldn't believe it!" said the owner as he stood there with his son. "There in a parking lot filled with the latest shiny vehicles, my heap was gone!" He was almost complimented. The police were watching us all carefully for a setup of some sort.

It turns out that Glenn, with his excruciating headache, had stumbled out of work, looking for the "heap" he had rented, and chose this car. Being a British engineer, raised "up to his ass in grease and machines" he knew out how to start any car.

The police acted tough and suspicious. "I'm sure. His birthdate please!"

"Well, it's today. June 29."

"Yah, sure lady!"

The story unfolded. Our friend Pat, worrying that Glenn would be sentenced, said to them, "Excuse me. My husband is a judge." She'd possibly pulled a trump card? The policeman rolled his eyes.

The car owner was amused. "Actually, I am flattered that he chose my car." No charges were filed. The police wrote their report finally, with their own almost-humor. They see

221

so many strange stories. The rent-a-wreck was found in the sprawling parking lot, and we returned it for a hearty fee.

Back to Glenn. By July 3, there had been no change in him. His folks were arriving from the U.K. the next day. I wasn't weeping on the drive home anymore, just emotionally paused as I drove the freeway on the third.

Suddenly, Glenn arrived in my car. Even though he was "see through," I knew he was still alive. "Far out!" I said in my Sixties vernacular. "Your etheric self can travel!" He was all dressed in gray clothes. That color always represents an odd self-containment. "Hi, Glenn. How are you?"

"I've decided to stay."

"Oh, great, Glenn. Why?"

"Because I need you."

"Oh, heavens! That's no reason. Maybe if you want to have experiences, or a life, or you love us?" I remember feeling irked.

"But you have to let me climb the mountains."

"Glenn, I didn't stop you. You stopped yourself. And that was before my time. Susan [his first wife] didn't want you to climb anymore. Susan — not me!" I couldn't believe it. There we were bickering multidimensionally with all the sounds and visuals you would expect on the 'net these days! It was a "you-and-I-tube event!" He disappeared, and I wondered if it had been a creation of my affirmations and vigorous imagination.

Early the next morning, off I went to the hospital. I planned on picking up his folks at the airport a little later and take them to see him.

"Hullo," Glenn said as I walked into his room. He was sitting up, smiling. That was the first time he knew I was there since he had arrived at the hospital. "Hullo," he said again, and his cute, crooked grin grew. He was awake. He was aware. I was startled. It was true — we did have that visit in the car!

The doctor shrugged behind me. "We have no idea what happened. Suddenly, last night, he changed." I didn't tell the doctor that he had made a choice.

At the airport a few hours later, my waves to his frantic-eyed yet composed folks, coming through customs and the airport rabble, were joyous. By the time we reached one another, they knew. "He is going to live. Glenn is going to live!" Shedding tears of happiness, his U.K. family surrounded him in his room in the huge Philadelphia hospital.

"Hey, Glenn," I said. "You stole a car!"

"What? I did?" He loved it! He laughed and laughed as I told him about the fishing gear and coffee cups, the man and son, and the police.

"How did you get it started?" I asked.

"I hurt so badly that I would have lifted that car and run up the freeway with it on my back!" The image of him galloping up the freeway with a rent-a-wreck on his back was hilarious. We all laughed.

His recovery was slow but steady, his crooked smile was impish. He walked with a cane and mixed up right and left, for which he blamed the plumbers with his famous line "and their piece of shit" work as he endured cold showers. He didn't notice the times he put his shirt on backward. But each day he was better.

One day, his Boeing managers visited. "What can we do to help you, Glenn?"

"I want to go back to Washington."

"Right you are."

I groaned. Within weeks, we were packing our household. Back to the wetlands. So much for programming for the Southwest — the warmth, the dry, and the desert.

"Alright everyone," I announced. "We need to get wellies [rubber boots]. We're going back to the Pacific Northwest."

Little Bridget was edgy and becoming difficult in the ambient turmoil. Lucy told me a few days later, "Bridget is very upset." But our little actor/comedian's eyes were twinkling.

"Why?"

"She's worried. 'Lucy,' she said, 'if we are all going to Seattle, why do we need to get willies!'" Lucy and I howled with laughter. Poor Bridget. Why would we have to have a willy (the British slang for penis) if we are moving? And how does one get a willy?

Soon, after a series of lurches and some heavy hops, skips, and jumps, we were in Seattle in one of the longest rainstorms they ever had—well over forty-three days. Glenn's stroke was a stroke of good fortune for him, but a wet one for me.

Finally reassembled in rainy land, with Glenn back at work, his younger sister came to visit. We were getting ready for an excursion with her one Saturday when Glenn, hair dryer in hand, fell to the bedroom floor writhing—his first grand-mal seizure in a series. Having your six-foot, three-inch husband on the ground writhing in seeming pain is terrifying. I immediately started crying and apologizing. All right, that was helpful!

Hmmmmm…it was the old fear that my power was out of control. But it usually happened just after a disappointment or an altercation. Plus we did live near power lines. It has been suggested that they can leak charges that exacerbate sensitivities. And after all, he did have a scar in his brain.

Seizures are frightening, so I started a series of seizure drills for the girls. They never actually witnessed a seizure, but I would tense up until I shook and show them how it would look. They would try, too, plus Bridget's dolls had their seizures, as well. And we learned, thanks to our counselor Richard, an ex-priest who combined spirituality, meditation, and visions, that Glenn could interrupt a pending seizure with a magical, specific kind of breath. Little Bridget added the special breath to her healing work with her dolls.

Our marriage was now stretched in every way. I started looking for help. One day, en route to my first visit to that same counselor, Richard, I noticed that a woman was sitting in my car, annoyingly right behind me, making it hard for me to "see" her as I drove. But when I did stretch to see her, I noticed how like my mum she looked. Messages flowed through my mind. She was my mother's grandmother. "I want you to know," she said, "that I was the woman who set up the resistance to men in our lineage."

Was I crazy? That familiar question rose. When I arrived at Richard's office, he asked, "Who is that who came in with you?" Further research explained that her bitterness and resistance to men arose because of her experiences, mostly of the authority that they had held in her family and in her marriage.

Because of his seizures, Glenn couldn't drive, so each morning, I drove him to Boeing. I was getting the girls sorted out with preschool and college as well as establishing a flow for my own healing work. My brain was terribly scrambled at this point. These five-AM drives were in traffic, often in pouring rain. Glenn was generally enraged, often at strange things. For instance, it annoyed him that I would take alternate routes along the lake that were more beautiful than the clogged freeway, I wasn't working, I kept getting pneumonia. My resentment at him and our life was billowing. We

225

hadn't put gratitude for one another into our daily routine. Money was still terrible and cranking up more tension.

I decided that a vacation weekend away could possibly save our marriage. The nearby Olympic Peninsula is beautiful and quite idyllic, bringing oceans and forest together. I called the Bed and Breakfast Association. A British voice said, "I have the perfect place for you in Port Angeles. A Tudor-style inn, and it's stunning."

"Great! Thanks."

But then a day later she called, "Oh, sorry, it's fully booked. But I have another idea in Dungeness."

"Okay." But I had started to think more about it. B and B's are basically in someone's home. Maybe we needed more neutral territory. I called the Tides Inn in Port Townsend and booked us there.

Canceling with my new British B and B friend was hard work. "I have already booked you."

"Thank you. But please cancel. I have booked us in the Tides Inn."

"You can't cancel. This is a nice woman." Her British voice was harshly motherly.

"Heavens! I feel like I am wrangling with my mother! I need to cancel....."

"You can't just go around canceling!" On and on and on she almost shrieked at me. I held the phone away from my head, rolling my eyes. She was tough. But sometimes I remember to get smart: I flipped my eyes and mind upward to access my Guides, unhooking our challenge. "Is this a good choice?"

"Excellent!" streamed through me. In the midst of her word flow, I said, "We'll take it."

"Wot?" she said, obviously startled. "What?"

"We'll take it."

Her papers rustled as she confirmed our booking.

I told Glenn about it. He loves mountains and oceans, so I thought it would make him happy. But, "I want to go to Winthrop where my climbing buddies and I used to go," he said. We hashed it around. I was trying to find us a new place, a place where we could enjoy one another. The idea of his old drinking, climbing haunts with memories of his buddies didn't feel to me like a balm for our relationship. He stormed outside—I had nicknamed him Heathcliff from *Wuthering Heights* because of his intense presence or "heavy presence" as he called it—and had a huge seizure. Again I wept and felt guilty. It was the old power issue, but I also noticed that the seizures seemed to punctuate his anger.

But there, on the Olympic Peninsula, we had a delightful weekend in the best B and B I have ever been to. Wandering around Hurricane Ridge and the spit was healing for both of us. It was a suddenly snowy weekend, and we were the only ones who had braved the driving. Simone, the proprietor, made great breakfasts. She and Glenn talked most of the time. I was very quiet, contemplative, not wanting to leave my marriage, but feeling so confined and confused—alone, though in a crowd.

As the weekend ended and we were paying the bill, Simone commented, "Ronni, we haven't talked much. What do you do?"

"Radio. I do radio. Don't have a job right now. Oh, and I do readings."

"Readings? Wonderful. How about coming back in exchange for readings for me and my family? And I can get you people from the neighborhood. Don't leave it too long — you know what happens." That was a turning point for me.

Within a month, we had set up my first weekend in Sequim. People were lined up all round the B and B. With income and a growing reputation, finally I had a viable business! I returned home on Mother's Day that year with a stack of cash, a new, dear friend in Simone, and true happiness about my work. The girls were so pleased, but Glenn was angry and unimpressed. He made it very clear that he wanted me to get a regular job at Ernst Hardware. More and more grit rose between us, and I couldn't seem to rekindle the closeness we once shared. The depression, the seizures, money issues — it was just so much. Once a contract is done, it is impossible to sync into one another again. Yet Glenn was a good man, handsome, kind at times, and beginning to get his work on track. When I first met him, he had been complaining that he wanted to leave engineering to become a photographer. But that leap was too scary, and he was less and less inspired by my own seemingly evanescent journey.

I went back and forth to Sequim where I developed a following; even more thrilling was that my telephone market with clients from around the country magically expanded. I was coming into my work, delving through the murk of my old self-esteem issues, and embracing the healing of my central nervous system with the help of the revitalizing energies the Guides brought through. I was also incorporating nutrition, channeling, and renewing and recognizing my entire personality. The buzzing in my head, that strange, twisted, tangled electrical circuitry that I could see sitting in my head on top of my brain, still took me over at times. But I was on track.

I was still driving Glenn to work at five AM in the rain and traffic, though. He was managing fewer seizures, but he was still depressed. Money was just beginning to grow.

"Simone, I have to leave," I told her when she called to talk one day

"I have an idea," she said. "I know someone who just died and his house is mostly empty. You can get it for about four-hundred dollars a month!"

Glenn joined me on my trip to see the house. "I feel like I am shooting myself in the foot," he said as we looked over the vacant place. Mr. Wilson, a relative of Simone's and a dear man, had been a hoarder. His cute, little house was packed with junk and newspapers, radio stuff, old World War II memoirs, and some torn furniture. The yard had been beautiful. The kids and I moved over and left Glenn in our little townhouse.

We garage saled and stored a lot of things—I would say meaningless things—from both the new house and the townhouse. I think we were getting beyond just having lots of things for the sake of having things, including relationships.

So began our new chapters. I was relieved but angry, saddened, and disappointed that Glenn and I couldn't find a way to support one another, and I know it was hard for the girls. In some ways, though, life lightened up. Lucy went off to Peninsula College and Bridget went to preschool.

I was skitterish as I took on this new phase of supporting myself and two daughters as an intuitive and doing healings and energy work. Wow! I was afraid in the night, so I took to sleeping with a spray bottle of 409 house cleaner under my pillow. If there were any marauders, I would spray them in the eyes. What an ad that would make for the product's company! Hmmmm…fortunately I never did need to test my theory.

We three enjoyed the adventure of this move, though Bridget, now four, missed her dad a lot. Lucy advanced swiftly through the little college, immediately acting on stage. She knocked people's socks off in her theater roles, one of which was her performance of Ruby Bertle, a British maid. It was a small part but stole the show, cracking people up and making a bit part a cameo role. Still does!

Things were perking along. Friendships blossomed, people came for sessions, the kids were emerging.

One night, soon after we had moved in, the old man who had died there showed up, sitting right beside me on his tattered, old couch. I panicked. "Oh, my gosh, a ghost!"

"Oh, stop. You are a psychic," my self said back to me. I laughed as I remembered dear old Archie and the wall scratching.

"You are right." So I turned to my see-through friend. "What would you like?"

"Just want to watch a little TV here on my couch."

We sat together in ease through a couple of programs. Then he was gone.

In retrospect, I look at the ways I was carried through these changes. They sound so easy! But despite serendipitous support across various chasms, being nudged to open more and more, I was still timid, even reeling from the amazing influences from the Guides, finding myself having to change, expand, and grow more and more multidimensionally, accepting the sometimes even painful stretching and ripping of the usual human boundaries of thought and feeling. During readings, I would watch the number of levels of being that began to show themselves within my clients. I could "see" gargantuan waves moving through the universes and watch as streams of frequency came through to be a part of our vibrational makeup.

That is the awakening process, and it is painful at times. But also, I still had to unravel some of the programs in myself, abuse programs and old lineage attitudes. I still longed to be acceptable to my family of origin, which created a lot of pain in me. At night, I would often go into what is called "process," exhuming old programs from my history, maybe past lives, or imprints of other existences floating around in the universe and on this planet. These old programs act out in my feelings, such as terror, or the sense of being hunted, or taking on the insecurities of the people closest to me. My body hurt and my brain felt drilled as vibrations electrified channels throughout my body. If I could, I would do yoga to keep things moving through. Back to my dear friends — alternate nostril breathing and good old meditation — I'd go. These awakenings/clearing processes continued slowly and dramatically for about four years, helping me realize more and more of myself and guiding and improving healing sessions with a growing number of clients.

There were times when releasing meant I cried for hours on end. I just couldn't stop. It was like flushing old thoughts and feelings through. I didn't know where to go or what to do with myself. I was too sensitive during this period to go to the school with my daughter. The experience was hair-raising. I became dizzy, feeling as though I was being bopped right, left, and center. Volunteering there was impossible, as I was unable to handle the energy of the place. I couldn't concentrate on earthplane demands much of the time. I could only concentrate on what was going on — *me me me* — discovering what it was that I was trying to birth. I was afraid of other people, competition, being seen. So insecure and shaky, I was terrified of the judgments that were supposed to "straighten me out." I had felt thrown to the floor during my time of initiation. Initiation is a time when nothing we hold on to will work and, denuded, we are left in a state of surrender and reconstruction from the inside out. Judgments felt like they were shredding my right to be, while they were actually reflections shredding old, unconscious programs until I could re-create my inner self. I couldn't even admit certain faults to myself because *I* would then shred me further. Yet I always knew I had a goal: to be really me. I always knew there was more of me in there and I would find it through the craziness.

I was faithful to my emergence. On a greater level, I watched the tapestry of human consciousness unravel in the amazing changing universal fields. To me, the fields here on the planet were moving upward. Some of the universal energies hold much more dynamic light that, once ingested, or even just included in the atmosphere around us all, push everyone's ability to hold more light. The process is helped by avatars and the radiances of willing students, including myself and many "lightworkers" here at this time to consciously bring the fields into our species. I became more and more familiar with us all as "vibrational beings of light" first and foremost, downloading influences into the physical second. It has been said by a number of teachers that if people from two-hundred years ago arrived here today, they would see us almost shimmering. I'm not sure how to put the political greed-and-grab fest into that mix, but that would be another book.

As I watch the world these days, I see people awakening. Their processes are so fast, much faster than mine, and many have far less dramatic pain and craziness. We are an empathetic species; many of us broke through with great effort, which has made it easier for others to just burst open their own cocoons. Remember the "times they are a-changin'" as Dylan sang during the Sixties? They haven't stopped changing. That, combined with the fact that the references to awakening, emerging, evolving are so much more accepted and shared around the world, has sped up the process.

Oh, yes, I seemed and felt truly crazy at times. I watch so many homeless on our streets, lost, and I hurt that many of them might just be going through something, not simply being mentally disabled as society might think. They need guidance through their own distressed neurotransmissions and soul journeys. Being on the streets probably isn't going to do it.

Thank God, I had breathing, yoga, movement, nutrition, and the love of my Guides and friends. Thanks also to Van Morrison and others as well as the clients I was privileged to work with who validated all my shifting perceptions and incoming lights and wisdom with their own healing.

At that point, I had another subconscious plan on a lower rung than my commitment to my awakening: to never make anyone mad at me again. Never. The screaming, crying, attacks, shunning from the family all threw me into wanting to die. I was already so shame-based and self-deprecating. I was doing everything wrong, acting out—they knew this out loud.

To stay harmonious is insane, however. I found myself in a box, a self-judgmental, defensive box. At times I was even scared to go out. But that was just another kind of façade I had to wear until I caught on.

CHAPTER FOURTEEN

Dimensional Explorations

And then came a Special Delivery by the Universe: a new man, Bryce. We were unlikely, me with my thrift-shop clothes, he with his California material finesse, and each of us a stretch outside of one another's typical attraction. He was also recovering from a divorce, so his finances were tapped. A real-estate mogul on the Peninsula, however, he soon regained his financial composure.

His knowledge and practice of metaphysics was a relief to me as he was hugely supportive about my journey. But just as Steven panicked about my being raised Catholic, Bryce panicked about my revolutionary experiences in the Sixties — and my clothes. But I must say here that his concern with material wealth was also a boon, as he could help me learn to ground myself on this planet and to dress with a view to my outside presentation! Finally! Many of the people who had gravitated to the Peninsula, like him, had followed the Ramtha School of Enlightenment, which is located there. From his loftier perspective, Ramtha had counseled his followers to move to a "safe" part of the country, gathering a two-year supply of food and water, preparing for "the end." I remembered those nights on that train to Vermont, I had spent many an hour shaking as I listened to his dire predictions.

Many of the times Bryce and I spent together were fun. We'd try out new meditations as well as explore energy from my own channeling. When the searing pains of awakening, the drilling into my head and body amped up, he'd comfort me. When I would rise, weeping, in the middle of the night to relieve my agony with yoga, he would get up and do some poses with me. I was so grateful. He calmed my fears of being crazy. "It's just a process. You are getting enlightened!" he would encourage me.

Bryce was hilarious, running through the house, ripping his shirt open, and yelling, "She can't take her hands off of me!" He wanted to marry me. He loved my daughter, too, and she loved him as he ran around playing Barbies with her. He enticed her to eat, despite her resistance. I just "knew" I couldn't marry him, though. He was always in terrible physical pain, which he never did release. Whenever we prepared to go out somewhere special, he had too much body pain and too many headaches. We often cancelled.

More and more strength emerged in my energy work. "I've got the money, honey, if you've got the time," he would say. And I worked on him four or five times a week. It was a rich class for me as he was like a living cadaver. He could tell me and show me where the energy impacted him. After a day or two of relief, his pains would recur. But we learned so much about the rapport with his hidden emotions and his pain. Finally, I experimented by building up a team of healers to enter his body's fields from different perspectives: hypnosis, energy, chiropractic, past lives. We set up to do a series of sessions in just a couple of days—too quickly for him to slip back into his old process. It helped for a few days. Then he would be pained. I loved him, but the sickness and pain, and always seeking a route through the puzzle, was relentless and draining.

We did a spiritual business deal—he put a downpayment on a little, easy-to-manage tract house for me.

We thought we would make a great profit when we sold it, and he would get his downpayment back. I would pay the monthly as if it were rent to him, but, he assured me, it would be my house. *No* contracts—just a spiritual contract. Later, I found out that he'd had a plan: I would simply marry him, and the whole thing would be "in the family."

Here is a story about good intuitive or psychic information being badly filtered through my desire. Strangely, the entire time I was with Bryce, five or six years, I "saw" another man in my visions. He went everywhere with us. If we were cooking, there he was in the kitchen. Then he was in the car with us, or even the bathroom—wherever...just like Harvey, the huge invisible rabbit in that classic movie who accompanied James Stewart everywhere he went. Harvey had less of a personal story than my phantom man, but still, he kept everyone scratching their heads. This see-through phantom man kept me feeling crazy. Finally, I knew that he was breaking up with someone, and they were both crying. He also looked angry. He was very creative and emotional. At that point, I was also having wonderful conversations with my first husband Steven's spirit self, who was finally learning to speak instead of dragging things out through games of charades.

I told Bryce about my conversations with Steven from the other side as well as about the invisible man who was in most scenes of my life, as I didn't want to deceive him. We even went to see a wonderful, famous therapist in Port Townsend. She'd written a mesmerizing book on entering and following the visions of a schizophrenic in order to successfully lead her out of her nightmare. She was Jungian and said, "It is just your male side. Make an appointment to meet him. He is just a part of you." Maybe that was true, but that wasn't all.

I kept channeling about it, plus just praying to be shown. Spontaneous visions were a little like today's FaceTime. I found myself thinking of that old limerick about "the man who wasn't there,"

> *When I was walking up a stair*
> *I met a man who wasn't there*
> *He wasn't there again today*
> *I wish that man would go away*

I nonetheless kept learning so much about him, his life and his relationships, as if I were talking with him. Guidance said that it was a relationship yet to come. I didn't ask if it would be wonderful, loving, great, supportive. I assumed it would be.

Hmmmmmmm...I didn't let go of the concept that this invisible man would be my husband, that soul mate I dreamed of. Bryce and I were a transformational relationship, my Guides told me often, setting one another up for better relationships in the future. I trusted that the words coming through were not skewed by my personal mind or my desires—a powerful lesson in purification! I trusted that Mr. Invisible was my man. What a surprise!

The Guides advised me a number of times about Bryce: "It is time to leave this man." Bryce wanted Bridget and me to move in with him. At five or six, though, while Bridget loved Bryce and loved playing dolls, laughing, and eating great meals with him, she also had insight. As I mentioned, I am still waiting for her to emerge, but that is for a later story. So despite the fact that she loved him, she would say, "Don't live with him, Mum. He is troubled." And those words came at six years old.

At times I did want to live with Bryce in the beautiful home he was building, to continue to be with his humor and his enthusiasm about my talents. But I always knew something. In many ways, it couldn't work. Vibrationally, I "saw" a glassed-in chest, a heart enclosed behind something. I think that this is a common shield with people who have been abused. Also, that relentless pain throughout his body often happens when people's emotions are deeply repressed. Of course, I could be quite annoying as I let go of many old emotions that flowed out in my tears, emotions that had piled up, plus old fears and programs. What about my intention to let them express and move through? I thought people would welcome my honesty, but it just charged up their disgust or fear of my weakness...or their own, really. I laugh now, as I'm not so naïve any more.

In the older days or in India, during the emerging processes of hallowed gurus or beings of light, expression was blessed. With respect for their spiritual awakening, they were supported, helped, mopped up, washed, and fed so they could continue with their emergence, which was for the sake of all people. Not so in the single-parenting, 3D world!

Maybe Bryce's pain was from another lifetime, as we couldn't find the abuse in this lifetime. He had an unmistakable warmth, and he made us laugh. I became a great cook as he loved to eat. I continued to work and work on him, but outside of small gains he would return to his pain level. When we were out visiting and there were other luscious young women present, he would slurp loudly. I tried not to mind, but I couldn't quite trust him.

Following the Guides' advice, I would break up with him. Then we would see one another and, like magnets, we'd snap together again. That parting dance was wrenching. It was so hard to be apart. But, for me anyway, it was also hard to stay together. The Guides kept pushing me to break up with him. Warning, warning. We broke up three different times. Soul connections are the hardest. Over how many thousands of years had we bonded and over who-knows-what unfinished business? The love was unmistakable, but the addiction part was unwieldy. I found that when there is something deep to learn, the Guides don't just tell me. I had to experience, to choose, to grow.

As I was reeling from the pain of our final breakup, my Guides said very loudly, "We have asked you to leave this man!" Why couldn't I? They spoke of "soul bonding and soul bondage." This was soul bondage — for him, too. We loved each other, but shouldn't have stayed together. If I had listened when they first advised me, if I could have stayed away from him, I could have kept my little house, continued the payments, and eventually taken over the deed. We might have even enjoyed the long-term friendship we had heard about from the Guides and planned together so many times, once we realized the benefits of our transformational relationship. But I just couldn't let go of the relationship.

As Bryce and I writhed on the ancient cords between us, one day I received a call asking for a reading. The call was from Wyoming, and I "knew" who it was immediately. "Hello, Ronni," said the phantom man. "Jan told me to call you. She said you might be my woman." Ironically, his name was Steven. We called him Steven 2. I did his reading, and I remember saying as it opened, "You have a lot of wonderful light. But if you don't do your emotional work, you'll bypass your belly — your subconscious." I could psychically "see" little squares of angers, defiances, and defenses bouncing out of his belly, which reminded me of the challenges in an astrology chart.

Forewarned isn't always forearmed. I told Bryce soon after that phone call. He shot out of the house, shaking. "I need a month," I said. I didn't meet my phantom man in

239

person for three months, though we grew our relationship with frequent phone calls. After our month apart, Bryce and I arranged a conscious parting. We would meet at my house (well, the house I thought was mine, but which turned out to be merely a rental from him) every morning at seven to meditate. Despite our desire to part consciously, his head kept turning into the head of a devil or a demon. I thought it meant that I had to poop, as I knew by then that a toxic intestinal tract darkens visions. Or was I simply being negative? Once again, I overrode the strong warnings.

It turned out to be a three-way nightmare. Slowly but surely, what emerged was that the three of us were in a karmic triangle. Steven 2 hated Bryce. When Steven 2 was angry, he stayed angry for days and days and even more days. He felt duped that there had ever been a Bryce in my life. I was hurt by his constant competition with me instead of the support from Bryce that nurtured Bridget and me. Bryce was hurt. He who'd always said, "There is nothing that cannot be resolved by communication," stopped all communication. Our last connection was a session at our friend's acupuncture clinic, where I worked energetically throughout his body, opening it to healing at myriad nerve intersections.

"Why can't I come to the house for this?" Bryce demanded.

"Steven 2 can't handle that yet." I explained — thoughtfully, I thought. "I just need a month to settle him in, Bryce."

"No." He was determined.

We continued the session, which turned into an energy lesson on the underlying emotions of our pain. Bryce had always loved going to the doctor, even as a child. Somehow it is where he found love and comfort. That day, right after he said, "No!" I watched as all the receptors, where his pain nested, shut — slam, slam, slam — deep inside and along the nerve intersections. Mesmerizing! It was as if all those times of him letting me see into him and his vulnerability had been a treat for me. But he was taking that treat away from me as he renewed his armor in the face of Steven 2's fear and his own feelings of betrayal.

"You have to know you just refiled all your pain, Bryce. You have the ability to open up to release them as well."

Our last kiss was cold.

"You don't trust me, do you?"

"I will always love you," he said. "I trust you as a healer, but not as a woman. I am going to find a woman as fast as I can and marry her for the rest of my life." He did.

We had made a verbal commitment that we wanted to clear all the karma between us. We didn't. He sent a note to my daughter while still not speaking with me. "I'm coming to pick you up for the weekend. I have a new family now, and I want you to be a part of it."

I panicked. The Guides said, "No. They will go through a very intense time, and your daughter doesn't need to be there." Was that true or was that filtered through my own mind and fears? I will never know.

The relationship with Steven 2, my phantom man, was also skewed. I was reliving our karma, emotionally trapped everywhere I turned. That's why Steven 2 was intrinsic in my relationship with Bryce, appearing in my visions the minute I started dating Bryce. I just didn't ask the right questions and made huge assumptions. I am aware that we don't have to live out all of our karmic urges. We can just be with them, knowing that all the tings and dings are from leftover reactions. His rages at me, mostly because I hadn't explained to him that my house was actually owned by Bryce, were endless. Bryce was leaving vitriolic, poisonous messages on my voicemail, which Steven 2 also heard.

241

I had jumped to the wrong conclusion. Steven 2 was my soul mate—or so I thought. And maybe he was. But what does that mean, to find your soul mate? Our immediate attraction and bonding was deeply embedded with past-life or subconscious reactions among all three of us. Through the years, I realize that what we were all talking about, soul-mate-wise, could actually be someone who is deeply aligned with us at the soul level, but well out of sync at this time or in this life.

Our wrangles seemed interminable and felt abusive. Finally, I had to ask Steven 2 to leave. Bridget was crushed. She loved him and actually had seen him coming as well: "Mum, we are going to be a family with a new man. He is looking for us, too!" She told me this when she was eight. And even though she had loved Bryce, too, she'd still given me that warning back when she was six.

Despite warnings, I had tried to move in with Bryce anyway, but each time I would feel an odd holding back. Guidance was trying to stop me from going further. "No. Don't do it." Bryce knew what the Guides were advising, but he forgot all that in his hurt and anger at my betrayal.

As I told Steven 2 he had to leave, losing the dream of home and family broke all of our hearts. I knew by then, by the long-lasting rages, that there was an abusive quality to this relationship. We separated with an agreement to work on ourselves. Then, in a few months, he'd fly in for a weekend to retest the waters, give it another try.

Simone commented wryly as I was preparing to drive to Seattle to meet his plane, "Why on earth are you doing this? A leopard doesn't change his spots."

"I believe in transformation?" I said hopefully.

Weaving my way through Seattle traffic, I sighed to my passenger Anna, a metaphysical friend and wonderful bodyworker. She and I were headed to a flower show on the way to picking Steven 2 up at the airport. "Simone doesn't think it can work out with Steven 2. She said the leopard doesn't change its spots! But you and I know we can all change. Right?"

The Universe spoke up. A car turned right in front of us. It had a leopard-skin roof! Soon—very soon during that retest weekend—the relationship wrangled itself into a confining rage again. Steven 2 continued to be disgusted that I had ever had a relationship with Bryce. Bryce raged by phone. My relationship, the man whom I had "read" as my man, was just an old karmic tryst looking to express.

Bryce never spoke to me again. All of our channelings and preparations for the ending of our relationship hadn't worked. Why? He told people I had ripped him off, which startled me. I hadn't. And in all the gossip, there was no accounting for any of the work I had done on him. And I lost my house entirely. A friend had warned me that he was making money on me and my house, and I would never receive anything from it. I didn't believe her. Again, a spiritual contract had been in place. He immediately rented my house out to a friend for two-hundred dollars a month less than what he had charged me!

Periodically, maybe once a year, I would write to him. "Let's heal our karmic stuff, Bryce." In one letter, startled at the wisps of gossip about how I had ripped him off, I detailed the financial exchanges of our years together in an effort to soothe what I saw was out-of-control and untrue gossip. Folks love to tear up reputations of higher-profile people like us. No response came from him.

So many life-shaking circumstances had come my way — all of these dramatic changes happened as I was turning fifty. Mum passed that year, after a few years of mini strokes and serious mental deteriorations. Just before she did, I learned another new level about empathy. I was walking into the grocery store with my eight-year-old and her friend and thought I was about to have a seizure. Heavens! Not my style. Not here with the girls. I stomped my foot and commanded that the feelings released. A little later, I received a phone call. My mum, four hours away, had just had a number of mini strokes on the same part of her brain.

"You can die with her if you want to," the Guides explained to me. "Learn to disconnect better." I hopped to it, quickly.

I felt the odd freedom that so many feel when the mother, whether the relationship was harmonious or difficult, passes. I needed to leave the Northwest. I needed to expand into a bigger world. Bridget didn't want to do anything, although she was quite a dancer, albeit a reluctant one.

Bridget and I left the next year, when she was nine. Poor Bridget so heartbroken that both Steven 2 and Bryce were gone and that she and I were on our own again. Lucy was on her own now, too, but working on her degree. We left our little town. I needed to be in a warmer climate. More than that, I wanted to live where the fields of the earth were more electric and transformative. I drove and drove, working via the phones in motels, feeling the land for quickening frequencies.

That whole time was so hard for Bridget. She was an inward child who, as I said, didn't want to do much of anything—just be left alone. Yet she was pretty attached to me. I assumed, naïvely, that she would just go along with me and everything would work out just fine. The third month, September, however, I put her back with her dad on Bainbridge Island. We had traveled a pleasant summertime route, throughout the hinterlands of British Columbia visiting relatives and friends, then heading down to Missoula, Montana, to stay with more friends. I did many, many readings, and we would move on. I considered living in Missoula, but if I had the choice of living anywhere in the world, would I pick an area that had a hard winter? And on I went.

My journey stretched to four months in total, becoming more and more grueling to me. I needed home. I loved and missed my daughter terribly, although I had found single parenting hard. Obviously, I had ripped up our male support. I was questioning myself, longing for a deeper rapport with my Guides and Angels. They whispered to me, "Go here." "Go south." "Feel the energies." In retrospect, I recognize the value of feeling so much of the vibration of land—from mountains to prairies to seasides, from cold-weather areas to deserts. I had turned myself into a traveling Geiger counter. Amazing! Some environments were terrifying. Some were uplifting. The mountainous environments around Jackson Hole were forbidding. My journey was intense.

When Bridget was with me, she didn't have much fun. It was hard on her. By nature she is inflexible, so when we stopped to row in paddle boats, play miniature golf, or go for a walk, she would resist. She told me years later that that whole period was a nightmare to her. I was doing what I thought I needed to do. I learned a lot about frequencies, about turning myself into a radar as I drove, sensing and feeling the energy of the land. But as I write this, I wonder. What was I doing? Was I a nut case? What kind of a mother puts her kid through all this? And actually, I wonder what she learned.

I found myself touring places with strange names like Truth or Consequences, New Mexico, expecting some kind of answer. In beautiful Taos, my Guides clearly told me to

245

stay in a specific hotel. "It's expensive, isn't it?" I questioned them. I called there as I had been told, found an exceptionally inexpensive room, and booked it.

When I arrived, the front-desk manager told me there had been a mistake. No room was booked for me. But magically, to make up for it, she put me in a suite, the room number 555—Christ Consciousness. It was beautiful, and I was thrilled. There I did my dance workout and a powerful meditation, plus grounded my heart and spirit. With such gratitude, I felt *homed* with kindness and love.

The next morning I was told, "Now leave." As I headed out of town, there was a beautiful metaphysical shop. And like the wanderer in a dream fantasy, I went right in and met a couple of women.

"Oh, you can't leave Taos so soon," they advised me. "You must see this museum and that gallery...."

"Okay, that'll be fun." I like to have fun. I checked into an inexpensive hotel. The rest of my time there was horrible. The hotel was frightening—sounds in the night, the water taps didn't work, an odd feeling of danger. I asked the Guides, "What on earth is going on?"

"Why don't you ask ladies in a shop?" was their quick retort.

I left early the next morning and cruised across New Mexico, finding it beautiful and quite exotic. Finally, I found myself in the wonderful environment of Sedona, Arizona. I sat at the base of the Grandmother vortex and began to weep. I felt held. I felt loved. I felt known and made safe, as if I was understood. The energies rose through me and filled me as I wept and wept. That night in a room rental in the home of a spiritual woman, still weeping and weeping, I begged my Guides, "I have to go home now. I need to be with Bridget. I can't do this anymore I am *done done done....*" My anguish rose in a huge cloud. I was going back to Washington. I couldn't handle any more.

"Go south."

"What?"

"Go south."

"All right." I shuffled my inner feet, not wanting what could seem like the great two by four over the back of the head from not listening and always questioning their wisdom. "Alright, but then can I be done with this?"

Silence. Unfortunately, they frequently punctuated our talks, especially when my questions were demanding or the journey was to be a part of the self-exploration, with silence.

South through Phoenix and onto Tucson I drove, and there it was: the deepening feeling I sought was in the soft, purple, flowing Catalina mountains, the funny, desert-y Spanish buildings, and the feeling of space. My energies quickened as the land sparked. Here is where I will make our home, I thought. As quickly as I could, I obtained an apartment for us — ironically on Oracle and La Canada. Here I was, the oracle from Canada, I chuckled. It was near a school and had a swimming pool for Bridget. We could be here until we found a different place that we could afford. And off I went to be with my daughter again, so very grateful that my ex was willing to let her be with me.

CHAPTER FIFTEEN

Time in the Desert

We learned. We grew. We merged with many people who were also drawn to the electrical fields of Tucson, the lightning capital of the country. And each of us rippled through energetic processes that were at times unwieldy. Bridget, at eleven, developed Grave's disease, chronic fatigue, and other symptoms as well for a grueling four-month process. She was so thin, with huge circles under her eyes and no energy. People stayed away from her and kept their kids away, too, fearing AIDS or some other contagious condition. She hardly moved her body, so weak she was. We took up bowling, learning to go to the bowling alley when things got too weighty and stuck. At the local bowling alley with air conditioning we would sit, then pick up a ball and roll it slowly. Sometimes she would have a hamburger. It is still a default although our scores are still low.

Finally, desperately worried, I called her dad and asked him to come down. "I don't know if Bridget is ever going to get well. She's so skinny, so lost."

Glenn came, and together we had some wonderful excursions. We rode the little train up Sabino Canyon, wandered around picturesque villages, and just relaxed in charming cafés.

My pale and exhausted Bridget nobly wandered through our experiences, happy to be a family for a few days. At Mission St. Xavier down near the border, however, after each

248

of us lit candles and focused our prayers, she turned to me. "Mum, I was supposed to be sick for a long, long time, but I just had a vision. I am going to be better soon."

"Hmmmmmmm," was my wise reply.

Three mornings later, for the first time in many months, she jumped out of bed and called out, "Hi!" My sensitive, creative, feisty girl was almost back again. In fact, soon thereafter, she was given a homeopathic remedy called brionia, and—pop—even more of her returned. That was followed by a dose of arsenica, and she experienced more healing.

Lucy, then twenty-two, called us from Vancouver. "I'm lost. My Guides say, 'Go to Ronni's.'" My sweet, beloved, fair-skinned, red-headed stepdaughter was coming south to live in the sun with us.

"Of course you can come. Of course you are always welcome," I said. "But, honey, you can't complain about the heat, not even once. You have to take tons of vitamin C with bioflavenoids and drink more water than you can stand. Eat little or no sugar. And no complaining." In Israel, even with her albino Bedouin look with her huge, wet towels wrapped around her neck and head, the heat there had been too much for her.

Her living with us was a success. Lucy started her own improv troupe, creating unforgettable shows she was to launch later in the San Francisco Bay Area. With her softer nature, she calmed the storms between us all, and helped us keep the house running smoothly as we pushed our careers and school demands, at least for a while.

Around that time, Mum began visiting, from her home out there in the realms. "Hi, Mum," I said nonchalantly.

"Please talk to your father for me."

"Okay, Mum," but I ignored her and just carried on. Then she showed herself again. I was becoming accustomed to seeing spirits, but reluctant to engage with them. The second time she came, she was crying. "Oh dear, what is going on over there, Mum?"

"I have asked you to call your father!" she wept.

"But Mum, he'll be mad at me!" She looked defeated. "Okay, Mum. He's always mad at me anyway." I was always the child who did things my own way, no matter how much he said, "You will conform."

I called him in Canada. "Hi, Dad."

"How are you?" I could almost see him toss his shoulders back and forth, establishing some kind of inner comfort.

"I am fine, Dad." Big breath. I know I always worried him with my odd forays into an alternate world; it was all very insecure to him. "Dad, I have been hearing from Mum."

"You did? What did she have to say?" His sudden enthusiasm stunned me.

"That she is fine now, and she loves you so much."

He wept. "Thanks. I miss her so much. "

Intermittently for the next year or so, she would come in again and again to say hi to him.

"Mum says you are going to marry again, and it is fine. She wants you to."

"That's hard to believe. She was pretty jealous. Besides, that seems unlikely. I am pretty lost. Not sure I ever want to do all that again—and to feel like this again!" He wept but over the next few weeks, he began to keep a file folder of her comments, which lifted him.

Mum came to me in different manners. On the one hand, she wanted her messages to go to her husband, and I would be her interlocutor. On the other hand, she would let me know about what I was doing wrong in my own life! "I kept telling you to go back to teaching school. You don't handle your finances well. You don't earn enough money. You would never listen to me."

Finally, I realized I felt victimized. Spirits don't always know better than we do. The evolution and perception embodied by some of them seem to be the same level they were on here in good old 3D. We have to choose our growth. Although I'm not sure how, I closed off her calls to me. "Sorry, Mum. I am not taking your judgments or your calls anymore." So while I was happy to send messages to Dad, I rejected any to me—a magical, new, invisible skill. My dad and I began a new kind of relationship in which he had a toe in the ocean of my world. He found it intriguing and it did help him. Just for fun a few years earlier, when he was living on Pender Island and before Mum became infirm, he asked me questions about relatives—aunts and grand-parents I didn't know.

I apparently read them accurately, and he was impressed at news from his mother, my grandma, as well as his own grandmother. His dad, my grandpa, was clearly off exploring and wasn't available for interdimensional discussions. But others answered at least some of his questions.

"I didn't believe at all in life beyond. You just die and that's that. You've got me realizing that there is something beyond my thinking, way beyond. It's changing my life," he said with a little wonder in his tone.

In Tucson, my rapport with the unseen continued to become much stronger and richer. So did my world of service with new clients and fellow readers. Six of us, three men and three women, gathered weekly around a vortex we designed in our visualization and which we called the Crystal Table. We six did some fledgling out-of-body travel, actually periodically even sharing each other's explorations out there in the ethers. Transported by toning — there is the toning again — and our common intentions, we pushed frontiers of our world to learn about healing and out of body. One member of our group, Fred, had studied at the Monroe Institute. It's a school based upon the experiences of Robert Monroe, once a radio personality who suddenly had spontaneous out-of-body experiences. Finally, he carefully followed them so often that he was also able to guide others out of their bodies. My favorite of his many books was *Far Journeys*, which recounts his soul travels out of the body. He made a huge difference to the growing community of people waking up to their own multidimensionality. Every Tuesday morning, we would arrive at Fred's home in the desert, pillow and blanket and a box of cookies in hand, ready to snuggle into a trance. It was so fun, so inspiring to push to our edges of trust and perception. I did the channeling, and we were guided into our own self-recognitions.

Dramatic learning curves arose. We quickly saw that our inner space could be filled up by someone else. Once we recognized that, we learned to mobilize our inner muscles to claim our own space. Someone else could actually take over our energetic body/mind and steer it. That startling discovery pierced the veils of our innocence.

My own work grew and grew — people from all over the world were calling for appointments. Our household rustled as we prepared tapes for mailing, addressed envelopes, planned groups and gatherings, made flyers, hosted regular meditation groups, and finally brokered time on Tucson radio. My daughters were proud of me. Then came the Energy Spot, a KTUC call-in radio show at seven on Sunday mornings. My daughter, usually reluctant to awaken too early, arose at six to handle calls for me. She complained, but she did it.

I believed that as a family we should pitch in to help one another's projects. But Bridget was getting angrier and angrier. I still don't quite know why, but it probably stemmed from my unusual pursuits, her loss of the men in her earlier years, as well as her innate resistance to doing anything. Always, she preferred solitude. Even lots of counseling didn't touch the pain in her and her frustration with me. What with her articulate, angry, and sharp tongue, the tension between us was almost too painful for me to handle sometimes. My fear, of course, glowed in the memory of my history with Naomi. Then, of course, my own childhood reactions and beliefs still kept me twanging and deeply insecure.

The radio show even included someone in the process of dying. The ratings for the Energy Spot were the highest of any program on that station, but no one told me that until a year after I had stopped doing the show and the station itself was defunct. By then I had encountered the arrogance and competition among many media people. The station was in trouble and the gift of expanding one another with support or even compliments was very restrained. The typical fear of being diminished by someone else's success is a prevalent, huge reason for people not seeing the value in others. I was sad that I hadn't gotten anywhere with my show, but I actually had!

It'd been twenty years from the camp nights 'round the fire on North Pender Island to Tucson, from popping open so I could "see" inside of so many: the fully spectral lights spiraling up through people (people who were there or in the distance), the lights moving through the chakra systems, carrying morsels of transformational experiences up through the beings. I could see a rapport between their goals, their life drives, and their daily routine with all its attachments and resistances. It'd also been twenty years since those electric and radiant triangles pulsed in the middle of my sight. Triangles, as I found out later, are actual portals to awakening and building blocks for reality. Even now, over thirty years since my awakening to our being or seeing us as vibrational vehicles of light, I am still fascinated.

It is an intricate dance, obvious and subtle, between our human potential, the soul's fulfillment, and the healings or illnesses that can reflect our resistances, to me, in colored forms of matted, dense pockets of energy. It is intricate but still intriguing—even more so after giving many thousands of readings. When we direct the flows of the subtle energy or simply free them to run through the body, our vibrational vehicles of light pulse as they forge releases and transformations. After years and years, I still learn more about our bodies, both the physical and light bodies, about our personal dharma, and about the flows of consciousness in the collective body of humanity. Also, as in the current style of talk, everything is a choice. But just as when I kept notes of readings to figure out the level of consciousness or multilevel intelligence the readers read from, choices can be made on many, many levels, some not that easy to access. Onward go my discoveries.

A few months later, my dad started talking to his neighbor Georgina. "I've seen you in my visions," she told him.

He spun his finger in circles at his temples, that familiar gesture of calling someone a nut. Fortunately, he is a funny man. She laughed. He carefully explained that he wasn't going to mate again. "Okay," was all she said.

She couldn't drive, and he began to take her shopping once a week. I visited him and the Northwest every few months—which were the most precious times of my experience with my dad. I stayed with him, and after the first day of adjustments, we would get into some wonderful conversations about him, who he was, and who I was, wrangling thoughts and philosophies.

One time, I was sitting in his kitchen drinking tea and chatting with him while he stirred his cookie dough. "I looked at Georgina last week after a shopping trip," he said quietly. "I realized I am tired of being alone. I don't want to be alone. I kissed her—on the cheek," he added quickly.

"That's great, Dad. What's she like?"

"Irish," he said. "And Christian Scientist. Crazy stuff."

CHAPTER SIXTEEN

Desert Healing

Back in Tucson, my friends and I did the Whole Health Expo, and we did it with élan. What a blast! Besides booths for the Crystal Table group, we had another booth that we called the Energy Garden where we sold energized clothing and did readings and healing work. We set up a performance, too. I took the mic in hand, and mimicking Oprah's hosting style, I introduced our song. Again, three men and three women, after hours and hours of practice, sang good old doo-wop. For the Expo performance, we took questions from the audience, which I answered like a good psychic; then, in harmony, the six of us spontaneously serenaded our audience with an appropriate song—mostly old, easy-to-sing songs, like "Love Hurts" for a broken heart, "In the Still of the Night" for romance—"Shoo doo shooby doo!" With the women dolled up in long skirts and the men in lawyer's clothes, it was unique, different. Our audience (well, half of them) stayed and rollicked with us. Question: "How am I going to know what to do?" Answer: "Please come to Boston." "When will I get the answer?" Back to "In the still of the night…." "Where will we move?" We toned, "Down in the valley…." It was fun and brilliant, this "reading" the ethers and giggling. The show barely paid, but we had fun, the practices were hilarious, and it was all about serendipity and mostly about lightening up.

At the amazing desert park called Tohono Chul, we tracked the night-blooming cereus along pathways lit with Mexican luminarias (candles in paper bags), flickering lights that led us through the dark to the mysterious, stunning flower that emerged for that day only. Fortunately, there were many of them emerging for one day only, and we stalked them among the huge cacti in the desert darkness.

And I had very few dates there. My fear was of hurting my daughter anymore, after she'd been caught in the karmic turnstile with Bryce and Steven 2. She loved them both, and how I lost them hurt us both. My caution was deep. But one day, as it would happen, I met an interesting man at the bakery coffee shop where Lucy reigned as the star of cappuccino brew. He and I chatted about life, metaphysics, and our love of the desert. It sounded like a great idea to meet in Pima Canyon at five AM one Thursday to hike. As I donned my shorts in the rising sunlight, at about 4:30, Guidance said, "Don't go!"

"Don't go? Oh, dear. I can't stand this man up, just leave him there in the canyon at five AM." I have been thoroughly marinated in the juice of consequences when I didn't heed warnings. I listened but, as was typical, bargained—just a little. "Okay, I'll just meet him briefly to tell him I can't walk today," I told the soft voices that flow through my mind. Off I went. After parking in the lot and moseying up to the arranged meeting place at the trailhead, there he was, smiling.

"Hi. I'm so sorry—I can't walk today. But I didn't want to leave you in the lurch!" I rushed my words through an apologetic smile.

"Oh, too bad. I was looking forward to walking with you...and to more inspiring conversation. We were just getting going there at the bakery. Before you leave, can I show you this amazing cactus? It isn't far up the trail."

When smooth meets naïve, things change. We walked for about fifteen minutes up the rugged trail when I got the first message. "I often come here with my wife."

Oh, crap! He's married. Not my style after my tryst so many years ago. Then I tripped, wrenching my right ankle between two rocks on the path—truly the rock and the hard place. I hobbled back to my car. Its window had been broken. Business cards, mine and others, even a little purple energizing plate I carried, plus other bits and pieces from my purse were strewn around. Fortunately, I was able to easily re-create the important cards missing from my purse and have a new window installed, but the pain in my ankle was more permanent. I had to chuckle in my pain, though. "Okay, okay, this is the two by four again. I am sorry." I asked my Guides, "Am I over it now? Am I out of danger?"

"You are," the Beloved voices sighed in my mind. "But pay attention."

The erstwhile date, after watching me lope to my car, disappeared, but a few days later went to the bakery, hoping to find me. Lucy told him she had no idea where I was. I didn't look for him, ever.

But my ankle required a lot of attention. I still limped after a chiropractor realigned the little bones inside several times. Knowing that underlying emotions are a huge proportion of illness in the body, my healer friends and I worked through my issues of balance, power, and money, and we moved the distressed energy out of my ankle. What were my feelings when the rocks grabbed me? The right leg stands for stepping forward, the dominant leader; the ankle represents flexibility between one's own history, one's own understanding. I had learned that from my Guides.

Walking with friends became easier after a few weeks of energy work. But about a month after I was injured, I got the *click*. As our walking conversations would roam through our experiences and other people we knew, suddenly the conversation would hit pay dirt! "Mary is a wonderful intuitive." My ankle went out—not only "out," but I collapsed and couldn't walk at all. Upon exploring, being as honest as I could within myself, I would find fears and competitions, and for this I had to be vibrantly honest. "Does she have more clients than I do?" or "Is she really that wonderful?"

"Okay, what's the feeling?" a friend asked as I sat, pained, on a rock.

I paused and felt inside of myself. "Insecurity. That's what it is! I feel insecure."

"Hmmm. Insecure...about being acknowledged?" Sometimes a very short investigation would pop the hidden feeling lurking in my ankle. The feeling was probably already there before I hurt my ankle, but the injury gave it a nesting place, an expression.

To be a psychic requires being exceptionally sensitive. We can't blunt it or hide it. To be on the spiritual path, we also have to awaken to our hidden fears and beliefs. Then we learn to use the sensitivity as a tool, a gift—conscious empathy, attunement to new growth, clearing of the old fears within...it all starts to work like radar. Insecurity itself is required or we find ourselves tamped down, held safely in the cradle of our self-definition, with little or no room for learning and growing.

Here's another example: I might tell someone, "I have a date! I might go out to the show with Eric next week." The pain was excruciating.

So here was my ankle, a mighty tribute to my willfulness, to my resistance to my Guides' advice. I often pushed the envelope. But now my turned ankle is a tuned ankle, a kind of test strip, a teaching tool to show vulnerabilities and hidden feelings in a broad array of situations. And I didn't go out with Eric!

That was about sixteen years ago. My ankle still collapses if an insecurity-triggering subject is brought up. Usually it is about stepping forward, having to find confidence in an up-and-coming episode like dating, comparing myself to someone, or setting up a new project for work. It used to hurt so much I literally could not walk. I would drop to a rock on the hiking path, a car bumper, or a chair in a room, grabbing someone's arm just to stay upward. Then my job would be to go inside and ask questions of myself—myself and my rollicking neighborhood of Guides, Angels, and higher self— what was it about. I'd feel through the insecurity, always including the possibility of other attached feelings like anger, frustration, or wanting to hide. Neither detailed discussion about the story nor apologies about the baser nature of feelings are necessary. Just the feeling. Usually less than five minutes in, even at times just a few seconds in, I could recognize where it comes from. In the understanding and soothing, my ankle would release, and I would be happily walking again as if nothing had ever happened. A bit dramatic, but fascinating, huh? This great example shows that it doesn't matter if you hurt a limb or an organ; a whole emotional and psychological, maybe even spiritual, story lives at the root of your injuries.

My Tucson group was a blessing that spawned long-term connections among several of us. That whole time I had actually "gone to the desert"—that biblical image for deepening to truth without any cacophonous labeling by the social structure. It was an electric experience that, like acupuncture, can send electricity through a person, exhuming old, stuck beliefs and emotions with a little help from our intentions. We grew. And the desert touched my spiritual heart.

CHAPTER SEVENTEEN

The Desert Moves Through Us

My daughter didn't do as well. After her bouts with Graves, chronic fatigue, and other illnesses our doctors couldn't name, all of which were terrifying, she was skinny and wild looking. Her bowels would evacuate so fast that I had to use a dustpan to catch the fast flow. Her recovery was slow and dubious as the months stretched on. People were still afraid of her, as she still looked like she had something contagious. Our frustrating explorations with doctors and energy workers were finally laid to rest with the help of homeopathics, but always strong willed, she became more and more impossible for me to parent. My fears, of course, made me totally question myself, my ability to parent, my whirling brain, my penchant for becoming so easily ungrounded, my own childhood, and, always, what had I done to Naomi. The lingering heartbreak ripped through me as I remembered her pain, my inadequacies, the terrifying events of her running away, the police, the craziness of not being heard, and not finding enough help for either of us. At times I was ungrounded and confused.

I was so afraid that Bridget would start running; indeed, as we know, fears will surely manifest, and this was no different. She started running. I thought I would simply die, if not crack into a million pieces. This little one who was a psychic, who had done readings for me when she was four, became almost feral. During this phase of her life, her rebellion was thorough, wanting to be left alone, raging at me, and choosing only friends with the least likely possibility in life. I remember calculating and saying to myself, "I can do this for eight more years. Sure I can." I love my daughter so much and used to feel that my life made so little sense unless I was doing my spiritual work *and* had her to love and care for.

Bridget always wanted to work—not at home, for sure, but out there. She wanted to be an adult with an office and a briefcase. At age eleven, she was blessed with a babysitting job for a rather large family. No briefcase was required except the one in her heart. The children ranged from newborn to nine. I would pop over with cookies or something for all, making sure all was well. She seemed proud of herself when I did, and I loved the kids. You could feel her love for those children and see what a responsible sitter she was, and the experience gave her the power she needed for a while. She also made the Junior Achievement Roster.

A year or two after that time, Lucy had moved on to the San Francisco Bay Area to work on her master's in drama therapy and to light up her career in improv and acting. We missed her balancing force, her always being there for Bridget. She was a huge part of our family, and with her gone, Bridget and I struggled further.

I didn't know who to talk to. Regular therapists didn't touch the issue. My Guides were loving, but I couldn't get clear direction beyond "she needs to be left alone." I couldn't leave her to her own devices as a thirteen- or fourteen-year-old, however. I tried to set up classes that she would enjoy, including horseback riding, dance, and a church youth group. By fifteen, she just wanted a job. We worked hard to find a place that would hire her. As I mentioned, she did nothing around home, but in the world, this was one adept young being, one good worker.

When Bridget was only twelve or thirteen, Lucy had a grand-opening performance of her improv troupe. Bridget had taken on the entire refreshments stand — ordering foods, setting it up, organizing, selling, working hard, making money for Lucy and her crew. I stayed away, but watched from a distance. She was amazing. She almost got the job at the bakery where Lucy had worked, but it fell apart because of the danger involved in hiring a then-fifteen-year-old. The law said workers had to be sixteen. Okay, next life I would like to be Chinese or Italian or another culture that accepts the talent and wisdom of children to take a significant role in the family business. This kid wanted that so much. Right after the bakery job collapsed, she went wild and would run away again.

We had an increasing series of therapy appointments to deal with Bridget's building rage with me and life. Was it her thyroid that was making her crazy? Was I simply a horrible mum? The Guides were loving and supportive, but I wanted them to illuminate something — anything — that would help me keep our pending Titanic upright. Pubescent rages are powerful. One day, Bridget actually picked me up and stuffed me into the laundry room. She wouldn't help me with anything. I said, "I wish I was just your friend instead of your mum. One twitch of an eyebrow, and you interpret my look as a venomous reflection. Even if it wasn't." A flick of some kind of reaction and off to her room she went, usually with the swinging of an intense, vituperative verbal machete.

My tension and fear, plus projecting from my experiences with Naomi, didn't help either. "What have I done to create this in you?" I asked her one day. Flounce.

Yet, there were soft times, deep times all the way through. When she was about seven, she wrote me a note that said, "I went way out there to pick you, because you are different and I need that, Mum. I love you." One midnight, when she was about thirteen, she called and asked me to come pick her up across town. She was afraid to do an overnighter with her group of Rainbow Girls. I went, then stopped for gas on the way home. As I got back into the car, she said, "I don't know what I would do without you, Mum. You are always there for me." She wept. I could feel that something in her was suffering deeply from her own inner self…past life memories?

Yet I also remember chasing her up the road, her pony tail bobbing in its scrunchy. "Please, please don't do this to us. We don't need to do it this way!" I called after her as she loped up the hot, dusty lane from our house.

Abraham, via Esther and Jerry Hicks, came to Tucson at that time. "What do I do with my teenaged daughter?" I asked them. "She is angry. Willfull. Courageous. Creative. I don't know how to handle her. I am scared of her and for her as she runs away."

Their answer dismayed me—it dismayed many of us, actually. "She has to do her own life. Let her go as far as you can. Let her explore and experience everything."

A lot of parents rustled in the wake of their advice. My inner self double-dipped into unnamed panic. "But her safety. I can't handle it!"

"She has to do it her own way. She is a courageous soul, strong, determined. She has light."

I writhed as I tried to incorporate their wisdom. But what was I to do with the wild fears inside of myself? Again and again, I revisited the memories of a wandering Naomi and the multiple visitations by police. My own family didn't even believe me. My healing wasn't complete. Trust of myself often fell into a void or drowned in the huge waves of judgment. I was reeling. At night, I would drive around crying, looking for her or a sign of any of her friends. These friends were all the kids with no real advantages, kids far from their essential selves. I was conscious most of her life that she was an empath, but I hadn't taught her as much metaphysics as I could have—I'd wanted her to feel she could have her life and not be spiritually ruled by me. I knew she was talented and probably a psychic if she ever chose to be.

As I write this, I realize that I was just too weak to mother anyone, given all my own quirks and fragilities. The empathy that filled her was the stickiness of shame and pain in others, a reflection of the pain that Bridget had experienced with—just for starters—my men and her own dad's reluctance to spend time with her. The missing dad was a common theme for every one of these kids.

She told me one day, "We all sit together and talk about how abused we are."

"But, honey, you aren't abused." But she felt abused since she empathized with them all and was surrounded by their vibrations.

I begged my Guides to tell me how to work with her. "Love her. Don't confine her," they said. Maybe my situation with Bridget was too close to my own soul for me to hear more. Or, the likely thing is that she was on her soul path, exploring and discovering as she went. Me, too. It was tearing me out of the numbnesses I had used to recover from my own breakdown—or "nervous breakthrough" as I learned to call it. Extreme emotional pain is hard to work with, so many feelings jockeying for position, for expression, for reflection. Friends still remember a point, hilarious to them all, when I had said desperately, coming awake, out of my trances, "I just have to learn to prioritize my emotions." My emotions tended to be a tumbling ocean—except when the Guides were at the helm. Then all was peace.

CHAPTER EIGHTEEN

Working Away from Tucson

Ironically, during those days my work grew and grew. I know that the pain, the questions, the prayers refined me and helped me develop more and more of my rapport with my Guidance. New clients graced my living room. My phone took me farther around the world, shifting more and more frequencies, making essential detachments from old ways, old selves, old beliefs—all during the denouement of my family life. But Spirit works that way. Or, as I say, purification works that way. Intentions on a soul or personal level that are aligned with our true connection can tear us away from the setup of our lives. The learning curves were rapid. If my anxieties about family mounted up, I would have a series of clients working with family issues. Together, we would learn more about our souls and the kinds of intricacies that brought us together in family. It helped me unstrap some expectations and connections with my own family.

The subject would be abuse. Or romance. Or finances. In sessions, the issues I worked on with my clients were always pivotal, releasing their old selves to prepare for the emerging new. My work took me into higher levels of talk with my Guidance about the many levels of psychological patterns that rule us, that rule our futures.

The true nature of our spiraling inner energy is always to carry the rich, vibrational resonance of our life experiences to another level so we can experience its wisdom from a different perspective. I have known this since I was a child. Whatever happens will often recur, but with a perspective that can help us neutralize its pattern in the soul.

Take the skeletons in our closets. We all have them. Do they spiral up just to be seen and known, so we don't leave their drives lurking and haunting from deep within our subconscious only to play out into our lives? Or are they seen so we can heal old, defensive attitudes and beliefs, birthed in our deep, dark shadows? Or perhaps it's to heal the lower frequencies that come from abuse? We are learning to evolve or free ourselves from enacting the suppressed depths of the human collective. We see the suppressions all over the news today: fears such as not winning, not getting enough, others getting more—lack, lack, lack—or hatreds that consume people. In that muck, there is the possibility of neutralizing and releasing primitive survival reactions. It meets an emerging drive to be ONE, to come from our true nature and from love.

When old patterns or hatreds rise, with intention and with focusing honestly on what we feel inside, we can neutralize them. Or maybe, better said, we can neutralize ourselves so we don't just take on, store, and pass on debilitating feelings through our actions or our radiances. Each of us can find our beloved self under that sludge of old reactions. Or we can keep our empathy and sensitivity shut down in the presence of influences on one another, or on life on the planet—that cold state of being that says, "Oh, what does it matter if we kill the planet?"

Hmmmmmm...that is a whole long discussion on sociopathy. As we've heard in the healing world from ancient times 'til now, nothing on the planet—no evil, no brutality, no greed—that affects a country, a family, a village, a group of any kind can be resolved until every one of us resolves it within ourselves. Each of us is a microcosm, containing an entire arsenal of healing tools.

Onward with my daughter, my precious daughter, my Indigo daughter...how did I know she is Indigo? Because flashes of purple light came through her since birth, no matter how Goth she became. I also knew because of the big heart she hides, retracting its love when she sees inequities. She is a watcher who can never just play the game. I didn't want to believe the Indigo descriptions, mostly because I was afraid of dealing with its enigmatic, enormous power in my child. But, in retrospect, I was given many an opportunity to understand her from that perspective. I know now how I blocked many concepts that would frighten me, always remnants of times with Naomi or the stringent and unyield-ing rules of authority and family life during those years of the 'forties and even 'fifties. I blocked things, but they were there anyway.

Always, the option to open to my own power to love, to forgive, to change, to realize the incredible Presence of Spirit has been right beside me all along. That's why I refer to it all as "near life." The empowerment of these experiences is easier when time has buffered the situation and the pain is no longer red hot; the lessons we receive are clearer. If I had to do it all again—hahaha, that great, old line!—I would breathe, be still, and watch more, helping to install in us both a greater sense of self. I'd also spend more time easing my tension and hers.

Often, I see in my sessions, and even in my social life, that a girl child is enraged at the limitations of her mother, angry when she see her mother modeling the crippling influences of fears and inadequacies, roiling under unhealed pain, vacillating between being fierce and strong, and fading into weakness in the role as a mother. Maybe the weaknesses anger the male child, too, but I think it is different. And some girls have to do things their own way no matter what that would be. Their soul journeys are just to express.

In her early school years, Bridget would come home and tell me little stories of how she sent bright pink bursts of light to a sad girl on the playground. And she continued to do readings for me. Very intelligent, she also had to learn her own way. And it continues; now in a rather high-level corporate world, she is the "go to" woman—efficient, careful, underpaid, beautiful, and overworked as a mum.

But back then, as I've mentioned, I would turn to my Guides in despair. "What can I do?" "She has her own path" was all I gleaned. Apparently, it was my path to have children who will do life their own way, children whose souls have some karmic healing with me. And in many ways that is me as well. Mars in Pisces in the Fifth House....

Once again, my heart desperate and sinking, I tried to live through my daughter's disappearances. Finally, I called her dad. "Glenn, will you and Gail take Bridget? Can we get her to you?"

We planned it carefully. Twice, she was missing for ten days at a time. During her second disappearance, we set up an arrangement with the family she once babysat. The mother, Julie, had remarried, and the family now lived in Phoenix. When Bridget phoned, I offered her a bus ticket to Phoenix, which she accepted as she loved Julie and her children. Julie would pick her up. What Bridget didn't know was that while she was there, her dad planned to arrive and take her north. When I saw her after her time away, I was shocked. The skin on her beautiful face was taught, tight against the bones. Her beautiful blue eyes were adamant. She looked at me with such distance, such coldness. I shivered and ached. I wanted to hold her and make everything all right. It wasn't possible.

I couldn't go to Phoenix to say good bye. I knew it would be hard for Bridget and thought my presence would just twist things. She called, heartbroken. "Mum," she sobbed over the phone, "Dad's here. He is taking me to Washington. I don't want to go." Her tears tore at me. "I want to be with you. I want to be in Tucson!"

"I am not making you safe. Dad needs you."

"You can't do this. It's entrapment!"

"I can't do this anymore, Bridget. Dad loves you."

In all the spinning trauma, I was angry with my Guides. "Why, why, why, why?" I asked them. "Where are you when I need you? Why, why, why did it have to go this way?"

I was torn. How much would the seeming abandonment hurt Bridget? Once again, I was getting rid of my child. Lordy, Lordy! What kind of a woman am I? The question was poignant and familiar. My family was sure to judge me again. I had nowhere to turn. My mothering had been too soft. I'd thought that hearing, understanding, even feeding her carefully would work. She was — and still is — a strong being. I felt guilty when I didn't work, guilty when I did. Was I working too much? Perhaps there'd been too much indecision on my part. Fears jabbed at me: I had caused Naomi's demise, Steven's cancer, even Baby Margaret's death. My good, old, hidden phobia, that somehow I had a destructive power, was in full force. And, oh, my, I loved that girl. And, oh, my, I love the woman she has become.

In retrospect, I appreciate the courage it took for them all, her dad and the family she babysat for, to do what they did. Julie and her children welcomed Glenn with a family barbecue, and soon father and daughter were en route to Coeur d'Alene. The hew and cry was there, but not as loud as my passing Naomi on to the system. After all, Bridget was going with her dad.

But, her dad, wanting her to love him, was unable to curtail her running, her ongoing attendance at raves, her involvement with dubious youth. Her stepmother managed to get her a job at a large grocery store and she worked. At nineteen, she was pregnant. Perhaps her baby would ground her, just as she had grounded me. Yet, I was horrified. She was finally working at a good, steady job in a bank. Magically enough—and magic or Divine Intervention has been there for her over and over—her job covered all the expenses of her three-hour birthing experience, which topped my twenty-nine-hour style! Having a baby was a mistake, I thought, but I am truly grateful for the feisty, creative, talented son she brought into our family and deeply into my heart. My grandson is a bright boy, a true communicator and performer, who also has to do things his own way. He's adept at the computer, filled with light when he is "on," and capable of deep understanding. He and I have many playful adventures as we explore life together. Oh, the wonders of the alternative generations and the friendships we can forge.

As I told you, the benefits of Tucson's electrical land, the sparking of the fields and frequencies that drove awakenings in me—and in so many other healers who had been drawn there at that time—were tremendous. But a full year before I sent Bridget north, Guidance started whispering, "It is time to leave now. Time for a larger city."

Hmmmmm. A larger city? Oh, great. Where do I start?

When Bridget was still with me, I packed her and her friend Nic up to see our friend Brian, encsonced and studying in Colorado Springs. We explored and camped in bountiful nature. The kids had an amazing experience during our camping trip: a young deer played and played at our campsite. They would imitate it dashing around; then it would imitate them. The game went on for quite a time, with other campers watching the wit of this young buck — a touching experience. The resonances of Colorado were not mine, however; I just didn't feel that it could be home.

Onward.

CHAPTER NINETEEN

Big City Transitions and Love Again!

I was angry, hurt, and in rebellion now. After sending Bridget to her dad's, I decided to move to the Bay Area — that was certainly a "larger city," just as the Guides had been promoting. By this time, my stepdaughter was graduating with her master's and her acting career was shining brightly with the creation of her improv troupe in downtown San Francisco...courageous being that she still is. I wanted to be near family, and I picked Lucy.

As for me, I told the Guides that I was done with this crazy career. I longed for home and family. I felt more alive, more purposeful no matter what work I was doing when I had home and family. If I couldn't have it, what would be the point of my life? I know I was working tremendous things with clients all over the world. I know I was on my spiritual path. But I needed that feeling of heart connection, of domestic routine.

I went to the Landmark Forum, the evolution of EST, hoping to find myself. I didn't find me, but I met Giovanni. He was a creative contractor and...Italian! Hey, maybe family will count here. Giovanni was coming out of a long marriage and had three young-adult kids. We became friends, helping and supporting one another. Where I had been lurching through waves of insecurity and uncertainty, he had his own version. So much was in transition. He wanted to launch a career as a singer. Also, as a builder, he was marketing a special kind of small house. We had some fun, but mostly it was about work and building the courage it would take to do our next steps. Through him, I found a job as a secretary — although I proved that I am terrible at that kind of work. I have to laugh at the concept of my being a secretary...what a ruse! My talents are better used "seeing things." Some gifts just don't file well in 3D. Still and all, Giovanni lined me up for that job for a few months, and I began to stand up financially again before I was fired.

I did explore some of life in the Bay Area, with all of its strong spiritual centers. I needed that sustenance as well. Where were "my people" or a spiritual support of sorts? For years, I had been a student of how everyone's mind creates everyone's individual reality, although my waves of emotional turmoil swamped me. I needed to learn to surf the turmoil to give myself my clear focus at times. I made appointments to interview Christian Science, Unity, Science of Mind, the I AM Temples, and on and on it went. Interestingly, there in my pothole between roles and commitments, I experienced judgments and arrogance. I was out of my station, or lost. These lost months would become some of the most transformative spiritual periods of my life. This was also my Saturn return, as I was fifty-seven — a time famous for intense reevaluation of life patterns. I sought inspiration, upliftment, teachings, and even teachers (although always reluctant to truly follow any one teacher or guru) who would boost my consciousness. For many years, I had studied the I AM Discourses, high-frequency, beautiful teachings channeled in the 'twenties and 'thirties, but I was obviously snagged on some deep beliefs, or maybe disbeliefs, or I wouldn't be in this space between worlds. Karmic leftovers? All of my meditations, treatments and affirmations, violet flames, and constant Spirit loving weren't working—at least as far as my home and family were concerned. I made an appointment with one of the teachers at the I AM Temple. He asked me if I had been involved in the Sixties.

"Oh, my, yes. We sure grew."

"Were you involved in any drugs?"

"A little marijuana and one acid trip."

"We don't want you here. When that energy gets released, it will cause problems for our practitioners."

In several of the new-thought churches, people turned away in judgment of my wandering, prodding, "What have you done to create this?" I floundered, perplexed. What was love? Where is love? That's been a lifelong question for me. I was used to feeling it and giving it in my service, even when on certain levels I didn't like a client. What was wrong here in the hallowed halls of spiritual growth?

My Christian Science experience was different. I arrived at a Christian Science Reading Room in Oakland tense, frightened, and desperate. Yet Georgina, with her radiant steadiness and wisdom, her nonjudgmental approach to life, her ability to research and study and allow herself to change, had kindled a great respect in me. So I went anyway. Right away, I was embraced and directed to the concordances, which include biblical quotations and Mary Baker Eddy's interpretations. They gave instructions on the in-depth wisdom of biblical learning. I am not a biblical scholar, but as I said before, I read the entire Bible in an interest in God and what it all meant. I examined their truths, their style of new-thought mind over matter. Tuning into teachings of many types allows us to see that Spirit flows through and between all kinds of seemingly different words. The Bible was not always my favorite source, but I could feel it infused with Spirit. I could feel that Mary Baker Eddy's language was infused with Spirit, as well.

For a while I loved it, especially because the tone was set. People were kind, and not because of a hairdo. There I experienced a tremendous mélange of well-to-do and home-less people embracing one another in the circles. "You don't know what each person is learning" is an oft-quoted piece of Mother Teresa's wisdom. Through people I met in the reading rooms, I was offered housesits, then dogsits that took me through an amazing homing path that lasted nine months. I was humbled and yet honored at receiving or needing to receive, but I surrendered to it as well as the joy of being validated with the consistent presence of offerings of Spirit through these people. Housesits were met by more housesits. My only angst besides my old friend, loneliness, was that I felt I had to conceal being an intuitive and quite a good one, or I could be judged and rejected. I worried.

Back to that job: being a secretary was interesting—I, who am terrible at detail; I, who have trouble sitting still; I, who am preoccupied with visions all around the job at hand, prolonging the time-sensitive chores. I was dragging my feet, not great at Word Perfect or any of the other details in the office. In my three-month review, I was lovingly let go to find myself, to do "the work of your heart." I had done healing work on a few of the people who worked in the engineering firm. For that I received kudos.

It was a cold, cold winter, the winter of the rolling black-outs in California. The various housesits I bounced around to were cold. I needed a home of my own again. My income from my secretarial career, short-lived though it was, had built up, so I rented a room with a woman who was in recovery from the death of her husband. That was a very, very cold period for me—even colder than the outside. On the positive side, she was about my size and gave me clothes from her overflow. I still had a trickle of readings in the evenings. One evening, in preparation for a call, I lit a candle to purify the atmosphere and, with my mind, focused on expanding the warmth from its tiny flame through my mind and body.

"What? A candle? Now you have given me bladder cancer. I am allergic. You have to leave." Three days later, I was packed and out of her home.

Miraculously more solutions came. Remember Simone from the B and B in Sequim? She arrived in the Bay Area to visit friends and called me to join their party. The segue was immediate. Once again, Simone, with her huge heart and gift for nurturing, played the role of Divine Intervention, and suddenly I was at home in her friend's room rental in her house in the Oakland Hills. My life started to warm up again.

After my disastrous secretarial career, I shifted to data entry at a college for a few months. That would have to be easy enough. The Universe peeked through in its loving humor one day. My creative friend Randy Masters, sound healer and sacred geometric wizard who currently leads tours to sacred sites like the pyramids in Egypt, whom I'd met when his tour brought him to Tucson, called me. "Is it true? I hear you are in California, and you haven't even called me. Why?"

"Oh, Randy. Sorry. I am embarrassed. I am broke and doing data processing work." He knew my work as an intuitive reader in Tucson.

"Oh, come on," came his get-over-yourself response. It isn't unusual for people on the alternative and self-actualizing path to go through sparse times. He wasn't buying that I was worthless. "Look, I am giving a workshop in Santa Cruz. Please come."

"I have no money, Randy."

"Come anyway. Stay at the house and come for free."

I didn't then, which was February. But in August I did. In the meantime, I did a couple of Marsha Morgan's *In the Company of Angels* morning shows at KNRY in Monterey, plus a downtown show on Terrestrial Radio, hosted by Bonnie Colleen. I was gathering up steam and picking up clients as I went. I even did a housesit for Marsha when she was holidaying. So by August, I was ready to face Randy and his crew.

The first morning of the workshop, I arrived early with a grand bouquet of colorful dahlias to adorn his workshop.

"Hi!" A freckled and eager face with a long ponytail greeted me. "Hi! Trevor Bissel."

"Ronni Entwistle." We shook hands.

How strange! Immediately he began, "You are dealing with your mother, have a lot of shame...." He was giving me a reading! Nice change. I was fascinated. On he went until our conversation collapsed behind the din of people arriving, and the healing sounds of Randy's gongs and chimes began the workshop. At breaktime, I sought out my new friend, curious to hear more of his perceptions. It turned out that he was an old friend of Randy's and was also staying at the house. He was pleased to be basking in the increasing vibrations, the magic of resonance retuning, and fantasizing with Randy about projects that could change the world. Amidst the tremendous flows of information about sound, physics, and sacred geometrics that Randy taught, Trevor contributed detail.

The three of us, Randy, Trevor and I, went out for meals together. Trevor and I always ordered the same meal, which is rare in these days of diet explorations. As the workshop ended in flurries of farewells, he asked, "Do you mind giving me a ride back to the East Bay?"

Odd, I thought. "Sure."

As we drove, he asked, "Would you mind stopping at the Alzheimer's home so I can see my mom?"

"Sure." That was a bit strange. I scratched my curious inner head.

After sitting outside the Alzheimer's care center for twenty minutes or so while he visited his mom, we drove to his house in San Carlos. Trevor regaled me about me. What a treat! It was an unusual indulgence for me who was more used to informing others about themselves.

"Let's go for a walk or something soon. I'm going to a conference in Florida, and then in two weeks I'll be back. Let's connect."

"Okay. Here is my number." I handed him my business card as he got out of the car.

He looked at the card. "What? Are you an intuitive?"

"Yup."

He looked shy and amused as he wandered off to his little house.

Earlier that summer, I had purchased a Dell computer. Now that I had my rented room, I was going to write a book. My book. This book. That was over ten years ago! I had so much trouble getting that computer going. Oh, no, not for that entire decade. But I tried and tried to follow instructions—my least favorite skill—to learn to use this dynamic machine. Every day, I plugged away at it for an hour or two, sometimes even longer. My frustration grew as it just didn't seem to yield to me. I started calling Dell for help after the first week or two, and they gave me some advice. I still couldn't get it to work. Finally, I called again: "I need to return this crazy machine. It won't work at all."

"Sorry. You have gone past our return policy."

"Wait a minute." My ire was rising. "I started calling you well before my return date expired. You have that on your records."

"Sorry, there is nothing we can do."

The computer wouldn't work, wouldn't go online, wouldn't do simple tasks — like allowing me to write a book. I even conscripted my techie sister and her husband on the phones from Canada. After hours and hours of work together, we were nowhere. No matter what we tried, nothing worked. I called Dell again, but they just sloughed me off. The patience I had been practicing on my path slipped into rage. "I want someone here. I want you to send someone here." My voice was piercing.

"I don't think we can, ma'am."

"This is ridiculous. Send someone! Send someone! It has been three months now and still no computer. Send someone to help me." I demanded.

"Okay, okay. Calm down, lady. He will be there on Friday." I gave him my address.

That Friday, no "Dellerator" showed. In the meantime, Trevor had returned from his Florida seminar and called. "Let's get together. I have been thinking of you since I left."

"You have?" I was surprised — pleasantly. My hostess was away, so I could cook upstairs. "Would you like to come over for dinner on Friday? Simple chicken and vegetables?"

"Okay, great. I'll be coming by train. Can you pick me up at five?"

How odd, I thought again. Friday afternoon, I put the chicken in the oven and toodled on down to the station to meet his train. Soon, the slick train pulled in, and there he was. I waved, but he didn't seem to recognize me. He just looked anxious, peering around, glancing down. Lordy, Lordy, I thought. He doesn't even remember what I look like. But he perked up as soon as I spoke to him, obviously happy to see me, and off we went.

I told him about my technical plight. When we arrived at the house, Trevor went right to my computer, lifted his leg over my chair as if he were a cowboy mounting a horse, and looked into the screen. Really, he peered into the screen. Right inside of it.

"Oh, my gosh! You are psychic with computers, too! What are you doing?"

"No mechanical brain is going to beat my brain," he quipped. Well, it still wasn't that easy. It took even this technical wizard a couple of weeks. It turns out that Dell had initially given me the wrong password, but, the Universe again chuckling, sent a computer man...a man named Trevor, an upgrade by far. And here was a man who would have to spend time — weeks — discovering the glitch they had set up in my technical access.

Dinner was fun. We began spending time together. I learned why he seemed a little odd, a little disconnected. He had lost his sight a few years earlier, at forty-two, to macular degeneration, and he was legally blind. Aha! So that was why the odd ride requests, train rides, as well as not recognizing me at the station. Otherwise, he managed so well, really, that most people couldn't tell. He had been worried that his life was over, as his vision was an acute tool for inventing and for working with the ever-shifting frontiers of the percolating Silicon Valley. But he loved healing work, too, and was—and still is—an adept metaphysician. His vision just shifted to another plane.

283

We walked and talked, ate in great restaurants, and toured the Bay Area in all its majesty. We swapped stories about how we had both "seen" that we would meet someone around February. Synchronistically, we had both missed the date for Randy's February workshop and instead met there at the August class. Commiserating about it later, we laughed at the Universe's flexibility. I had been asking my Guides who my next partner would be. I was shown a man lying down. "Lying down? Oh, please! Not another sick or dying man please — too traumatic. Haven't I had that learning experience already?"

Then I saw it. With his limited sight, Trevor was always lying down on his bed to work. He had attached a scissor-like arm to his computer so he could pull the screen closer. He loved crystals and, à la the teachings of Lazaris, the channeled consortium he had been studying with for years, he created, tapping universal wisdom to manifest the next levels of his life, using huge crystals. I was fascinated. The wanna-be writer, the filmmaker, or something in me would peer into his room when he was working. He was a character right out of a movie — long hair, thick glasses, layers of goggles wrapped around his head, doubling the strength of his thick glasses. Huge crystals sparkled as he programmed them and turned them. No makeup, no costumes needed!

"I need a driver," he said one day as we walked along the bay. "I could pay you to drive me, probably more than you are making in that ridiculous data-entry job. You are an intuitive! And a good one! It's time! Get over your rebellion. Get back to work."

Next thing I knew, in November — a mere three months after we met — I had moved into his wee house. In addition to being his driver, we were both working in this seven-hundred square foot home, me at the tiny dining alcove end of the house, him in his bedroom. The kitchen was practically virginal, rarely used. But the rest of the tiny house was piled high with bits and pieces of things he planned to use. In addition to pyramids, there was a huge dodecahedron, a geometric made of copper piping, which creates a loving atmosphere to sit in to listen to music. Grand speakers sat on the sides of the structure. I loved lying on the mat inside of it, in the ocean of music. Trevor dreamed of creating the best sound system in the world. The tiny spare bedroom was also filled floor to ceiling with pieces waiting to become something. In a heartbeat, he shifted some of the wires, piles of books, little boxes, and tables with a single bed and a lamp, and there I was. Voilà! I had a new home.

But then, safe again, feelings seemed to flow out in the night. After bouncing around in the housesits, the new stability allowed my inner volcanoes — the buckling up of deep fears and losses of and for Bridget, along with the experiences with Naomi and Steven — to erupt and overflow like boiling-hot lava. Tremendous nightmares ensued. I would wake up making terrible whimpering or stifled screaming sounds, shaking at the vulnerability of my home and family, stifling panic. Trevor would tiptoe into the room and talk me down. He was so kind.

Trevor loves to talk, and he uses his words to "process" people. And I am one who loves to be talked to. The human voice, in particular the male voice, can calm me. His especially made me feel safe. I chuckle as I think back on one old boyfriend in particular. When I was insomniac, I would ask him, "Tell me about your life." As he launched into his "bedtime story," I would drift off. I wonder if he was offended or if he just felt useful, or is that why he never talked to me again after we broke up?

I also channeled for Trevor and me most nights, and from the Guides flowed amazing information that lit dark corners of our lives, told us where each of us was going, revealed what soul blocks we were writhing against, and taught us more and more about the moving energies of these days. At times, we shimmered in their wonderful light. I began giving workshops, and the readings mounted up again by phone or in person in the area. I was back at work, the work that made sense of my life.

Trevor had his own fragilities. Losing his eyesight was devastating. As I mentioned, he didn't want anyone to know, especially his Silicon Valley peers. Courageous, and a strategist, he set himself up in that cute, tiny house, from which he could take trains to the airport, with its access to any place he would choose to go. In different ways, though, he was hiding and in his own recovery, as well. We helped each other grow. Together we'd laugh, explore, set goals, and cook. I busily whirred greens in our juicer for our hearty liquid salad. When we drank it regularly, he could see better, even get keys into locks more easily. It was obvious he'd had acute eyesight before, along with a penchant for detail, which returned to him when we partook of the greens and faded when we didn't. We were getting stronger.

One late afternoon, though, sitting on the side of my single bed and looking at all the wires, pipes, poles, and bits and pieces of stuff in the tiny bedroom, I said to myself, "I need to move along! All this stuff is exhausting."

Less than two minutes later, Trevor popped out of his bedroom door. "Can you help me?" he asked. "I want to put all the wires under the house and need some help." Wow! Wow! That was within minutes, or maybe even seconds— hmmmmmmmmmmm. He'd picked up that I was planning my exit. And in a few short hours, my little bedroom had some of the peaceful ambiance I needed.

We were a working friendship, another transformational relationship. Obviously I, a transformer (so sayeth my Guides), was using relationship to unearth my true nature and heal so many leftovers, loosely called karma. We were very close and always very, very supportive. Trevor began developing his speakers, which would offer "the best sound in the world." And I was increasing my confidence to reach out into the community with my healing work and my radio shows. Trevor has always loved media, and we had fun developing my online-radio ideas. I still have clients from my early radio appearances in the Bay Area.

Trevor is magical. And his tiny, old, cute home was on a corner lot in a high-demand area. He thought he would sell and move us to Marin with its expanse, so we started fixing the house. I put flowers in the errant garden and paid for the removal of some big but sick trees. We contemplated all kinds of fixer-up things when his friend, a real-estate agent, popped by. "Are you willing to sell, Trevor?"

The thought rang out, and the Universe answered. The timing was impeccable, just like those wires suddenly moving out of my bedroom.

"You bet." He was given a grand amount for the house and lot by a young man who was a contractor and wanted it just as it was so he could fix it up for his bride-to-be. As I say, Trevor is magical. He spoke it, and it happened. Off we went to a delightful two-year rental in Mill Valley as we looked for a place to buy in the high-priced neighborhood. Unfortunately, or fortunately, we weren't earning the kind of money to sustain the lifestyle of a multi-million-dollar-house purchase. I wasn't even earning a clothing budget, although I was helping a lot of people there.

Several times a year, I headed to the Northwest, sometimes alone and sometimes with Trevor, combining sessions with visits with my daughter and my grandson, my dad, and even my siblings, although I still made some uncomfortable. That, I know now, makes sense. It took me some more years of individuating to value the importance of separating from the family vibrational fabric in order to shake myself free from the intricate web of beliefs often inherited or in one's lineage—like what was security, what we should be like, what was success, or anything about self-realization. I had to break free in order to transform, to touch my dharma/purpose, to express, and to contribute to the freedom and love of a new reality—a new reality that I could create. I had to. It was my soul's drive. I wrangled with feelings of guilt and despair and self-judgement, still thinking that to evolve or be a better person, I should sort old mistakes and resolve or even atone for my craziness. Friends found my emotional angst, as I longed for my family's approval, bizarre or rather boring. I would catch on eventually. My efforts to be a better and better person, to get over my own foibles and defenses, just kept tweaking everyone around me. The good part was that it kept me working on myself.

Faithfully, I drove the thousand miles up I5 to heal myself in the family, to be involved with my aging father, and be inspired by my stepmother. When I was in town, Georgina would say, "Sit!" Out would come the Christian Science magazines. And we would explore spiritual principles, examining the hurdles we set up that blocked creating the realities we would rather choose.

My dad, despite being a hilarious, musical, fun guy, was famous—or actually infamous—for his resentments. Maybe they were about politics. Or about how people talk, or lash ion, or the sounds of rock music, or Goth looks. Discussing with him concepts and expressions of change in our world was a challenge. But he was well read. I remember one special time when, in the heat of our discussions and his resistances, Georgina pointed out my dad's resentments. With the Irish tilt of her vowels and the lovely lilt of her voice, she cautioned him, "Grant, you had better look at your resentments."

I gasped. No one addressed my dad's behavior, ever. But she did. His silver curls, overdue for a cut, seemed to emanate from his churning mind. He actually laughed at himself and admitted that he had a lot of resentments. And he talked about how it created problems in his life. She kept him accountable for his judgmental behavior, probably for the first time in his life. And he loved it.

She treated me as though I were wonderful, intelligent, making a difference. She actually honored and admired me. I loved her and was pleased she was sitting as a matriarch at the head of our family.

But Georgina passed. All of her treatments and prayer work couldn't pull out the roots of or transform her advancing health problems. My dad's love for her was growing deeper by that time. He read all her books, trying to understand her healing process. And she loved him, so she finally accepted medical treatments. It was a humiliating nightmare for her, but she did it for Dad. My dad's second widowing experience was hard.

Talk about resentments, Georgina's niece, who would inherit all her wealth, had resented Dad's presence in her world, sure that he would intrude on her inheritance. He had his own money. He didn't need Georgina's, nor was he that kind of person, but this niece had been counting on the gains she knew were coming through her aunt. The day after

Georgina passed, she began her attack on him. Poor Dad. He was completely unaccustomed to having anyone emotionally attack him. He had had no time to rebalance, so my Dad came apart, with anxiety attacks and blood-pressure problems. We were all concerned that he would die. My brother and his wife stood guard and dealt with the niece while my dad was sent to his sister's home in Calgary to feel safe and recover. Finally, he began to ground again and announced, "That bitch is not going to kill me!" and he began to get stronger.

After all the painful action died down, perhaps six months or so, Dad returned for a while to being pretty cynical about my work. Yet by then, he had already received so many messages from Mum. Back in California, the phone rang.

"Hello, Vereo...." His voice hung down, exhausted by his grief.

"Hi, Dad. How are you doing?"

"Well, (pause) how would you like to give your old man a reading?"

My heart thumped. "Sure, Dad," I said, praying at the top of my inner voice's lungs for nonattachment and clarity.

We set up a time and my preparation began. I was hilarious. I did alternative nostril breathing, whined, and released old resentments between us. "Please let me be totally out of the way. You do it all," I begged my Guidance. "Please, please help me to keep myself and our history out of the picture. Please give him a vaulted perspective in which he can feel the amazing unconditional love that comes through sessions." I prayed daily both in preparation of and for neutrality among the tangled webs of the family politics. It was both intense and funny. My Guides call it my antics. I sweated, danced, meditated, breathed vehemently, and cleared chakras as well as anywhere else that clutter would linger, blocking me as a conduit—all the usual stuff. I wanted so much to honor Dad and to help him through his grief.

I am sure I looked like the Tasmanian devil/angel. Trevor pretended not to notice, but he was very aware and quite bemused. All that sweating worked. It worked! Dad's sessions, and he actually had four or five, honored him, honored my mum, honored his life journey and his time with Georgina, gave him some solace, and sorted through some of our incomprehensible family dynamics. Plus, he was relieved to know that his middle daughter wasn't crazy after all.

During the chapters of his life between Mum's passing and Georgina, and then after Georgina's passing, I spent a number of two- or three-night visits with Dad, and these were extraordinary. The first day was always a little tense, as I mentioned earlier, but after that we would talk about all levels of life, his and mine, old days and new dreams, at a level we had not shared before. I treasured these glimpses into my dad, his disappointments, and his dreams. Living in his domain for those few days helped us get into sync, and we really began to appreciate each other.

CHAPTER TWENTY

Back to the Northwest

While searching to buy a home in, as I said, a tremendously expensive market, I was also making those regular trips to the Northwest; my Guides encouraged me to look in that market. We decided to look there, to be near my dad, my daughter, and my wonderful grandson, plus maybe do some healing between me and the family. I'm like a bulldog, huh? Trevor loved the damp, rainy climate. It would be a respite where creating and having pieces built for his inventions would be much cheaper.

"You will find a triplex," my Guides whispered.

"Oh, a triplex?" I responded sarcastically. It sounded preposterous. Work was growing again, but I didn't have that kind of money. Then again, the word from their reality often is magical and can seem preposterous. A triplex. On we went, wandering around the Bellingham area checking out multiple-family dwellings, including row-house-looking duplexes that seemed starkly plebian. Both of us loved space and light, and that wouldn't be in the rows of upstairs/ downstairs uninspired places we toured.

"It won't be on the market," I heard my Guides say.

"Oh, great! Sounds like a needle in a haystack! We may need a *little* help here!" We sent our etheric decree "out there." Guidance is funny sometimes. And hints can be subtle. Well, our haystack glinted with perky road signs. One major one was when we were driving past a metaphysical store called "Wise Awakenings." I screeched to a halt, and in we went. It was a haven of spiritual accoutrements: sounds, jewelry, sparkling crystals, books. In the back was an intriguing, outer-space looking machine, with a number of geometrics surrounding a healing bed. The owner, Diana, lived out on the Lummi Peninsula. "Call my landlord. He is a realtor." We called him.

"Would you like to live on the Peninsula?" he asked.

"We have no idea, but we'll listen."

"One of my agents is thinking about selling her holiday home, acreage on the water. She's just thinking about it."

"Can we take a look at it?"

"Sure. Let's go now."

Off we went. As we entered the house, a grand vista of evergreens, myriad birds, a bay view and the tiny skyline of Bellingham across the water greeted us. The house was cottagey with a homey upstairs along with a roughed-in suite downstairs. For me, it was a potential to spread out and enjoy guests; for Trevor, it was an inventor's haven. Plus, there was an apartment over the three-car garage. It was potentially a triplex! The two acres stretched out into a magical fairyland—over half the acreage included an orchard, a third of which was virgin territory. Eagles perched in the three huge evergreens that stood forty feet tall at the front edge of the property. Others chatted to one another atop the tall evergreens around the back. The water in the bay rippled silvers, blues, and greens in the soft wind. Huge bushes, some loaded with rhododendrons, and a variety of other trees dotted the property. It was so peaceful.

Trevor and I looked at each other.

"I could live here."

"Me, too!"

With stars in our eyes and caught in the magic of it all, we really didn't spend much time checking out the details of the house. We visualized, prayed, and programmed to create our purchase that weekend. Our prayers were answered. The owners found a cruiser they wanted in place of this second home, and soon, furniture included, we bought the house on the water. Yes, the house that wasn't yet on the market, just as Trevor's San Carlos house had not yet been on the market. Our new home had renters for a few months, so we returned to California for a few months. But our prepa-rations started in our hearts and minds rustling with dreams of settling.

"This will be great for about six or seven years," my Guides told me.

Oh, my. Wouldn't it be for a lifetime? So far neither of us had lived that way, but we had that dream — you know, the happily-ever-after one. Our souls had greater plans or dreams, however. "Okay, this and then something better," we said as we accepted what we were told.

"Great" it was. That house filled up with our work. Trevor was in the basement where he worked on his inventions — speakers, amplifiers, servers, and who-knows-what else. Upstairs, I did many readings by phone or in person, conducted radio shows online, and channeled for us both on most days. We grew and transformed. Life felt vaulted. I added the goal of learning to be sustainable.

The family enjoyed it, too. The kids, along with my precious grandson, learned to experience it as their home away from home on holidays. Once again, my dream of home and family was alive and well, at least some of the time…but it began to wobble.

Then there was Junior, a little Maltese, that, at first anyway, lived in the upstairs apartment His owner, our renter, had to move to town. Her workdays would be very long. "Will you take Junior?" she asked.

He was a sweet dog and my grandson, age two at the time, loved him. But, heavens! I knew little or nothing about dogs. I tried to give him away to my daughter who couldn't have him in her townhouse, then to a few older single women who needed companionship. But one of my wise California women friends was a dog lover. She said, "Stop! You need the love." And she was so right. Junior and I became attached, and for the next eight years he would be a core of love for me and a cohesive force for our entire family. He was a love pivot. Summer and winter, he and I took walks on the beach.

I also knew next to nothing about gardening, but learning to garden started off wonderfully. In the summertime, we'd pick fruit from the trees and vegetables from our garden. Our neighbors were kind and warm-hearted, and we developed friendships along our short road. Parts of that phase of life there on the Lummi Peninsula were a treasured idyll.

Best of all, I could be near my dad, who lived just over half an hour away, over the border. I visited him often, several times a week. After Georgina passed, Dad pared down his living accommodations in stages. Trevor and I and a U-Haul intercepted some of Georgina's beautiful furniture and dishes that were en route to the thrift store. We plopped the huge, green recliners at the picture windows, to watch the eagles and the water. Those chairs stayed there for the duration, a site for inspiration, my healing work, channelings, readings, the radio shows, and grandmothering. I was so happy to be surrounded by Georgina's things, even though the elegance of her feminine, pristine taste was miles from my fashion. I felt so nurtured by her presence.

295

Multidimensional visitations from Mum and Georgina amped up, and my work grew and grew during that section of our life. Besides Mum and Georgina, many more from the "other side," or the vibrational realms, arrived, always seeking to rebalance their relationships with clients. I objected at first to what could be construed as flakey woo-woo of the spirit world. But my objections quickly ceased as I saw the huge, amazing shifts in clients—programs unraveled almost instantaneously in the light of experiences between a spirit and a client.

On the domestic front, our relationship was shedding, maybe molting. Our work stretched into two separate businesses, although Trevor's dreams became laden with debt. My business was growing, but my focus of family, driving, and garden spread me out too much. I wanted to write and do television and other forms of communication. Trevor was clear that there would be no marriage, which hurt me. I let my garden and the dream of home slide while I focused more on my work and spiritual path.

Along the way, I inherited some money that I put into some television programs through KVOS TV. The shows perked my creative flow and turned out all right. I ran out of funds, however, and KVOS changed hands.

Our home situation became dire. Trevor and I were both spinning. Somehow I knew it was time for me to emerge—I was nearing seventy! Trevor's debt was crushing him, and his inventions weren't selling. Too much time in isolation seemed to strip his credibility with him-self and potential clients. Or was the universe pushing us out of our hiding places? Perhaps, we muse today in our daily phone chats, we had a contract to lift each other up to carry our talents to new levels and not hold one another back. He was actually looking ahead when he said no marriage. He was carefully assuring us that should his debts crash, they weren't both our debts. I didn't understand that until later.

On one hand, I felt as if my ship was sinking. On the other hand, I had an exhilarating feeling that my self was stepping forward. Though we kept helping each other, I felt Trevor's isolation as a rejection. The home demands were claustrophobic, drowning my own ambitions or even my right to have them. I fantasized that my own work could support our entire world, but the income of an intuitive — at least this intuitive at that time — wasn't enough. Trevor couldn't fathom that if he put himself fully behind my work for a few months, maybe it could support us. He pulled farther into himself. The dizzying losses unraveled our home. I couldn't allow myself to feel my heartache as he became more unreachable.

The inevitable started again: I found myself looking for where to go and what to do. What is belonging really, I asked myself. A part of me was saying, "Oh, no. I'm not leaving again!" But I had to and I did. Now, at seventy, I was striking out all over again. Just as with Glenn, or leaving Sequim, Edmonton, Vancouver (multiple times!), and Tucson, I was leaving for the next phase of my path.

That must have been our contract. But there had been great gifts there among the trees, the eagles, and the bay.

The very first day we were living there, sitting in the huge, green recliners by the grand windows, I began a channeling.

Through me, Guidance said, quite loudly, "This is beautiful, yes. Yes. Now let's get to work." And thus began the gold-light drawings called "the structures."

"About two miles above your head is a radiant, golden ball. Forty feet below your spine is another golden ball. From the upper golden ball, down and through your spine, draw a gold filament of light. You are essentially on a spit. Now, from the upper golden ball, drop a three-sided pyramid with golden lines to about waist height. Push its base out, widen it, so there is room to play underneath it.

"Upside-down is another golden pyramid, its point touching the lower golden ball. The bases meet to create a large, golden, diamond shape, a tetrahedron.

"Inside of the diamond shape, create a crystal ball that touches the inside edges of your tetrahedron. Notice the spectral radiance of the ball.

"Inside of that, see a star tetrahedron. And inside of that, you are. Now spin and spin and spin. And as you do, see in front of your eyes a screen, a movie screen on which you are going to create movies."

And then the powerful manifestation tool begins. "On the first screen, create a movie of you, becoming what you want to become as a being. As you see it unfolding, wrap it in light and move it to the side. On the second screen, see a project you want to create. See all the resources flowing to you — money, time, place, and on and on. As it unfolds, you see it coming to fruition, and as it does, you applaud. Then in come all the resources it will take to keep your project going to its natural conclusion."

The final phase was what they called *the galactic healing center.* "Call forth a healing team from your huge consortium of guides and healers. Have them surround a fresh healing table, on which you lie. And you ask for the healing you need. If you don't know what you need, ask them. They will tell you. As the energy of your healing builds up, wrap it in light, then move it to the side. Now bring in a new healing table. Your team replicates itself — magic you know — and someone comes in to lie on the table. It may be someone you don't know or someone you do know, but it is a person going through something whom you choose to put on the table."

Oh, my. These structures have been a mainstay on one of my radio shows, *Radiance by Design*, and often I get calls ahead asking me to put someone in the structure. Of course, there have been so many changes and added options to the structures, but it still builds even now after seven years of steady use. The consciousness of us all creating coherent fields into our communities also increases. Trevor and I worked faithfully in their light.

For many years, as I had been conscious of the fact that conventional, mainstream media sends suppressive frequen-cies out over the airwaves — a glut of soul-diminishing news and depressing messages of *spend spend spend*, painful drama, and lobbying for power. My longheld desire and intention to bring higher vibration and consciousness around the world, to infuse the collective with transforma-tive frequencies, is what initially brought me to radio in the 'seventies. One day in the mid-'nineties, I walked past the television as *The Little Buddha* was playing; I clearly felt the frequencies of that conscious film rush through me. I simply had to be more a part of that kind of work: sending out very high consciousness on the airwaves. Most people just don't realize how the fields of a lower vibration — in sounds, pic-tures, colors, even processed foods — dull human conscious-ness and blunt our lives. When we're asleep, we are actually quite enslaved, dominated, limited. We don't realize how uplifted and healed we can feel when the emanations are of a higher frequency. We can wake up!

Bless Internet radio—I started a series of interviews, interviews that are illuminating, highly charged, and an educational portal for me and for listeners. Well, I certainly started at the right time, just like those days in Vancouver, pre-social network, pre-Internet, when just at the right time I was on a growing tape circuit of so many healers. Books and more books poured in the door from publishers, books that broadened my awareness of healing: Pleiadian realities, Arcturian existences, ET worlds, mind over matter, transformations that enable greater creating of our reality, and wisdom about ancient sacred beliefs and structures.

I'd started off doing my shows in Tucson, then Monterey, then the Bay Area. But hiding out far from the madding crowds in our eagle's nest, I had two weekly shows. One was the interview show, and the other was a call-in show where I got to be a psychic, teach meditations, and make connec-tions.

Trevor, as both my wonderful partner and the "sound guy," tweaking volumes and balance, always joined me. To Trevor, who had studied physics, music, media of all types, Lazaris, and so many other metaphysical realms, this work was an enjoyable accent in his world. He enjoyed being present for these interviews and sometimes interacted with these amazing artists who push out human boundaries.

Randy—Trevor's and my guide to one another, since we'd met at his workshop—was my first interviewee. Heralding our discussion with rich music from his trumpet, he then set the tone of our talk with his sacred resonance. Another interview I loved was with Peter Calhoun, an Episcopalian priest who had spontaneously opened to visions,

He was "shown" that our planet is surrounded by a kind of skin created by an elite power, not Creator Spirit. It weighs us all down, and the people on the planet walk under it with stooped shoulders. He also was "shown" that humans have an amazing potential to fling that skin, the yoke of the elite, off and become powerful creators themselves. Although he was told he would tap to his own knowing and wouldn't have a specific teacher, at times he studied with greats. One of these was Rolling Thunder, with whom he sped up his learning to manifest, create rain where it is needed, consciously attune with animals and nature, and teach many others the same. He could even perform spontaneous combustion. After my interview, I just wanted to talk with him more. He called me and asked to be on again. I chuckled at myself as I found I was in love with his vibration and his empowering sensitivity, but he crossed over shortly afterward. His messages and their frequencies are still radiating and held in the intentions of his wife and his students as well as in his Presence.

Yet another wonderful interview was with Juliet Nightingale, who had had near-death experiences, wrote about the wonders of their perspectives, and developed a community, mostly online, to help others sort theirs. She was a sweet powerful woman! While I was speaking with her, an enormous rainbow unfolded across our entire view, reflecting itself on the water. It was beyond radiant.

I interrupted our conversation. "Juliet, as you speak of 'the beyond,' the most amazing rainbow is decorating our skies." Trevor took a cellphone photo, which we sent to her while on the air.

Juliet passed over a year and a half later. I know she is missed. Interestingly though, with all this experience across the veil, she became even more free to continue growing and exploring. One day, perhaps a year after she passed, I randomly relistened to her interview. It was vibrationally inspiring and answered so many questions about near-death experiences that I decided to air it again. As it was rerunning, a rainbow as bright as that one of several years ago arced across the sea and the Bellingham skyline!

My own Guidance keeps giving me expanded awarenesses of life in different realms of consciousness, and we can all dance around on the moving frontiers, on the cutting edges of our empowerment, from frequencies both inside and outside of ourselves. My healing work becomes more magical. Subtle levels of resonance, from which we create our realities, has become more apparent. Willing purveyors, whom I call my Paradigm Shifters, which is also the name of my second radio show—whether they are talking about sound healing, color, multidimensionality, channeling, diet, or other keys to empowerment for each of us individually— can infuse and inspire the entire consciousness of our species through their interviews.

It was a huge deal when one runner broke the four-minute-mile record. Once he did, lo and behold, so many more were able to break that record and create new records. By the same token, we literally breathe new possibilities every day. The courageous explorers I interview, for example, are people who break through limitations over and over, even if those seem to be barriers to possibility. Their teachings are contagious. Many, crushed by loss, depression, or illness, have had to surrender the identities they thought they were. Then they'd had to come apart, like I did—what we affectionately call a "nervous breakthrough" as I refer to it above. Usually, the crisis of money, health, or home pulled them apart until they relinquished layered attachments, even to their lineage. A breakthrough thins and actually tears the vibrational fabric of self so that deepening wisdom and empowerment can burst through and outworn wrappings of identities melt. Often, then, higher guidance and higher consciousness becomes easier to hear. It directs them with nudges, whispers, words, synchronistic opportunities as their identity redesigns itself from the inside out. Sometimes the process is painful. Sometimes so slow, while goals and realities begin to redesign themselves in concert with values and true nature.

These include people such as Jack Hawley, a successful businessman who, with his wife, became a long-term Sai Baba follower after coming apart at the sudden death of their young-adult son, then made connection with their own Divinity. Through their evolution, the rising of their consciousness in harmony of release and intention, they radiate a loving presence. Jack's book, *The Bhagavad Gita: A Walkthrough for Westerners*, "walks through' this ancient epic poem, a story of a warrior in battle, who, with his avatar friend, Krishna, learns to choose his true nature amid this embroiled reality. Ancient works like *The Bhagavad Gita* or the Upanishads are filled with analogies of our inner struggles, conquering our baser responses to life and others. Always, the message that when we choose evolution, our ability to find happiness and love no matter what the churnings of society put us through, life after life, is the gift. The soul's goal, says the *Gita*, is to feel and radiate love no matter what circumstances we find ourselves in — no matter how grueling, how depressing, how hard. The battle is always within each of us. And what are called the seven deadly sins in the Catholic teachings form the core of issues to resolve for our evolution — such as competition, jealousy, pride, covetessness, murder...you know them. They aren't a surprise.

303

Each interview leads us to new levels of self-creation and the sorting of deepening goals, stretching our reality. We are, in fact, empowered deeply from within.

We all have special and unique roles as human beings. But many don't consider that, or even seek it out. Sometimes, if we are lucky or blessed, however, it seeks us out! But when the breakthroughs occur, they can seem like illness, mental-health problems, and craziness as the person is forced to feel her beliefs and perceptions break apart or the scaffolding of a familiar life is dismantled. And the process continues with some deepening focus from our subject here, *dharma* (I use *dharma* as our unique contributions to humanity, our own purpose, our gifts). Awareness awakens, and after a period of confusion or chaos, for some anyway, the demand to answer the rising call from within becomes insatiable.

Marianne Williamson, who writes about the Course in Miracles teachings, says in *A Woman's Worth* that we are more afraid of the light than the darkness within. People are terrified to have to mine their own truth, because there can be a lot of wreckage—mostly from one's understandings and senses of security. "If I cling to these thoughts and beliefs or this status and lineage, I will be secure." People can't tolerate our changes erupting from within because, once again, humans are empathetic or contagious beings. Many feel the danger within themselves when faced by our vulnerabilities unless they themselves are conscious of the possibilities for themselves in these changes. It does awaken the potential of becoming available to the greater good, including the evolution of our species.

Judy Carroll from Down Under had her world literally break into layers of reality before she finally caught on. Judy, after the discomfort "being different" as a child, through some ethereal visitations directed her to discover that she is actually an ET, functioning in a human identity: human by day and Zeta by night. Zetas are those almond-shaped-eyed beings so often depicted in ET pictures. Like humans, they come in many levels of integrity — some dangerous. Many are a force of healing, love, and support.

I always see fields in people as packages contained by vibrational membranes, holding various programs that run our unconscious programs: patterns of health or finances, or emotional programs like depression, self-esteem, or rage — all kinds of responses from old experiences. As I see them, they almost float throughout our being, and as we work through various problems, we move, disband, or clear them. They forge our personalities with resistances, expectations, and feelings that are mysterious or that even contain pain and limitation. But when we move them, we quickly catch on that many of them are changeable. That in turn creates healing.

Judy's life story, *Human by Day and Zeta by Night*, reads like a science-fiction novel as she tells of leaving her 3D body asleep on her bed while she goes aboard Zeta ships at night. There she meets fellow Zetas from different levels of consciousness and power, including teachers/coaches. She also sees Earth people who are brought to the ships, often terrified, in their sleep or in trances, to be worked on. Her books are fascinating. Her conscious multidimensional explorations, infused with her kindness, help people manage energy and discipline for their own healing and transforma-tional flexibility. She teaches about subtle energy, and its not-so-subtle influence on us all, for healing and manifesting, and moving to higher and higher consciousness, and the iconoclasm it requires. Breaking out — or through — is like a death. It empowers us and gives us new ways to be in the world. But we leave behind many aspects of identity.

"Change your energy, change your reality" is a quote that keeps me prying myself or clients off of stuck places in life. It comes from the *Arcturian Star Chronicles*, which are channeled messages of how subtle energy works in our world. We add a proliferating flow of wizards like Steven Pollitt, who measures and amps up energy fields with frequency potions. Then there's Deborah Stuart of HighChi, who designs, creates, and energizes beautiful jewelry as well as machines that radiate higher frequencies throughout life for our living and health advantages. Deborah, once in the international fashion industry, is now designing clothes charged with higher frequencies. Charged-up jewelry gives people and their auras a huge lift. So, even in fashion and beauty, we can enhance our rate of evolution. Beauty is one source, and she adds the technology. Won't it be great when we can deck ourselves out while we boost our evolution! I wanted to create that years ago, but was too timid to push through all the details of clothing as I tried to balance my world as a three-dimensional single mother. Blessings to Deborah on her path.

And then there are more musical maestros like David Ison, Jonathan Goldman, and Diele Ciele, and my dear friend Randy Masters, whose sound potions in the form of beautiful music, chanting, singing, and toning, plus his own line of energizing and exquisite jewelry teach us to enjoy living in the resonance of chosen fields for healing of ourselves and others who see us. We are an empathetic species, so as we send out higher frequencies by choice, we can then resonate with possibility that is, again, contagious. I wear one of my two resonant pieces of his jewelry most days.

The channels I have grown to love are Galexis, through Ginger Metraux, Ashtar through Terrie Symons, Lazaris, with the beauty of metaphorical language that works through our subconscious as we resonate while we listen. And of course there's Esther Hicks who has brought Abraham to a wide audience with the Law of Attraction. They speak on so many levels, touching our radiance and helping us gain access to what we are hiding within our beings — hiding in the subconscious and yet experiencing it playing out in the form of repeated patterns. As with Peter Calhoun, we feel bathed and nurtured in their love. And the power we have can emanate a radiant, conscious, loving "I AM" existence. These and so many channeled beings show how amazing the universal flows are, how intricate and infinite consciousness is, unfolding through the willing receptacles who continuously have to purify their own thoughts and feelings, and their ancient and current reactions to allow the messages to flow through cleanly. Some of them, during our conversations, use their multidimensional awarenesses to give us a grander perspective of the political power flows. They show how to rise from the collective of individual evolution out of the old tangles of competition, jealousy, possession, greed, and separation. They help us see, at least in our imagination, a species that can enlighten itself out of the murder and war consciousness, as old as mankind. They teach us that we can grow beyond this.

The Oneness Blessing Givers, in massively growing numbers, are also busily purifying their own reactions, getting to know their own inner divine as they pass on the deeksha or transmissions of awakening through the heads and eyes of many. I have interviewed a number of them on various stages of their awakening journeys and always feel their radiance. I am kind of a calibrating tool; I listen to my interviews often to "feel" how much resonance they stabilize and also how I can interact with it. Oh, I often feel jealous of myself as my podcasts of conscious guests lift me.

Recently I interviewed Baptist de Pape on "The Power of the Heart." He was a lawyer who just didn't feel right about his huge opportunity as a corporate lawyer. So he walked and talked to himself: "What does life want from me?" Or he'd ask the old Ramana Maharshi mantra, "Who am I?" He was told to create a film on the power of the heart. He did. And as he grew, his innate love frequency took charge of his vibrational being. So his interview radiates *love love love*. When I hear people judging him and others, I trust his resonance more than the vibrational level of their words. The love radiating from him and others is contagious.

Profound and uplifting information on healings, integrations, and evolution come from Jim Ehmke and Caroline Sutherland on nutrition; Barbara Hand Clow and Carl Calleman on the flows of consciousness through our collective; and channels like Sondra Sneed and Salacia — all experts on the changing fields throughout our universes.

I find myself growing, headed inside of myself under their tutelage. It is as if the ashram I live in, with its dancing fields of awakening, is the playing field of the consciousness.

Essentially, each interview leads us to new levels of creating the self. The speakers survey possibilities and access ways to create realms of expansion in listeners. Hey! I love this part of my life as I still have the luxury of speaking to these givers, writers, energy wizards, inventors, explorers. My own understanding of this swirling vibrant mass that we share as *me* accrues greater and greater levels every day. The world is enriched with knowings as much through the Internet as through our broken education systems. We are still learning and learning, and I've had the opportunity to speak personally with so many of these change agents—all from our big, green chairs with their view of the sea, alongside trees dotted with numerous kinds of birds while the moving ceiling of moody clouds shifted the colors of the water. And windows in the small cityscape off in the distance winked back at us on a sunny day.

These are just a few examples of the ways we were touched and lifted. The radio shows and the phone interviews built up more and more. These days, we are now up to three-hundred recorded interviews of purveyors of consciousness. The rich spectrum of topics, layers of consciousness, and awakening vibrations spread wide, and I am meeting my goal to send out heightened frequency energies more consciously than marketed media does.

Think about it! Mass media can hold us down and keep us vibrating at lower levels, tranced into a lower consciousness until we shake ourselves awake. Changing our frequency through media could be a wonderful gift for humanity. To know which shows are for you, just turn your Geiger-counter self on, sit by a radio or television during a normal broadcast, and you will feel the push-pull of vibrations emanating from the various sources of energy. You can learn to choose the shows by the energy it inspires.

As I have said, I've never been much of a sleeper; over the past thirty years or so, I have set up recordings of teachers and healers, or often my own radio interviews, to listen to while I'm lying awake. Now the interviews are on my iPhone. I run them in the background so that if I drift through pockets of being awake, I absorb wisdom that allows me to improve my vibrations and the quality of my work. I also receive something I long to "see" and "know" — the greater view of the collective of humanity. But, also, mostly I feel the fields that record life's experiences moving through me. More and more, I can feel them moving out; they don't stay stuck in pockets of pain.

Manifestations — because of the overall rising fields and increased frequency flow in the universes, in the atmosphere, on the planet, and among all of life — occur more and more swiftly these days, for good or not so good. When we see our intentions, our dreams, our visions, and vibrate with them as if they are real, they manifest more swiftly. There is a trick that can hold back your dreams and mine: it is that we share a low-vibrating subconscious. Subconscious programs tend to be much lower, resonating with the collective's or mass consciousness' reactions to the past — like cataclysmic earth changes from thousands of years ago, or murder, mayhem, and wars from more recent centuries, plus personal abuse issues, and who-knows-what else from this lifetime. We don't need to know them all as we are learning to penetrate and transform those subconscious programs. Just feel the frequencies (weighty, pulling) or see the visions you create and the ones that just won't break free. Know the blocks can be moved and popped out. Otherwise they interfere with the intentions and visions we want to manifest.

I often muse that no matter what role we manifest in this lifetime, the inner core still faces the same inner challenges: finding our personal dharma or our true nature. So often we forget that. *Look at me,* someone says. *I am rich. Or married. Or employed. Or successful. Or famous.* But that isn't the true person. Those are labels. The journey to oneself, as I used to say, is the journey to no self. It's a journey of releasing and letting the love of being pulse through us. Still and all, the inner work moves on. And helping one another seems to fan the flames of the rising resonance of our collective, which in turn has its own purpose. Maybe now it is to find our true nature to live in harmony with the true nature of life around us. We can coexist with the awesomeness of nature as we launch rockets, aiming to explore the universes and expand far beyond the clutches of the third dimension.

I want to mention here that among Greek gods and Hollywood stars and intuitive healers and more, there is a zest in the marketplace for fame that has a competitive edge. Oh, not with all. But it is prevalent in many areas of human achievement—wealth, talent, appearances; people can be competitive and jealous of one another. I'm talking about *startling* competition and jealousy, which can be even more shocking when that green-eyed monster rises among, for example, spiritual people. It represents a deep fear, a huge lack in oneself. For example, "If Betty Lou is beautiful, oh, no, she took all the beauty and there is none left for me. I'm stuck with less, I can't get a husband or whatever." It is painful to see how this grips and confines human relation-ships and prevents support—so painful. And it also has a deep survival fear underlying it. Thus, when it comes up, always notice that it means, "Oh, *that* is what I want." Sometimes you will surprise yourself.

It hasn't been that long since a woman without a husband would have been destitute. Women learned to undercut one another: who has the most beauty, the best dowry, the greatest breasts? Feel it. Feel it—because when you can release the jealousy, you can give yourself the opportunity to be more of your true nature and radiate and shine the wonder of you. No competition is possible here as you are the only one in the universe that is YOU! Amazing, huh?

And guys, you also have jealousies, although maybe more about your finances and station in life. There are no simple rules. Bring up that feeling and let it flow through you. Notice where you are afraid, ask to feel the life-or-death struggle, and then command total release of it.

For all of us, our true nature radiating outwardly is our greatest gift to a partner, a family, a career, a world travel...it's our contribution into the grand collective of humanity.

Remember in all walks of life, those disquieting things will rise. Let yourself become conscious of those awful feelings, and again, take charge, release them. Watch your inner light RISE to the occasion. THERE IS NO COMPETI-TION.

In the midst of these times on the gray but beautiful, peaceful "edge of the world," as the new resident of our Lummi home calls it, my work amped up. In my readings, people's energy fields and frequencies were remolded and reshaped as if they were clay on the potter's wheel. Calling in the Guides, my clients and I would move along the pockets of density that they might have counted on as being themselves, but were the traps of self by lineage. "Oh, that is just like my Mom!" "Oh, that was like Aunt Jenny." "Oh, I take after my dad." Well, that good, old family issue in the form of energy density can be released.

For me, however, the proximity to my family was difficult in that the fields I recorded, let's call them karmic, were amped up by being near them and experiencing their resistances to me. As I said, I had assumed a welcome just because I belong. But I had to learn that I belong by not belonging. For a time, the writhing in my belly, the almost fainting, the relentless tears, the rejection I felt throughout my body/mind ripped at me. I wished I could just be angry. Over and over, I pulled up various feelings, so deeply embedded in my soul. I didn't have to find out exactly what the feelings were from, but I learned so much through that process. I learned the businesses of our souls that were being completed between me and the rest of my family: I learned about them physically; I learned about them emotionally. I had the courage and the inner foundation that helped me revalue them over and over until I could let them go…or let them let me go. It took decades, but I am finally able to just love myself, them, and carry on. I learned to be grateful for their rejection.

You might not have such an intense soul connection with your family. But some version of even the tiniest, most gentle clearings could work for you to individuate among them. And ultimately, I wouldn't be happy to be still attached in my original tapestry after all this work, exhuming myself out of our old, past, or soul connections or lineage. Part of that vibrational fabric or design is the drive to move myself out of the lineage clutches. This is a crazy and wonderful path!

We are vibrational vehicles of light, and that light is moveable. Highly programmed, acutely sensing computers, we can set ourselves free to receive huge, spiraling surges of light that move up through us. You can witness these changes by watching someone's face in the moment, soon reflected in his or her life as the energy is moved. And like the vibrational barrier that broke with the four-minute mile, we free ourselves from limitations as the folks around us pick up speed and free themselves more easily, as well.

I love my work. Even after thousands and thousands of sessions with people from all over the world, I still love the mesmerizing reality of our uniqueness. The gifts we each bring to the planet never cease to fill me with awe. The most fascinating part of my work is how love — the universal love that is each of ours — inspires confidence and manifestation.

CHAPTER TWENTY-ONE

Spirit Visitations, Reconciliations, and Juicy Rapport

My rapport is also expanding with beings on the other side. In turn, that expanded my vibratory fields, emanations of self and story, from the human dimensions off into multidimensions. Some were very personal. But I only accept ones that are transformational, not the spooky, sticky, controls we hear about. In my channeling, I learned about the layers and waves of frequency and the paradoxical dance with time and space.

I felt a new freedom after meeting Julia Assante. Her book *The Last Frontier* specializes in afterlife communications. She and I have some shared history, like our Catholic training. She told me that it was this Catholic training we had both received that curtailed my asking for specific spirits. I had learned not to, that it could interfere with their journeys.

"Ask for specific spirits to come. We can do that," she assured me, "as long as it's always with the intention for the highest good of all concerned. We are allowed."

I mentioned earlier that I had forbidden Mum to come and give me flak from the other side any longer. She didn't. I somehow had pushed a magical button and wouldn't let her buzz my brain with her judgments. When judgments come, there is always an energy of pressure, of control. Or if you see them in color, they are black/gray, even if very thin. If you think of each of us as a musical instrument, judgments can be a kind of clamping down, a dampening, on our strings. I somehow knew how to block her judgments of me.

But one day, seventeen years after she had passed and perhaps a dozen after I had planted my own flag of independence with, "I am not taking your calls, Mum," there I was, happily chopping veggies in my kitchen, when she came to visit. It was the day before Mother's Day. Through windows on my right, the green of the backyard rolled under the trees. Out the windows on my left was the start of the forest and glints from the sparkling water. Around the corner came a radiant, pink-lit Being with lots of gold and yellow shot through her.

"Oh, my gosh..... Mum?" I asked incredulously. "Mum is that you?" Somehow, we can still recognize the identity of beings who don't look like their earth selves. Tears of wonder sprouted.

"I want to tell you something," Mum said. "I am sorry. I know who you are now. I am so proud of you, so proud. I understand so much of what you are doing. I couldn't understand before. I am sorry. I am sorry that I didn't help you. You did it anyway. I am so proud of you.

"But I want you to know something else: Finally, I have broken through. Finally, I have broken through a huge barrier I had against love my whole life. I am so relieved. I learned. I *feel* love, Ronni." I could feel love surround us and fill the kitchen as she spoke. "I *feel* it." Again my visions were swimming in my tears.

"Please call your father. Please tell him that I made it through. And tell him for me, Ronni, please tell him that he was a good husband. He needs to know that."

"Okay, Mum. I will."

"And Bridget, my granddaughter. Call her, please. Tell her for me that I am sorry. I wasn't kind to her. I love her. I

316

see how powerful she is, and I love her and I admire her." Mum had been systematically judgmental of my unusual daughter from her birth on. I'd always entertained lots of guesses why — maybe because I wasn't married when I had her, maybe it was a past life, or maybe the Naomi story confused and hurt us all so much that she projected more pain onto this surprise child. "Bridget is an amazing woman, and my great-grandson is going to bring so much to the world. I love him, too."

I was busy, so I put off calling my dad until the next morning. Mother's Day was the perfect time. "Hi, Dad. Happy Mother's Day!" I laughed as I could almost see his shoulders roll, his eyebrows flex his sardonic wit.

"Oh, yes," his voice swooped in sarcastic humor.

"Hey, Dad. I have been talking to Mum." That got his attention.

"How is she?" His enthusiasm was suddenly childlike.

"Good, Dad! She wants you to know two major things. She has made a huge breakthrough, a barrier she had against love her whole life, 'whole life,' she said. She is free of it."

"Really? Is that how it works?" He sounded so happy and relieved.

"I don't know but that is what she is telling us. And, Dad, she said to tell you that you had been a good husband. A very good husband."

He burst into tears. "She did? Really? She knows, doesn't she? I have been pacing the floor every night this week, wondering if I had been a terrible husband. She was so angry all the time." He wept for a few minutes.

"She loves you, Dad. She just was stuck behind an old program."

"Her sister was so mean to her."

317

Immediately, Mum was in my head and said loudly, "She wasn't that bad. There was nothing she could have done. I just couldn't love then. I am done with that now."

"Is that how it works?" he asked again. "Do we keep learning things like that?"

"That's what they are telling me, Dad. She is freer now, and she sure feels different. She feels loving, supportive."

I called my daughter on Mother's Day, too. I half expected her to roll her own cynical eyebrows with an "Oh, Lord — Mum's talking to spooks again!"

But instead, when I started with, "I just heard from Grammy. She asked me to tell you that she loves you and admires you," Bridget burst into tears, too. "She is so sorry she wasn't kind to you. She didn't get to know you. She knows you now and knows that you are a wonderful and powerful woman. And she loves Dade, her great-grandson. She called him a wonderful spirit!"

"Mum, tell her I wish she could have a cup of tea with me." She sounded sweet and vulnerable. "I would like to talk to her, Mum. Tell her that for me — will you, Mum? And thanks a lot. Happy Mother's Day."

A couple of years later, when Dad and I were discussing it again, he put his hand over his heart and said, "That really touched me. That she is happier. More loving. She knows I loved her. It changed me. So much."

Her visit changed us all, releasing, shifting, and rearranging our energy patterns as well as unraveling some defensiveness and self-judgments. You've heard the old story "It's never too late to have a happy childhood!" Clearing these reactions adds to our freedom and self-esteem. But always, as we shift a held pattern — in this case the feeling both Dad and I shared that because of the fumes of Mum's anger, we had always been wrong somehow — as

318

we gain understanding, there can be a burst of powerful energy that infuses us so thoroughly. We then can live differently, with greater dreams.

As I said, though, I hadn't really been aiming for a profession of talking to spirits. I didn't quite believe in all that or know how to understand spirits. But over and over, they came. Their purpose was, clearly, a service to both our physical selves and beyond. I am loving it.

Here's one of my favorite stories. A girlfriend and I were enjoying some tea in pretty china cups and eating cookies that were set on matching china on the beautiful, golden oak table my mum and dad had had made for them years earlier. Joyce asked me, "Do you hear and see angels?' Her question, as if the sash on a curtain, drew open etheric portals. Suddenly, I "saw," right there, beside me, her mother, who had passed many years earlier.

I answered her, "Your mum wants to talk to you, Joyce."

"Well, I don't want to talk to her. She never was there for me, so tied up with her sisters and their grief over the early death of their mum. I don't want to talk to her."

Her mom just persevered. Spirits can have a staunch agenda. Remember Patrick Swayze bugging Whoopi Goldberg in the old groundbreaker movie, *Ghost*? She had no choice—a job had to get done.

I felt her mum's love for her. It was unfolding around us, and Joyce was moved to her innate, soft nature.

"Joyce, please go find your sister."

"Oh, Lord, Mum! God knows where she is!"

"Please find her. She is going to enter an abyss soon, get lost, and become irretrievably lost. Please, Joyce. Find Janna."

I felt her mother's tears slipping down my cheeks, and Joyce herself, always a giver, grumbled a bit as she said,

"Okay, Mum. But she was never there for me. You were never there for me...."

"I know. It was true. I am sorry, Joyce. Your sister was always troubled."

"She got all your focus, Mum. She was the family star."

"Please, Joyce. I know. I know. I was hurt. I am sorry." We could feel her care. "But I know you can help her."

Even now I could weep, knowing how guided we can be and yet our blinders of defense, fear or preconceived notions blunt emotional clarity.

Joyce still grumbled, but she did the work. She began her search. There hadn't been any connection with her sister over the years. She made the trek to Coeur d'Alene armed with an address that might be current, but might not. She found a tiny apartment at that address and a landlady to let her in. The tiny studio was appalling. Full to the brim, items of value were unceremoniously filed amid trash and even fecal material. Joyce asked the neighbor a few questions, persevering until, eventually, she found her sister roaming in the neighborhood near her home.

Her sister barely recognized her, but again Joyce persevered. It took a couple of visits before she could break into Janna's trust. Sometimes terrified, sometimes paranoid, sometimes just dull responses of her sister showed a mistrust of Joyce. But Joyce, always a contributor, did her duty: she found a way to enter her sister's psyche, to remind her how amazing she'd been in her life, what with being the first in the whole family of five to go through college, paving the way for Joyce. The compliments were crucial—the recognition was an energy transmission. Janna was a woman who'd been an international traveler, always beautiful, stylish, with a well-known and highly placed lover who wanted to marry her. She wouldn't marry him. No one was sure why. Joyce remembered her sister's jewelry and fine clothes. And here she was—filthy, lost, insane, mal-nourished. Those last two often go together.

Her mother acknowledged her, and was, for herself and her other daughter, so relieved. Joyce gathered her brothers, and together they sifted Janna's apartment. They found that she indeed had stashed enough money to support herself in full care. Her brother sorted it out. Now Janna, medicated and cleaned up, is living with a young family, calm enough to walk the baby carriage and feel like a participant in life again. She doesn't really remember her own family, but is well cared for. Her family checks on her regularly.

Good work, Joyce, and thank you to her mum. When spirits show up in my world, I listen. So do my clients and, often, my friends.

I had an aunt, a wonderful, eccentric woman, who understood me. My mum didn't like her, but I did and I even look like her. That I looked like her was hard for Mum, even enraging her. Traveling the four hours to Vancouver to join my family for my Uncle Art's funeral, I remember telling my boyfriend at the time, the illustrious novelist from the karmic turntable, that he would be meeting an aunt who truly did know me and enjoy me. "We'll spend some time with her as she is here from Ottawa for her brother's funeral."

After the funeral, I greeted her with delight. "I would love to spend an hour or two together with you, Aunt Tess, now that we are both in town."

"Sorry. I am going off with your two sisters."

My brother and sister-in-law were also verbally clear that they didn't want to spend time with me or with my daughter. I reeled. I sobbed and sobbed. Again? Again? The experience with the family and the loss of my uncle, my godfather, whom we loved, was shocking.

My aunt lived for a number of years beyond her brother and also beyond the life of my mother. I assumed after that incident that she was lost to me, so I didn't bother much with her anymore. She passed at age ninety-three. Just two days after her passing, we had our reckoning experience. These often happen right after the passing, within the first three days. It seems for some to be a time of reckoning if the person is awake. There I was in my galley kitchen with the orchard rolling out there on my right and the eagle-filled evergreens standing in front of the glittering water on my left. I heard, "Ronni! Ronni!" There it was, the unmistakable almost-British accent of my character aunt, who was born in Canada. "Ronni!" I could "see" her. Again, it was a see-through model.

"Oh, hi, Tess." I was uninspired, still feeling the sting of disappointment. But then I wanted to recognize and shuck old feelings. I wanted to be new, so I tried. "Hi, Tess. How are you?"

"I am fine, Ronni." She emphasized her vowels, as was her wont, and the cadence she used was familiar to me — it was definitely hers. "Ronni, I want to tell you something."

"Okay, Tess."

"I am sorry I, along with the others, isolated you. I am sorry."

"It's okay, Tess." I wondered if I meant that.

"I want to tell you what happened, why I did that."

"Alright." Was there an actual reason? I pried myself open.

"You and I had a special rapport. But I pulled away. You should know why."

"Why, Tess?" I was getting impatient. Remember, I had struggled for many years, running along the frontiers of sanity. Maybe most people do, but they don't admit it. I thought that that was the reason.

"Well, you have to know this. I also had 'the gift.' But I was terrified. So I turned away from you. I was afraid to be called insane, to be judged. Ronni, don't tell the others. They won't understand." There it was in a nutshell. Don't tell the truth.

My eyes sprouted tears, mostly of relief from her explanation. But the other part is that I had judged myself, as usual, for not being lovable, especially during all my breakthrough times, and my emergence in this strange world (the world of noses). But it wasn't that at all. It was that she was struggling with her own "gift" and didn't have the courage to use it. I felt released. I felt exonerated. I felt changed. Obviously, she wanted that change, too. Her vibration suddenly became clearer and was kind, loving, and so sincere. I could feel her love. And I felt my own renewed love for her.

Many people come to visit me soon, perhaps a few days, after they pass. Apparently, there is a light or energy around those of us who communicate multidimensionally. Some are sorting life and undoing old hurts or questions that are stuck. They seek that reconciliation. I think I know this—everything I really know becomes a question as I get older: Do I really know this? Truth changes with perspective, maybe in relation to details and circumstance. But I think that the great "judgment" we have been taught about from various pulpits is us with ourselves first. Then it's with Guidance when we have crossed over, a kind of experience of our effects or influences on the people we knew and often ones we loved or hated in our lifetime. And what I under-stand is, depending on the soul's truth and integrity, or perhaps love, there is a desire to unhook things left behind, or make sense, or cull the value from shared experiences. At least that's what I learn from the spirits who visit me. I'll let you all know when I get there.

Around the time that Mum shared her awakening heart, I went over to Sequim, the town I had moved to when I left Glenn eleven years earlier, the town I had left for the electrical warmth of Tucson. I was staying at Simone's bed and breakfast, visiting Jane, our good friend, who was dying. Jane was the proprietor of the first B and B I had been told about, the Tudor one that was full. She and Simone had become a strong foundation for us in Sequim. I went back to the Groveland Cottage that night, pensive. And just before going to sleep, I emailed Bryce—remember him, that key player in that horrendous karmic triangle?

"Hi, Bryce. It's been eighteen years since we talked. Our friend Jane Glass is dying. Don't you think it is time we at least have a cup of tea together and end the karma/tension between us?" I sent my email that Friday night, and accustomed as I was to no response, I left the next day, Saturday, and headed to Everett, a couple of hours away, to do a healing gathering. Sunday morning, I got a call from Simone. "Oh, Jane passed," I said to myself as I answered the call. "Hi, Simone."

"Are you sitting down?" Her voice had an odd angle in it.

"I am."

"Ronni, it isn't Jane."

"Really? Who, then?"

"It's Bryce."

I reeled. I still hadn't gotten over him all those years. I had felt an incessant pull, wanting a connection, of wanting... what? Something. Healing? Reconciliation?

"Oh, Lordy! I emailed him from your place on Friday night asking to connect." Initially, I wasn't going to admit that to Simone as my friends thought I should have just moved on years ago.

"Really? You did? Friday night? That's when he died."

My emotions swirled. I know our bonding—or was it bondage?—was very deep. That morning, I loaded my car to head back to Bellingham. And as I started the drive, there he was. Like Glenn years earlier, he was sitting right there in the passenger seat, "see-through." Only he was definitely coming from the other side.

"Oh, my God, Bryce. What happened?" I burst into tears.

"I know. I know. I was sick for quite a while." He looked humble and caring.

"Bryce, why did you tell stories about me, victim tales, that I had cost you money and other things that weren't true?"

"Because I loved you and you hurt me."

"Why wouldn't you communicate with me?"

"To get even."

From there it went on, vibrationally we shared a mighty reconciling of our years together, hashing out what each of us did. He kept saying he was sorry. He'd wanted to get even. I'd been trying to be honest about the pushes and pulls with my spiritual direction. He'd taken it as a purposeful betrayal of him. The accounting was detailed, more of he said/she said and expectations that were misinterpreted between us. I think it might have lasted half an hour. He had been in a state of betrayal all those years. Me, too, but mine was because I'd thought if everything was explained, he would understand. He'd thought he could woo me into a marriage no matter what I explained. I remember how he teased me years earlier, "Having a relationship with you is

325

like having a relationship with someone who has another lover." He was referring to my first love, Spirit.

All the pieces shifted around deeply within me. We were finally unraveling some of the unfathomable stuff that could have become more karma.

"Don't tell my wife about all this. She'll be furious!" I guess that could be construed as a betrayal, as well. But for me, it was resolution. Layers and layers of our beings were pushed and pulled as they cleared.

Actually, I received an email from her that Sunday when I got home. She had opened my email to him. "What kind of connection did you two have?" she queried. We shared a couple of emails and she offered me an invitation to his memorial. "Oh, he had compassion for you, finally." I snorted, feeling a judgment based on my skewed reputation. Reputations are a fabrication plot, reality creations often at a lower frequency. "He missed Bridget," she said.

"He could have seen her. They were close. After my initial fear, I wouldn't have stood in the way. He just wouldn't respond. And Bridget wouldn't call, rarely calls anyone, in fact." I could imagine how distorted the interpretations had gotten. And I just knew that I shouldn't arrive at the memorial in the little town. It could've caused a bit of a stir if anyone remembered.

Back in my car, both of us were crying—he from realms "over there," me while driving up the I5. The tears and our words felt like a huge inner bath.

"I love you."

"I love you" The fields unattached and flowed through our words and our hearts.

Then he was gone. I was fully changed. I know he felt the freedom, as well. Communication worked. We were unhooked. I have not felt that interminable and painful soul pull since our time together in my little Prius.

Over and over, whether with clients on phone wires under or over the Atlantic or Pacific Oceans or in person, beings who have passed come through, often unbidden, to tell of their connections to comfort and to release loved ones or, sometimes, hated ones. Humble in the face of life expanding, outside and through my defensive little boundaries, I grow, year after year—knowing that it will all be shown, knowing that the beauty and the true nature of each one of us is more accessible, more intricate, and greater than I could ever have imagined.

Spirits are either willing or not. Spirits seem to be simply multifaceted versions of ourselves in various stages of integration. Sometimes they come for healing—healing, that word that to me means unhooking some old beliefs or emotions or programs that prevent self-healing. Sometimes it's just for expression.

Experiences are subjective. That means only I have my particular collection of them. What do you experience? The realms beyond are rich. We can receive shots of wisdom or illumination, epiphanies, or visitations that can lead us away from binding, blinding tracks of our expectations, pushing us into new ways of being that can then lift us to a new or renewed generation of possibilities. We are the ones who are choosing to make it possible, aren't we? We are the ones.

My Guidance and many others have said repeatedly over the last few years, "You can release and step out of karma." I use the term *karma* as that grab bag to contain leftover reactions from the depth of our beings that form the subconscious that can blindside us, that are looking to be neutralized or maybe even for vengeance. They keep us running old, limiting patterns, like failed relationships, financial frustrations, and low self-esteem. We don't have to know where they came from. We can set ourselves free, be new.

Meditation is a true releasing process. And those rolling universal fields are of a much higher frequency lately. I can feel them bump up, coming through the collective. I used to "see" them like huge, white-capped waves, scooping and tossing even galaxies in their turbulence. Was it true? Did I actually see what I saw? I'm always questioning. Amma and Bhagavan, as a unit, the avatars who began the Oneness University, spreading the deeksha or blessings in ever-growing numbers around the world, are intent on awakening our species. Their work, blessings by initiates who touch the heads of many in a state of meditation, is activating the brain of many. People are moving into greater and greater states of consciousness with their influence.

But it's not only their work. Bhagavan and others say that our galaxy is moving into the central golden light of the universe, which can bring us into a time of love, healing, and evolution quite quickly. We are more and more able to incorporate higher frequencies and pass them on through our own work and intentions with others, or through energy and consciousness. More and more, I am aware of the movement of frequencies through my many clients and of our ability to transform more rapidly than ever before.

We are much higher frequency than ever before. The shift is slowly moving through us all on a smaller level, the earth and the universes on larger levels. Humanity can evolve. It is evolving.

We wonder, though, as we hear bought news, marketed "truths" about greed-gobbling resources, countries, money, all sounding more and more like the warring days of the The Bhagavad Gitu, with so many people heaving sighs of frustration, retreating, and stepping back from possibility. But it seems we are in the flotsam and jetsam of awakening to the massive hoodwinking and corruption that has propelled our systems of religion and government for thousands of years.

Watch the faces of people as they release old feelings, lineage patterns, fears, beliefs, resistance, and emotions such as anger. Watch them. Their faces become radiant, their eyes become much brighter. Rooms that felt murky, buzz. We, and that means the many people who choose to, are learning to corral frequencies consciously and use them to heal and lift environments. Through the Internet, news controlled by large corporations is right beside the news of real people around the world, with talk of extraterrestrials, tremendous healing abilities, ways of creating free energy — a gift that would have had inventors killed for the sake of the markets. But now with the proliferation of folks around the world presenting similar discoveries, it's harder to put out their lights.

And as people grow and change, open and expand, find more and more power within as well as the ability to love themselves — hence love life around them and feel even more love growing through them — there is a possibility of heaven on earth. I feel it as infused by Creator Spirit. But for us as individuals and a species, it requires free choice.

Those programs that resonate on lower frequency patterns like angers, resistances, jealousy, and competitions, programs that keep us slamming into dead ends in life, can disperse in the spiraling of the lights of our soul's evolutionary desires, moving through us. If it is true, and I actually believe it is, that we can step out of the edicts of karma or subconscious programming, we can watch it in the form of energy, lights, radiances in one another. It takes a conscious command from each of us to move the old, dense frequencies, but it is easy enough to test.

Like with my ankle and knee and probably your physical aches and pains as well, you can move a lot of pain by moving out the hidden emotions or reactions in the area. They call it healing as if it were a strange talent. It is just outside the so-called "normal" medical model. Call up the energy. Call up your greater being. Feel that emotion...even if it is ugly. Like most, you are probably quite reluctant to admit jealousy and competition. But admitting it, then accepting it, is the fastest way for you and me to disperse it along with other old programs that have kept us "less than" our amazing selves. Enslaved, actually. And competition with others is actually the old way; it's an implication that if they are better at some things than we are, we are nothing. We can admit our limiting feelings and recognize that they are showing us something we want but don't recognize yet.

The increasing shimmering of people is increasingly enticing. Step away from media for a minute. Feel. Soften and release tensions and holding patterns. Let yourself feel if it is pulling you down. Or use the downpull to experience your own reflections, then move those pulls. And you, too, can rise in frequencies, and your manifestations will change and improve.

Also it is all about love—loving ourselves...having the courage to absolutely love the self. Notice the word *courage*, which comes from *coeur* in French, the heart. It turns the meaning of defense on its head, inside out, and backward as that love vibration emanating through you does the job, expanding and touching others as well, creating a protective radiance.

Again I see the fields, those universal fields lifting and moving all of humanity, in fact, carrying our species to new levels of possibility. Interesting that our sparkling ascendance has met the frequencies of the Internet, of global communication, a true gift of radiating illumination for those who choose to ride the light changes. As Eckhart Tolle and others say, there will be two Earths. One will be the Earth and its inhabitants who awaken their consciousness, radiating to one another, to the powers of love and gratitude. There will be no frequency connection to the ones in the other reality where those who want it to be the same can play the same game, possibly to annihilation, or certainly in the old model of winner takes all. Or wars for God or resources. "They" say that the folks who inhabit the two different Earths can have little contact with one another, if any at all. The losses could be hard among family members.

I simply fall back on "change the energy, change the reality." Who will want to hang on and who will want to rise is a deep soul choice — maybe our deepest.

As the ancient Hindu scriptures talk about the shifting consciousness fields, they speak of hundreds of years of the grand flows bringing light and new information, moving through us, awakening powers within. To me, and as I see it in my intuitive work, time is a difficult thing to rein in. The frequencies move hugely, unfolding consciousness. Though many are feeling stirrings within, we may not experience it all totally. The shifting fields aren't really going to bring the old ways to a skidding halt and then move right into the bliss of awakening. It just can't happen. It might take a thousand years for the mass of humanity, but some are able to move the light through their being and experience that heaven on earth right now.

But we already see the tremendous shifts in many people around the world, even in war-torn areas, among oppressed people, among the diseases that afflict so many at times. We see the light in some eyes, and we know that they are receiving the gifts of these times.

CHAPTER TWENTY-TWO

My World and Godaddy.calm

Back to my own microcosm—the people in my world and my core family with all that we represent in one another's growth and evolution. We know now that the father instills the self-esteem of the daughter. I was struggling with mine, what with being a misfit and problem child. But things would become much better.

Around age eighty-nine, my dad's deteriorations increased. He went through some serious illnesses. One of the first big ones landed him in the emergency room. Trevor and I went to the hospital to see him. His mind seemed disconnected, and we were told that he was demented.

"Hi, Dad." I kissed him. "Is he really demented?" I wondered as we sat by his bed. "How can we know?" I know about being crazy, especially about nutritional sensitivities and craziness, and about imbalances that can get sorted out. Attending to the special needs that I had certainly worked for me! His medical group might not pay as much attention to such influences.

Sitting beside him for a few minutes, pondering, I came up with something. "Dad, I was doing some research for my radio shows, and guess what? I learned that some of your neurotransmissions are created first and foremost in your intestinal tract."

In a split second, he quipped, "So it's true. We have shit for brains."

Trevor and I burst out laughing. "My dad is still here!" I cried.

Shortly afterward, we found out that he had a bladder infection. When seniors have bladder infections, they can seem temporarily demented. After taking some antibiotics, he was better. Emerging body/mind information is miraculous. Soon he was getting strong again, and he moved to a wonderful room in a retirement center with an elegant dining room, a sports bar, and exercise instruction. It was lovely for a time. But then, after a few falls and a blood infection, he had to move to a place that provided more care. He had a smaller room, but still had his computer, electronic organ, iPad, Kindle, and tons of books he read voraciously. He was quite happy and busy most of the time, but quite secluded.

I visited fairly often, grateful to live nearby. We talked about his childhood, his fears, and a lot about Mum and Georgina. I took messages from them when they came. For several years, he had had a photo of each of them on his dressing table and always kissed both of them good night, every night.

He stumbled on a game I love to play with photos as well. He shrugged as he said, "You know something? I swear that I can see changes in their smiles. Then I think I know how they are right now. Maybe you think I am crazy, but sometimes one or the other or even both of their smiles are happier or sadder. Really! It's true!" He tossed his bushy eyebrows up and rolled his shoulder at his inner amusement that he should think such a thing! These visions truly ripped the fabric of his reality.

I also laugh at my memory of when Georgina first came to me from "the other side," which is really here all the time, just vibrating at a different rate. I was at a Lazaris seminar with Trevor. I raised my head and there she was, transparent, standing there in front of me in the huge auditorium filled with people.

"Alright," I said. "You had better give me a sign, Georgina. Remember, you didn't believe in spirits visiting."

We all have a unique scent, and suddenly hers filled the area. "Ronni, I want you to call your father. He needs you."

"Okay. But can it wait, Georgina? I mean 'til coffee break?"

"Yes. But he needs you soon. He is suffering terribly right now."

"Okay." I whisked back to the hotel room during the next short break and phoned my dad.

"Hi. Aren't you at a conference or something?" he asked, sounding quite normal.

"I am, Dad. Georgina just came to me, here at the seminar. She said you were having a little trouble and wanted me to call you for her. Are you okay?"

He suddenly wept. "I don't know what is wrong with me. I just feel ditzy and sad, and I just can't focus. I miss her. I miss her. How is she?"

"She's fine. Studying, she said. That makes her happy, as you well know. She says to tell you she loves you, Dad. She is so sorry about her niece—so surprised at her greed. She actually cried about it, how deceived she was. She watched it all happen, that horrible drama unfolding. She's so, so sorry. She knows your grief has been hard. She loves you. She wants you to know that you are doing well and that you have protection all around you. She will be there for you."

We chatted on, and I sent energy until he became calm again.

"Thanks, Vereo...."

"I love you, Dad. Will call you soon."

That was a couple of years before he passed. But that interim time for him and me was a learning curve, pock-marked with spirit visitations, including the time Mum told me to tell him that he'd been a good husband and that she had learned about love. We'd talk about the soul and what it was doing "out there." Then he would deny that he even had a soul, grinding his teeth on resentments about unmitigated spiritual domination. Then on again came the visitations. We had some quiet discussions about dying. He led these and became quite vulnerable; often, right after our talks, he would snap back and become the resentful curmudgeon cynic: "It's all over when you die. I know that."

"Okay, Dad." I let him lead. I had been a challenge, the nonconformist, the one who was resentful of his ignoring or even denying the pain that his daughters, especially this one, had been through under his watch. Yet, I loved my dad and earnestly wanted to be there — to get to know him, which can be easier when one is ready to die, and to offer what I could. Maybe we could complete what we could between us and for ourselves, or at least him, during his last period.

When he was about ninety, my sister called me. "Dad wants to talk to each one of us. Come and hear what he has to say." It turned out he had a near-death experience. He was sure he was dying, so he called each of his four kids into his room. I couldn't get there until the next morning and fretted that by that time he would no longer be in the magical mind-set of the event I knew he was experiencing. But not so. "Have the other kids told you what I want to say?"

"I think so, Dad." I wasn't sure, but was certainly ready to hear.

"Well, I had everything in boxes. Do you know that there are no boxes? We are all one?" Tears graced both our cheeks as he went on. "There was so much light. All the boxes

336

melted into one—a kind of flow. There are no boxes," he repeated. "I learned so much, including that I really love my family. I never knew how much. I've decided I am not going to die yet because I want to enjoy loving my family." There was more, much more. Then his tone changed, and he truly looked at me. "Are you and I okay now?"

"We are, Dad. We are."

Dad did live for about another year and a half. Feelings weren't his usual conversational tool, but he talked to us more about his feelings and about each of us personally, with a new kind of loving. He seemed less and less resentful as he was truly loving his life and family, although his discomfort and limitations were increasing. He was nearing the end, it was obvious.

Dad always loved to play musical instruments and to sing, and the harmonies he had started us on when we three little girls were small enough to share the same bathtub had been seasoned. My brother, much younger, was a musical wizard like our dad.

So one day, to honor him, five days before he passed, we all gathered in his room. My brother brought his guitar.

"What's going on?" he asked. "Oh, oh. Something's wrong?" He looked around like a naughty child, and I saw he was relieved that I was included. He had expressed his concern about the family's split for years, but he had no courage when it came to bridging a gap. He and I had talked about it fairly often.

"We are here to give you a concert, Dad."

As we moved chairs and plants, I asked him, "Want a concert?"

"You said there would be one. Did you mean it or not?" He huffed and rolled his shoulders in impatience as we tuned our voices. Then, as if accompanying his legend, we sang songs from his era, songs from our childhood: "Rusty Old Halo," which had been background for many a Sunday breakfast, "Amazing Grace," "Hurry on Down to My Place, Honey," and "Sentimental Journey." Themes of time, woven through the years, unrolled for a couple of hours. He was quiet at the beginning, but then began to intone, "Thrum thrum oo boo boo boo...dum dum dad um..." as if he were a base fiddle. His head had often been hanging over the side of his wheelchair by then, but in this moment, it was upright. He came to life, even singing a solo. "You can bring Pearl / She's a darn nice girl / But don't bring Lulu....." and then came his finale: "'Cuz I'll bring her myself!" With the clicking and whirring of our phones, we recorded the magic of this last event.

His life was rapidly waning. Our musical revue touched him and made him proud of his gift of music and song to us all. We loved him, but were relieved that this feisty, creative soul might leave before he totally deteriorated. One day, my sister went to his room and there he was, sitting in his chair singing a verse from "Frankie and Johnny," the first song he had taught us. "Bring out your rubber-tired hearses / Bring out your rubber-tired hats / There are eight of us going to the graveyard / But only seven of us coming back." He always had a song to punctuate his moments.

After our performance, I went in every day. Friday he looked strong and still vital. "Oh," I said to myself, "he is still pretty strong. He'll probably last awhile yet." The next morning, though, while I was lying in my own bed about a half hour away, my "see-through dad" came to me. He flew on an arc around the bed where I was just waking up and said, "I am going now. It's time. Thank you, thank you, thank you."

"Am I really hearing this?" I wondered. A huge tunnel appeared. It looked more like a humongous slinky made of a lit-up fabric wire. Dad went into it, careening through it, banging off its walls. His was a humorous journey. I could see Mum, Georgina, and Grandma, his mum, at the other end. He threaded his way through it as it wobbled, bouncing off its pulsating walls, and then, jumping out of the end, he was rejoicing, "I made it. I made it!"

I thought it was strange that he didn't stop to hug his ladies-in-waiting, his wives and mother. He just kept right on going. "Hmmm," I said to myself. "That was fun, but did I make it all up? Shall I call Maureen [my older sister]? Better not, in case this is just my imagination. I'll just meditate."

As I sunk deeply within, in the next minute, the phone rang. A weeping Maureen said, "He's gone. Dad passed a few minutes ago." I felt a strange relief. I had actually experienced his crossing with him. He was free. He was rejoicing.

After his body was removed and we sorted out the room, Trevor and I returned to Bellingham, the eagles, and the sea. There, I saw Dad again.

"Thank you," he offered again.

"Why do you keep saying thank you, Dad?"

"You told me to keep my eyes open! It helped me. There's so much for me here. It is so wonderful. Thank you, thank you."

Then later, maybe a few days, maybe a few weeks, I don't quite remember now, he came with a commitment. "I just didn't get it. I do now. I know what you are doing and I am proud of you. I couldn't support you at all. But I will be here now. You'll know. You can feel me."

And I have. I truly have. Having my dad behind me as I take huge steps into my life is so strengthening. I feel him most days. Thanks, Dad.

A month after he passed, I went to Tucson to visit and work. I stayed with friends while I did tons of healing sessions, which energize my journey inside and out, visited, caught up with other beloved friends from our life there, and reinvigorated my old joy of walking in the early-morning, electrical desert warmth. I was and am still doing my twenty-minute wild dance to Van Morrison's "Wavelength" and other lively pieces calling through higher and higher frequencies, scouring chakras or parts of my body that periodically suffer from wear and tear—to keep relatively fit inside and out. But as I planned to return to Bellingham to somehow sort the next phases of my life, I was sad. I was dragging inside. My father was gone. I always feel deeply sad in the Northwest and vulnerable due to all the memories of my life falling apart, still not belonging to my family, my reputation that somehow keeps fomenting judgment. Thus speaks my Pluto line, the astrological line that resonates with the need to transform old patterns. What is the message here, you might ask—a drive in and through soul challenges? Or is it simply an invitation to leave?

Just before I left Tucson, however, my body spoke up loudly, much like the ankle/married man episode in Pima Canyon. I suddenly couldn't walk. It wasn't the ankle this time; it was my right knee. A quick look-up of knees in Louise Hay's famous *You Can Heal Your Life* reveals that knees hold programs about fear and insecurity, while the right side of the body is about leadership, taking charge, and stepping forward. My right knee was a mess. I walked funny, like I do when my mind is cracked as well. Actually, I could hardly walk at all. Hobbling, limping, I couldn't work it out. The pain was intense. I went to doctors and specialists in Bellingham and had tests and scans, bodywork, and whatever else they had in their arsenal. Unquestionably, they said, I needed knee surgery, probably a replacement. My knee had been hurt in a car accident back in 1966, so it was believable that it wasn't strong.

I hobbled with a strange gait that matched my relentless ruminations, juggling my vulnerabilities like age and fear of the losses of home, of Trevor's deepening financial trough, and my own sensitivities. Maddeningly, they circled around inside my mind, like a dance of eagles and bees.

I knew that, even at age seventy-one, I needed to step forward, to put my gifts to greater service, to be an inspiring, healing contributor right now—especially for these times of tremendous dark and light, of tremendous potential for transformation, of the rising of the feminine to balance patriarchal mania. I had to show up and be present to offer my gifts into the collective. These times, as we have heard, are likened to the end times of Atlantis. Can we change the outcome for humanity? I am here to be a part of the change.

I struggled and hobbled, then suddenly I would hear, "Keep going. Just keep going. It will be wonderful." Oh, it is often Spirit and my Guides—my beloved etheric neighborhood. But now the clear voice of my Dad chimes in, too. "Keep going. You will do it." Each time I hear him, I feel him—so much stronger. I always like to check out my personal connections, have a second opinion, as desire can truly steer our perceptions. I have sure learned how subtle that can be. So I spoke to my intuitive friend Julia Assante. Her confirmations were delightful.

"Hello, Grant. You know, Veronica, I have never met a being who crossed over so recently that was this spirited. He is having a wonderful time, exploring, reading, making sense of life from his new perspectives. Your dad wants to be there for you. He says he will be with you for a long time. He is sorry that he did nothing to protect you. He was afraid. Now go ahead, even yell and scream at him. You can release all those pent-up self-esteem issues. Right, Grant?" she asked him. He assured her enthusiastically that he could feel it now.

Hmmmmm...is that possible? Her transmissions with him truly validated what I was hearing, complete with his humor and his love of music.

"Play music for him. Go back to playing your piano. It brought you peace even when you were just playing scales."

I laughed. That was the very phrase I used to say myself: "Even playing scales feels good." I will do that!

"I've never seen this before!" he told her with his usual curiosity and enthusiasm about life here in 3D.

"He's like a child, fascinated by how we look, connecting as intuitives."

We laughed and laughed, and it felt like we were laughing with Dad.

As I returned to the Northwest, Dad kept coming through me saying, "Keep going. Don't go back. Keep going. Don't tell the others. They can't understand. They'll judge you. I will be here with you. Keep going. You will do so well. Keep going."

You could ask, as I would as well, are you sure that is your dad and not your fantasy? Some unmistakable feelings move through my spine and I feel, truly feel, supported. I know it is my dad. But if we decided not to believe it, it still works

My own Guides are always lovingly coaching my growth through my changes in expectation, attitude, and home and what it really means to me. But there is also something about having my father finally know me and be behind me, deep in my psyche, that gives my 3D self self-confidence, strength, and wings. It is new to me and I treasure it. I have learned how our souls, his and mine, crisscrossed through several lifetimes, deeply etching the challenges between us. Those are healing. Resistances between us are melting. He is there.

I sorted my knee and leg, calling up and releasing as many fears as I could: Fear of no support. Fear of the vulnerability of stepping forward. The challenge of wanting to be safe and also wanting to be a contributor. Fear of being wimpy. Fear of my own dreams. Fear of being wrong all the time. Fear of judgment. Fear of being excluded from the family. On and on. I'd call up the fear and feel it wherever it was in my body. The pain lightened a bit at a time.

After I returned to the final stages of our eagle's nest home, I presented at a Healing Expo in Vancouver. I was extremely busy, and Trevor was amazingly supportive. We built up a booth, and I saw dozens of folks even though I was hobbling. On the final afternoon, I took a twenty-minute free-sample experience of lying on a Biomat with its strips of the magnet-and-amethyst-filled mat around my neck and my knee. Back I hobbled to the booth, where I worked with many more people. Trevor and I broke camp, I drove home, cooked for us, ate the meal, cleaned up, and fell in to bed. Next morning, my knee was all right. I mean it seemed healed! I was no longer hobbling.

Oh, another healing event was when two women came for a session there at the fair. They worked where my first husband Steven had worked. "Oh," I said. "My husband used to work there." Well, amazingly enough, one of those two women had taken over his office, even his books. I had felt so tossed out by those sections of my life in his demise. But she told me something different.

"We all talked about you and how hard it had been for you. Periodically, we would wonder where you are and if you found support."

Hmmmmmm. Really? Thirty-five years later, pieces of the puzzle fell into place. Similar to my discovery about my dad's unspoken love, I realized I had had support and recognition in what seemed to me a time of great deletion!

My knee threatens periodically, but only when I am headed back to a world in which I no longer belong or is in the wrong direction. If the body is a library, mine is an audiobook full of sound and fury! Its commentary squeaks and creaks with pain and limitation and then—after garnering the wisdom they brought—their release.

Trevor finished his speakers, "The best sound in the world," intending to sell them. Markets were thin. So was money. And for me, the magic had faded. I stopped many of the household duties, trying to keep the nose of my plane up—building my business, expanding. The Guides had been warning us that these days were coming: Trevor's funds would come to an end, the expense of the household would become onerous, as the increase of the debt to keep his inventions going would become overwhelming. I wanted him to focus entirely on building my business for a few months. He couldn't. I just didn't earn enough as an intuitive to shore up our family needs and our lives. Our light dimmed as we moved to the basement, renting out the upstairs to a music healer and putting Georgina's beautiful little tables in storage.

I then flew to Costa Rica to be with dear Tucson friends at their healing center, AmaTierra, in Puriscal. I thought maybe I would live there in the warmth of not only the weather, but also the hearts of my friends and the loving ambiance of Costa Rica. And I could be a support in their complex project. But the money flow is minimal there. I wanted to conduct interviews through the University of Peace with their UN reach, tapping the amazing ground-breaking minds and hearts that studied there. But practically speaking, I had to grow my income. Where could I write, host radio shows, conduct workshops, and—vitally important—have media? I wrote the first draft of this book there. My healing knowledge, both energetic and intuitive, is growing, and I wanted to expand my reach or contributions through media, through a television show. Costa Rica has wonderful centers, wonderful people, but at this point, I needed a more bustling business environment. Even Jill, my dear friend, host, healer, writer, singer, all-around talented wonderwoman, admitted that Costa Rica wasn't a great place for media or my sessions. My readings were hard to record, and clients from other parts of the world were frustrated with erratic and dropped Skype calls and recording difficulties. It just wouldn't work right now. Later? We'll see. Costa Rica, or maybe the camaraderie of my friends there, calls me still.

Back home, Trevor carried on, puttering on his inventions, walking with the dog. He rented out the apartment over the garages as well. My garden grew over, a denouement to our big dream and the end of a rich home chapter. The Guides said in our channeling sessions, "The marriage part of your relationship is over. This one"—they often call me that—"needs to move to where the weather is warm and business is active."

Once again I was on the road, this time headed to L.A. I would be near Lucy and in the warm weather. My many media dreams fit in here and L.A. was the place. I would miss my daughter and grandest one terribly, but Lucy and I made plans to gather him into some of the L.A. magic as soon as I settled in.

Trevor started his new incarnation. He landed a job as an engineer and began the process of rebuilding his life. He apparently needed me to release him to give him the leverage he needed to rise above his financial pothole. His speakers are still in the wings, or perhaps sprouting wings, with emerging accoutrements like servers and amplifiers. At some point, they'll enrich healing sound flows on this planet. And we are dear friends.

Some of my nights are filled with nightmares of all the losses. Trevor has his own. We aren't there to soothe one another's deep insecurities as we were fourteen years ago. Some days I am angry that our contract left us both vulnerable and starting over so late in life. But in our conversations, we hash it out together and unravel the mysteries of the emotions that rise from ancient soul stories, or childhood, or grief over the loss of our shared dreams. That helps.

I am finishing my book, the one you are reading now, and steering my media dreams to manifestation, watching wonderful performances, basking in the creative zest with all its ups and downs.

Once again, thanks, Dad. I actually feel these days, as if my Dad has my back and I have a confidence as I step into the world new, creative, leaning on the love and support of family and clients and Guidance to keep my wings functioning.

Throughout all the years of my work as an energy counselor, over and over I have experienced with and through clients that when a parent passes, whether the rapport with the parent was happy or painful, people feel an odd freedom, an expansion. I feel that as the parents depart, they pull away some of the vibrations, frequencies of some of the old programmed energies that we have woven into our identities during our life or lifetimes of connection to them. But then grief itself is at times a turbulent cyclone of emotions as we juggle layers of ourselves to create a new center. It helps to be able to consciously enter the vibrational reality of my dad, to finally be able to cry and express my hurt to him and have him respond. Over and over we, and so many others in different realms, can work to undo some of the limiting programs we hold on to. We can dissolve the leftover densities that come from old drama and no longer let them impede our ability to create our reality. At times the energy releases are thrilling.

Spirits, like people on the planet, come in full spectrum. Some are not at all awake, and others remain in the consciousness level they were in when on this plane. Some are awake and growing, studying, laughing, and always *loving loving loving*. I have had to learn to reject the ones who want to appease someone's ego or insecurities at the same level they were on when alive. My personal goal or job is to help empower people—unenslave us, really. For that we use subtle transformative energy, intention, and love. The ones who want to visit to maintain security can find someone else to talk to. You can reject any that bother you as well with a strong intention, a strong letting go. Assess carefully if the visitation is supportive. If not, well, just say good-bye, I am not available for this.

Subjectivity is a precious gold mine. No two people see, hear, and experience the same thing, even identical twins. We are all born with our purpose, dharma, urges, drives to complete, and yearnings to love, and we build recognitions and expressions, reactions and aversions. Spiritual teachers, especially of the Eastern philosophies, teach us that the release of all our attachments and aversions is key to our personal evolution. In fact, doing so can free us from the edicts or tantalizing familiarities of the subconscious that keep us running our old programs, or as I like to think of it getting the same old two by four over the back of the head — like relationships that don't work, fears of growing out of the security bases like identities or social placements we have set up, or resistances to new opportunities or new comprehendsions. My own fears, resistances, or forgivenesses of ways I have been in life just rise from infinite depths, always at a new level. Maybe that is an eternal job. To me it is slow, although I seem to whiz along in the eyes of my more traditional friends.

No matter from whence your myriad emotions spring — whether they are instantaneous responses through this life, born in the soul records of babies, or come from the absorption of emotions in utero from Mum's experiences — our lives roll out on those waves of reaction and belief. They can bring all kinds of limitations unique to each of us in the dance with our true nature. The work is to change through release our honest recognitions of our controls, resistances, and clearings. It's an inside job. It's this inner work that can catapult our empowerment as consciously multidimensional spirits: Transform. Become happy, grateful, nonreactive, and conscious/awake.

No matter what the experiences are on the planet during our times, in our lives, in our past, or in our future, our greatest goal is to be happy and to love. There is the gauntlet! I knew that as a small person in my ditch, but lo it has been a journey! Treasure all your experiences as a crucible, for the infinite possibility of transformation is there in the petri dish of your legend. You are the only one in the universe who is you, the only one expressing The Divine your way. And you can choose to catch the waves of consciousness moving through the universes at this time to help you burst into the real you.

Recently, as Christmas sparkled on the horizon, I was speaking with a being who transited about three years ago. "Happy Solstice, Merry Christmas, Happy Hanukkah, or other happy celebrations," I said. "What happens where you are now?"

"It is beautiful," he said. "There are stunning, spectrally radiant vortices here that build with the celebrations of your world. They are beautiful and the energy is...well...intoxicating!"

That perked my joy of the celebrative season as it reflects the consciousness and beauty of "as above so below."

Reach up with your mind as a sculpting tool and draw in the lights that are there for us all. Feel the essence of reality, LOVE.

ACKNOWLEDGMENTS

My Mum and Dad, Vera and Grant, thank you for bringing me into the world and, sometimes through adversity, helping me launch my perspective over life and all its conventional containers. I love you and my sisters and brother.

Ann Crawford for your friendship and kindness while editing this, my first book.

Trevor Bissel, my magical guide through technology. Patient. Kind. Loving. We shared radio, television, and a dream-filled reach. I resisted technology, but Trevor, you just kept creating with me. Step by step I learned. Always patient, you inspired my fledgling wings as we flew through constantly changing mysteries.

Terry Presber for your loving pivotal guidance through nutrition, media dreams, and friendship during my hardest time.

Rose Bortolon, Pat Hodgins, Jill and Bob Ruttenberg, Sue Newman, Ursela Gurau, Simone Nichols, and Anni Holtby —there are even more of you!—thank you for your loving friendships that weave growth and sharing through most of the chapters of my life.

Steven Holtby for your courage, for expanding my horizons over and over again, and for always taking an "unrealistic" and idealistic stand in the face of inequity.

Naomi for tearing apart what I mistook was the only "right" way.

Glenn Entwistle for your wonderful nurturing, and thanks for our feisty, powerful, beautiful and wise, creative daughters Lucy and Bridget, who light up my journey with their presence and love. Bridget for my "grandest" one, who charges up our family life with love and fun and wisdom.

Big hearty acknowledgments to my hundreds of radio interviews on Paradigm Shifters who continue to push the envelopes of humanity. Through your books and chats, I have had a vibrant education, one I can wear in my heart and soul. I love outflowing your radiant wisdom around the world online. Thanks for sending consciousness out, for free, for all. Here are just a few of my favorites....

Peter Calhoun, for your loving, multidimensional perspective of reality and for your empowerment of humanity.

Julia Assante, author of *The Last Frontier*, for breaking out of the organized bounds of religion and reality.

Juliet Nightingale for touring the power of the soul and perception through near-death experiences.

Nadya McCaffrey for courageously standing for veterans with her three-dimensional and multidimensional wisdom.

Joe Dispenza, Joe Vitale, Dianne Collins—quantum instead of quantity—for truly empowering our potential through dreams and understanding.

Stephen Pollitt, Penney Peirce, and Donna Eden—just a few Guides, besides my own, who lead us to higher frequencies.

John Grey who continues to awaken us to differences of the male and female...viva la difference!

Jim Ehmke, Caroline Sutherland, nutritional wizards.

Galexis, a fun and informative coalescence of channeled intelligence from beyond. Ashtar, too!

More channels—Lazaris, Norianon, Dashiai, The Team—who know how to be in touch with our human process and yet can lovingly awaken us to our multidimensionality.

Randy Masters of Universal Song for your "resonant living" guidance and friendship, and so many musical/frequency healing-sound wizards.

The Crystal Table, our special evolutionary group.

Plus so many great teachers, Oneness Blessing practitioners, and lists and lists of amazing gurus I study... one line at a time...wanting to be what I learn.

My thousands of clients who shared themselves so honestly as they transformed, grew, and practiced the arts of conscious evolution with me. Through you I have experienced layers and layers of the consciousness of our species, how inaccessible some of it is, and why change can challenge. How possible we are as a species! How able to transcend our limitations! I continue to learn HOW.

So many more of you who came in to my life to love me, laugh with me, dance with me, flick me, or carry me out of the potholes my mind landed in along the way.

Most of all, I am so grateful to my beloved network of loving consciousnesses. Thank you for clearly stating, when I whined about all the research I have to do in an effort to forge a greater perspective of human life, "You would never put up with just one answer. Dear One, you need a library to satisfy you. We have it. You are an explorer. We love you." Their abounding love light paints incredible and possible vistas with their radiant streams of information for you and me. As Mr. Rogers would say, "It's a beautiful day in the neighborhood."

I love you all.

Made in the USA
San Bernardino, CA
07 December 2015